# Toward
# A European
# Balance of
# Power,
# 1620-1715

# TOWARD A EUROPEAN BALANCE OF POWER 1620-1715

RAND McNALLY EUROPEAN HISTORY SERIES

**JOHN B. WOLF**

University of Illinois
Chicago Circle

**RAND McNALLY & COMPANY** • **Chicago**

*Cover Illustration:* Leopold of the Holy Roman Empire,
from Peeters, *A Set of Engraved Plates.*
*Courtesy John B. Wolf.*

*For Stanley L. Jones and Robert V. Remini,*
*good colleagues and good friends*

# Editor's Preface

It used to be thought that the sole object of history was to discover and set forth the facts. When the *English Historical Review* was founded it recommended such a procedure, for through it one "can usually escape the risk of giving offense." While much of this tradition has remained active in the teaching and writing of history, it has led, in turn, to a sharp reaction against such timidity and narrowness. History became a branch of philosophy or of the social sciences, and scholarship was in danger of being displaced by the search for general laws that might govern the development of all mankind. There is a hunger for history abroad in the land, but many of those who want to know about the past are rightly dissatisfied with arid narrations of fact (and turn to the historical novel instead), while others are bewildered by abstruse generalizations that seem to ignore the particular for the universal.

The books in the Rand McNally European History Series do not place themselves in either of these traditions. Instead, they recognize both the importance of accurate and detailed scholarship and the obligation to place such scholarship within a meaningful historical setting. They do not shun general ideas and assumptions; they test them in the crucible of research. This combination is always exciting, because it penetrates historical development; and this development, in each of its stages, illuminates a new dimension of mankind. A prominent historian once wrote, "What man is, only history tells."

Here "what man is" is told by scholars who have researched and reflected upon a significant period of history. They have taken this opportunity to present their conclusions in a manner that will attract and stimulate those who long for a lively account of the past. All of the authors in this series are specialists presenting their original insights, making it possible for all those interested in history to partake of their work.

George L. Mosse, *advisory editor*
*Rand McNally European History Series*

# Preface

Since the eighteenth century, diplomats, publicists, and historians have used the term "balance of power" to describe the political government of the community of sovereign states. The term is ambiguous and perhaps misleading; it was coined at a time when Newtonian physics dominated the intellectual climate of European men, and both the methodology and the terminology of the physicist seemed appropriate for all other disciplines. Political and historical "physics" did not seem as out of place then as it does now to men who have studied Darwinian biology, Freudian psychology, and Einsteinian astrophysics. In our time it might be better to speak of the "imbalance" of power, or the "evolution" of power systems, but the fact that the term "balance of power" has so many years behind it may justify its use today as long as we realize that in the political life of men instability is the only constant, and "power" is more important than "balance" as an explanation of high politics. No matter what term is used, the problem that we are studying is not difficult to identify: a community of states in which each of the component members refuses to recognize any authority superior to its own will, can find government only in some sort of system by which it is possible for states to combine to prevent any one or more of their numbers from dominating the entire community. This statement, of course, is an ideal structure; to implement it is quite a different thing. It required more than a generation of European men to develop the political and military experience and institutions necessary for the security and "liberties" of the states. The system that emerged from their efforts has been called the "balance of power" and in a general way it has been at the very foundation of high politics of the western world for the last two and a half centuries.

In this book I have attempted to delineate the process of development that seems to have been the origin of this characteristic form of European high politics. Before the seventeenth century, first in Italy and later in northwestern Europe, there were political combinations that seem to be embryonic of our modern systems, but a closer look at the century of Charles V and Philip II reveals that it did not achieve a political order whereby the Hapsburg hegemony was checked or thwarted by the concerted efforts of the rest of Europe. Nor indeed do we find the characteristic form of the "balance of power" in the first half of the seventeenth century when the "German War," as contemporaries called the Thirty Years War, raged in central Europe. In the second half of that century, however, when the kingdom of France emerged as the great military power of Europe, statesmen gradually learned the difficult art of coalition warfare, and as the century moved toward its close, the whole of western and central Europe became involved in the process. It was a hard lesson to learn, for successful coalition warfare compels disparate and divergent states with policies and goals quite different one from the other to unite in a common effort and to submit to a common program, at least until the important objective—namely the defense of the community against a dominant power—has been achieved. It can hardly be asserted that the process was perfected by the end of the War of the Spanish Succession, but the bold outlines of the form of international government that was to dominate the European world for the next two centuries had come into existence. Some may object to calling the system that involved so many terrible wars "government," and yet it was only by the formation of coalitions and the appeal to the sword that European, and later, world society could be governed.

By focusing attention on the early stages of the development of this process I hope to throw light upon its problems as well as to make the confused story of latter seventeenth century high politics both interesting and intelligible. This essay, of course, is only an introduction to the manifold complexities of European politics at a time when they were, perhaps, even more pluralistic than they are today. I hope that it will encourage the reader to delve deeper into the questions, and even more that it will provide him with insights into the form of the process of high politics that has so completely dominated the lives of men since the seventeenth century.

Like all writers I owe more debts than I can easily repay. This book is a by-product of the work I did in preparation for my *Louis XIV*, and, therefore, in a very real way I am as much indebted to the Fulbright Commission and the Guggenheim Foundation for this book as for the larger one. I also must thank the University of

Illinois, Chicago Circle, for its support and assistance in the preparation of the manuscript, and my friend and colleague John O'Connor, University of Wisconsin, for his careful reading of the text.

I would like to add a note to this preface, written almost a year ago, to thank Mrs. Naomi Donson of Rand McNally who edited the manuscript with skill and understanding, and suffered with me during the thirty-two days that it was lost somewhere in the recesses of the United States Post Office.

John B. Wolf

Bone Lake, Wisconsin
May 26, 1968.

# Contents

# Chapter 1

# France:
# The First Military Kingdom

When Cardinal Mazarin died in 1661 Europe was at peace for the first time in more than a half century. The Thirty Years War, or as it was called at the time, The German War, had ended with the treaties of Westphalia; the Hapsburg-Bourbon conflict was settled by the treaty of the Pyrenees; and the Swedish-Polish war, by the treaty of Oliva. Cardinal Mazarin could die convinced that his reputation as a statesman was secured by his part in forming these agreements so favorable for the kingdom of France. He left his young king installed on a throne that he had raised above the other kingdoms of Europe, and even though Louis XIV and his advisors still feared the rekindling of civil disorders like the recent Frondes, that throne was the most stable in Europe. It alone had military power capable of suppressing civil rebellion and guaranteeing its frontiers; it alone had a well organized government. The question was: what the young king would do with this political machine that he had inherited from the two great cardinal ministers (Richelieu and Mazarin) who had forged it.

Seventeenth century kings were still military leaders of a warlike race of noblemen whose fame and fortune depended upon military action. It was never a question whether or not a new king would go to war; the important question was against what enemy, foreign or domestic, he would fight. Every seventeenth century prince realized that by war he could fulfill his *gloire,* his destiny as a ruler, and satisfy the young men around him who clamored for action. Thus the peace that Mazarin created seemed a little too peaceful for this young prince of twenty-three who announced that henceforth he would govern the kingdom without a first minister. In the *Mémoires* intended for the education of his son, Louis explained that it was "unfortunate to have a peace more profound than anyone had seen in centuries ... at my age, the pleasure of being at the head of my armies made me desire for a little more action abroad. ."

What did he find? He wrote ". . no movements within or without the kingdom could interfere with my plans; peace was established with my neighbors evidently for as long as I would wish to maintain it . ." He went on to explain that the Spanish Hapsburg king was old, his heir was a sickly child, and his realm was entangled in a war with Portugal that could neither be won nor ended. The kingdom of France need no longer fear the Spanish crown. At the other end of Europe the Hapsburg Emperor in Vienna had his "hands tied in a thousand ways ... by the capitulations imposed upon him by the states of the Empire," many of which were allies of the French king. This ancient enemy was effectively checked by his own helplessness and by the league of princes that Mazarin had developed to guarantee "German liberties" and to prevent the Emperor from joining hands with his Spanish cousins against France. In the north neither Denmark nor Sweden could break the peace, and England, after two decades of civil disorder, had restored a prince favorable to France and completely engrossed with the problem of maintaining the tranquillity of his kingdom. The Dutch Netherlands, also an important power in the seventeenth century, was governed by men who had two aims; the extension of their commerce and the exclusion of the house of Orange from power in the United Netherlands. "Even a little war," Louis wrote, "would endanger one or the other of their interests." This left only Italy where all the princes, with the exception of the pope, who "still had rancors of hostility against Cardinal Mazarin," were friendly to France.

With such a panorama, it was hard to see how the young king could place himself at the head of his armies. Small wonder that a prince who had grown to manhood in a court where civil and international war had been the usual subjects of conversation and where soldiers were the hero figures for the young, should regret somewhat the calm that he found in the world around him.

What, really, was the situation of France and of Europe when Louis XIV assumed control over the kingdom? It was an important fact that the kingdom had just emerged from almost a century of civil disorders. From 1561 until the end of the sixteenth century the kingdom had been torn by civil rebellions usually cloaked as religious wars, that had threatened to disrupt the entire social structure of French society. The massacre on Saint Bartholomew's day was only the most dramatic of hundreds of scenes of murder, pillage, and conflict. The climax came when the crown itself became the object of the game and murder the ordinary expression of political life. Henri de Guise and Henry III were both assassinated leaving Henry of Navarre the surviving contender for the throne, which could not really be his without another decade of civil war. In the end he secured peace by giving the noblemen of the Catholic League hereditary governorships and other grants of money or privilege that gravely weakened the authority of the crown. The huguenots were even more handsomely paid. The famous Edict of Nantes was in reality a treaty between the king and the huguenot party; it gave them the right to have a political organization, to maintain soldiers in walled towns, to collect taxes, and to hold offices in the kingdom as well as to practice their religion. The huguenot party practically became a republic within the kingdom. It cost Henry more than a mass to secure the catholic consent to his rule, and the peace that he gave to his erstwhile friends in the reformed religion was something more substantial than mere toleration. The king's authority had been pillaged by men who were anxious to erect a new feudal order that would assure the great nobles and the towns important powers in the kingdom quite beyond the reach of the king.

Henry IV also made a peace with Spain that seemed to give him some security against further foreign intervention in the affairs of the kingdom; yet he was soon forced to execute one of his former friends who had been corrupted by Spanish influence and money. At the opening of the seventeenth century, the king of France quite rightfully remarked that he had little time to talk about his divine right because he had so much trouble persuading his subjects to do what he asked of them. Henry had to govern his kingdom much as a guerrilla captain ruled his band.

However Henry IV did bring peace to the land, and with peace the economy began to recover so that a later generation could propagate the myth that he had provided his subjects with "two chickens for every pot." Furthermore his superintendent of finance, the Duc de Sully, managed to force the tax collectors to turn over most of their take to the government and to cut down the amount of money paid to men who claimed that the king owed them debts. When Henry was murdered in 1610 his treasury had a "war chest" filled with money, and his government was gradually eroding the powers and privileges that he had been forced to give away in the preceding decade. Nonetheless almost on the day after his death, the regency government found itself exposed to the same pressures that had been such a baneful influence in the past.

For a decade and a half after Henry's murder, France had weak government. First the regency of Marie de Medicis and then the regime of the young Louis XIII who had his mother's minister murdered and placed his own incompetent favorite in his place. Again the kingdom witnessed threats of armed resistance and civil war. The great nobles and the huguenot party both were able to resist the king's armies with striking success, and in the treaties that followed their rebellions it almost seemed that the sons of the men who had pillaged the royal authority at the end of the sixteenth century were now insisting that they also be paid for their loyalty and assured of the privileges that their fathers had won. An observer in 1620 might well conclude that a new feudal order, replete with many centers of military power, was about to establish itself in the kingdom of France. The centralizing efforts of the Valois kings from the time of Louis XI to Henry II seemed about to be completely undone.

The disorders within the kingdom were reflected in the indecisiveness of foreign policies. After Henry's murder, in an effort to unite the two great Catholic powers behind the surge of the counter-reformation, Marie de Medicis reversed her husband's anti-Hapsburg policies and married her son to a Spanish princess and her daughter to the heir to the throne of Spain. It was a policy that outraged the "patriots" who remembered the wars with Hapsburg Europe, as well as the huguenots who feared for their future religious safety. Nor were Louis XIII's first advisors more astute. Confronted with a crisis in Bohemia when the Calvinist Elector of the Palatinate attempted to displace the Hapsburg prince as king, Louis XIII saw the whole affair as a part of a great international Calvinist plot; at that very moment he was fighting an unsuccessful war against his own Calvinist subjects, so he concluded that the same thing was happening in Bohemia. As a result, French influence in Germany, particularly among the Lutheran princes, became an important factor in the Hapsburg victory that allowed Emperor Ferdinand II to reconquer Bohemia and move on to power in Germany. By 1624 there were many men who understood that in 1619 the kingdom of France had served Hapsburg interests better than its own, and yet, considering the weakness of the royal authority, perhaps there was little else that could have been done.

It would be considerably less than true to say that Richelieu's entrance into the king's council in 1624 abruptly changed all this. It took several years before the bonds of mutual confidence and the strands of political organization that cemented the alliance between king and cardinal could fully develop. Richelieu actually entered the council against Louis XIII's will; as the agent of Marie de Medicis, Richelieu had extracted concession after concession from the king's weak counselors, and Louis XIII both feared and disliked him. Thus Richelieu entered the council as the queen-mother's creature, but once there he quickly united efforts with.those of the king, even at the cost of Marie de Medicis' hostility and anger. The alliance between Louis XIII and Richelieu was a natural one; both men knew that the rebellious tendencies in the kingdom had to be suppressed, both were determined to strengthen the powers of the crown, and both were ruthless and cruel enough to use any measures, even the executioner, as instruments of royal policy. Richelieu's famous and oft-quoted statement that it would be his policy to humble the great nobles, to undermine the privileges of the huguenot party, and to raise the prestige of the French crown in Europe may have been made after he had accomplished many of these things; for this was, in fact, his program for the king's government.

Richelieu uncovered plots of rebellion among the great of the land, and pleaded with the king for clemency in terms that precluded any such action. Special tribunals were set up to be sure that the guilty would not escape, and their execution followed no

matter what their station in the realm. Even the Duke of Montmorency, who was the first nobleman of the kingdom, the god-child
of Henry IV, the son of the late Constable, the brother-in-law of
the Prince of Condé, was executed for his part in a rebellion led by
the king's own brother. Pleas for his pardon fell on deaf ears. In the
preceding years noblemen had found immunity from royal reprisals
by associating their revolts with a prince of the blood or even with
the king's own mother, but under the rule of Louis XIII and the re-
doubtable Richelieu, there was no cloak that would excuse treason
or rebellion. Those who opposed the king by plots or by arms could
expect to face a special court selected to find them guilty, and order
their execution.

There were many ways to cut into the special privileges of these
men who sought to create a new feudal order even when they were
not taken in rebellion. Henry IV had first understood that if he
could persuade the great noblemen to exchange governorships he
could prevent them from forming strong roots in the provinces that
would reinforce their status. Richelieu continued this program and
in addition sent intendants to oversee and supervise the work of
officials for police, justice, and taxation in the provinces. He also
repurchased a number of important commissions, and at the death
of other officials no successor was named or admitted. Thus the important offices of constable, admiral, lieutenant-general of the infantry and of the cavalry ceased to exist as centers of power outside
of the king's authority. Richelieu also used churchmen for many
functions not usually associated with the clergy; we find bishops
leading soldiers, commanding ships, and doing other quite uncleri-
cal acts. At numerous points in their close association we see Richelieu and the king gleefully encouraging conflicts between bishops
and governors, governors and their lieutenants, and the parlements.
It is small wonder that several of the governors welcomed the royal
intendants who came to their provinces because these officers could
quell such problems. At another level Louis XIII made war on the
Sovereign Courts. He, rather than his more famous son, was the
man who could have told the Parlement "I am the State," and in
fact he did tell them not to interfere with the policies of "My State."
The parlementarians did not like to be restricted simply to the role
of court of justice, but Louis XIII was quite unwilling to have them
discuss or deliberate on questions of royal policy. The parlements,
even more than the tax officers, disliked the royal intendants who

could quash their decrees in the name of the royal council, remove cases from their jurisdiction, and presume to supervise their actions. Once Richelieu and Louis XIII were safely in their tombs, the parlements were quick to attempt to regain the positions that they had lost under these two formidable men.

The huguenots also fared ill when they raised the flag of revolt. As a boy-king Louis had experienced the humiliation of accepting defeat in his own kingdom before the walls of a huguenot stronghold; as a man he wanted revenge against what seemed to him to be an arrogant religious party. The history of the religious wars was still too green in the minds of men to allow any responsible statesman to provoke another era of religious conflict; the huguenot party was probably not as strong in numbers as it had been fifty years before, but the Edict of Nantes had assured it military strength that could not be challenged without peril. And yet when a huguenot rebellion compelled Richelieu to give up his intervention in the German War, both he and Louis XIII understood that this "republic within the kingdom" had to be brought under control. Rather than force an outright confrontation, however, Richelieu strove to divide his enemies' forces and to break them piecemeal. His first "victim" was La Rochelle, a great trading city whose merchants ranged the seas in the manner of the Dutch and whose walled fortifications made them practically independent of the king's officers. Richelieu provoked them into rebellion by building a royal fortification on an island where the king's cannons could control their commerce. When the La Rochellois reacted to this provocation by an attack, Richelieu could assure the huguenots elsewhere that religion had nothing to do with his quarrel with La Rochelle. Then the rebellious city committed the supreme folly of inviting the English to join in the domestic quarrel; even though the English were of the reformed religion, they were also the hated foreigners whose depredations in the past had not been forgotten in many parts of the kingdom. The conflict that we call the Hundred Years' War was not as distant in 1628 as it seems to be today.

This was a fight that appealed to the king; he wanted to be a soldier, he wanted to win military fame; even though strong political forces tried to dissuade him, he gave Richelieu full support, and in person aided in the military operations. The siege of La Rochelle took an entire year; only inadequately aided by the English whose leader, the Duke of Buckingham, was a man of third-rate stature, the valiant men of La Rochelle stood off the full power of their king for a whole year and surrendered only when starvation threatened to kill them all. All was not easy in the royal camp, indeed many times in that siege only the grim determination of the Cardinal prevented a considerable section of French nobility from frustrating his plans. There were noblemen who understood that victory at La Rochelle would place the king in a position to impose his will on them as well as upon that city. In the end the siege was successful, and the king's engineers demolished the fortifications of La Rochelle so that a plow could pass through the foundations of the walls. Never again would its merchants and magistrates be in a position to determine their own fate without considering the will of the king. But Richelieu did not take reprisals against the huguenot religion. He had assured the kingdom that the conflict was not a religious war, and when it was over he left the La Rochellois full freedom to practice the religion of their choice.

La Rochelle was only a start. Within a short time the huguenot cities of the south, fearful for their independence, gave the king and the Cardinal an opportunity to smash their political and military power. The Peace of Alais (1629) reconfirmed the right of the members of the so-called reformed religion to practice their cult and to hold offices in the king's service, but the whole superstructure of the huguenot republic with political and military institutions came down in ruins. All forward progress for the huguenot "cause" was checked; it would only be a matter of time until the gradual erosion of the type started by Henry IV would weaken the reformed religion to a point where even the right to practice the cult would be denied. Richelieu and Louis XIII, however, largely confined their actions to luring huguenot noblemen into the catholic faith by offering them offices or favors in return for their conversion.

While internal problems were undoubtedly most important during the first years that Richelieu sat on the king's council, the international scene also required careful attention. These were the years following the battle of White Mountain in Bohemia when the Danubian Hapsburg house made striking progress in both power and prestige. The victory in Bohemia turned that kingdom into an economic asset for its king, a base upon which new military power could be erected, and the invasion of the Rhineland by both the

Spanish Army under Spinola and the Catholic League Army under Tilly, and the arbitrary transfer of the electoral dignity from the Palatinate to Bavaria, signalized the new position that the Emperor had achieved. Not since before the Lutheran revolt had an Emperor been so strong. The intervention of the Danish king, subsidized by both France and England, and the petty North German principalities, subsidized by the Dutch, failed to check the onward rush of imperial power. Wallenstein's soldiers moved into the scene as an imperial army that could both win victories and free Emperor Ferdinand from his dependence upon the support of Maximillian of Bavaria and the Catholic League. By 1629, Denmark had been driven from the war and Ferdinand II proclaimed the famous Edict of Restitution which was at once a charter for the Catholic party in Germany and a flamboyant affirmation of imperial power. This new situation in Germany drastically altered the political structure of western Europe for the United Netherlands was now under serious military pressure from both Germany and from the Spanish Netherlands, and the kingdom of France might again find itself surrounded by the Hapsburgs on every frontier.

Both Richelieu and Louis XIII understood that it would be to the interests of the kingdom to check this Hapsburg progression, but there were strong forces in the kingdom and the court that considered it to be treason to the Catholic religion to join the heretics against the leading Catholic powers, the king of Spain and the German emperor. The French attempt to squeeze off the Spanish supply route by closing the Val Telline[1] had to be given up, and there was no possibility that the kingdom could intervene in Germany with its own forces for whatever power the king could assemble in France was needed to handle domestic rebellions. Richelieu did subsidize the Danish king and later Gustavus Adolphus of Sweden, but only at the cost of cabals against him, for he could not do even this without arousing great hostility. The Queen Mother, Marie de Medicis, who had inaugurated a pro-Spanish policy when she was regent could neither forget the Hapsburg blood in her veins nor the surge of the Counter Reformation movement in Catholic Europe. The queen, Anne of Austria, was a Spanish princess as well as a

---

[1] The Val Telline was the important link in the Alps between the Spanish positions in Italy and both the Hapsburg power in the Tyrol and on the upper Rhine. If it were effectively closed, men, money, and war supplies could not be moved from Spain and Italy to Germany.

devout Catholic, and around the two queens were clergymen, nobles, and politicians who in one way or another had been attracted to the *devôte,* Counter-Reformation party. Gaston d'Orléans, the king's brother, was a natural leader for this group of men and women whose motives ranged from deep Christian piety to selfish ambitions for power. For Richelieu this situation was often desperately dangerous; he usually found that the same people who plotted against his domestic policies also opposed his foreign policy; he had to contend with the intrigues of the two queens, of the king's confessor, of the king's brother and many powerful noblemen and clergymen in the court all seeking to destroy him. More than once the Cardinal was on the verge of disgrace, but Louis XIII seemed to realize that this ailing man who could propose a program of action so cogently, was really the only man who could carry out the policies that he also wanted. Louis XIII was sickly, morose, and immature, but in a stubborn way he was resolved to emulate his father as a soldier and a statesman and to maintain the office of king in all the power and prestige that he believed it had always had. This may have been a curious attitude for a monarch who supported the revolutionary policies of his Cardinal minister, but do not most revolutionaries insist that they only wish to reaffirm ancient rights?

One of the greatest problems preventing the royal government from intervention in Germany was the fact that neither the king nor the Cardinal wanted to trust one of the great French noblemen with the command of an army. In the past such armies had been almost as dangerous to the king as to the enemy. The soldiers wore their commander's coat and obeyed his orders; the king was supposed to furnish the money, but he could not be sure of the army's loyalty, especially at a time when so many noblemen felt threatened by royal policies. The fact that the Duke of Montmorency, son of the late constable, could lead his soldiers against the king, supporting Gaston d'Orléan's rebellion, was evidence of the unreliability of troops supposedly in the royal service. Neither Richelieu nor Louis wished to arm another such potential rebellion, and yet without soldiers how could they influence the course of the German War? This question became more and more pressing after 1634: Gustavus Adolphus was dead, a Spanish army joined with the Imperials and had badly defeated the Swedish forces at Nördlingen, and by the Treaty of Prague the king of the Romans (the heir to the Imperial throne) was uniting the Catholic and Protestant princes against Sweden. The new situation might not be as favorable to the Emperor as it seemed to be in 1629, but no one could miss the fact that the Empire would emerge from the Peace of Prague more united than it had been for over a century and that the Swedish army would probably be driven from Germany. Under such conditions, even though they could not trust a French soldier with an army, Louis and Richelieu had to intervene in the war or accept defeat for their anti-Hapsburg policy, and with it a dangerous political position for the kingdom of France. In 1635 Louis XIII declared war on his brother-in-law the king of Spain; the *devôte* party in France had lost its cause.

The military situation following this declaration of war strikingly illustrates the problems of war and politics at this time. An Imperial-Spanish army invaded France, and there were no French forces adequate for any significant response to the threat; indeed it seemed that the enemy would march upon Paris and force the king to flee. But the enemy was also weak; the invading army did not have the strength to take advantage of its opportunities; it could do little beyond raiding expeditions that pillaged the countryside and angered or horrified the French people. These mercenary armies that fought the Thirty Years War in Germany were ponderous machines involving camp followers more numerous than the troops, and a cumbersome supply system. Such armies were a menace to the land through which they passed, for nothing was safe from their depredations, but their slowness reduced their military effectiveness. Richelieu, however, had no alternative to hiring one of these armies. He took Prince Bernard von Saxe-Weimar into the French service; Prince Bernard commanded one of the Swedish armies left in Germany after the death of Gustavus Adolphus. Although he took French money, Bernard's own ambition to acquire the overlordship of Alsace was more important to him than the interests of the French king. As a matter of fact, Richelieu was unquestionably happy when Bernard died for he and Louis XIII also were ambitious to take over Alsace from the Hapsburgs for the Bourbon crown. This was the risk in hiring a mercenary captain: a Mansfield, a Wallenstein, a Bernard von Saxe-Weimar were all landless men who could hope to use their armies as a vehicle for the acquisition of a sovereign territory of their own.

Richelieu, with this hazard in mind, was determined to find some way to disembarrass himself of the dangers inherent in hiring a soldier of fortune to fight his battles. He began the recruitment of a new kind of army, smaller in size than the current condottiere armies, but better trained and better armed. More important even than the fact that it was an army made up of soldiers well trained and armed was Richelieu's intention that it should be controlled by the king's secretary for war. This was the real beginning of the army that was later to make the enemies of the French king tremble; Sublet de Noyers, Richelieu's first minister of war, began the organization of an army that would be loyal to the king. Goaded on by the Cardinal, he struck out boldly to bring order into the anarchic military organization of his day. The ministry had leverage because it was in a position to pay the troops and supply them with food and materials of war, thereby requiring the officers to accept the supervision of the king's intendants who took their orders from the king's council. As we write this, it seems easy to accomplish, for the twentieth century historian lives in an era when bureaucratic controls have been firmly established and few soldiers would dream of rebelling against the orders of the minister of war. But in the seventeenth century it was quite another affair; personal relationships were still more important than impersonal ones, and we find de Noyers and Richelieu securing control by promoting the careers of men related to them by blood or marriage, or at least willing to recognize their debt to them for their promotions. Richelieu gave high command to men who would marry his nieces; even the Prince d'Enghien who later was known as the Great Condé, started his career only after he put aside the lady of his choice and married a misshapen niece of the Cardinal. Seventeenth century government was an affair of the family or "team"; men had not yet learned service to an impersonal state. However, in the new ministry of war, progress was being made in the direction of this modern state.

Neither Louis XIII nor Richelieu lived to see their policies crowned with success. The Cardinal died in December 1643; the king followed him to the tomb some five months later. It almost seemed that Louis XIII recognized that he could not rule without the aid of his formidable minister. Fortunately for his program, a son had been born to the king and queen of France in 1638. After more than two decades of childless marriage, this prince did seem to be the gift of God, Louis *le dieu donné*, and wonder of wonders, two years later a second son Philippe was born to guarantee the succession in the Bourbon line.[2]

When Louis XIII died, his heir was less than five years old; obviously he could not govern. The late king's will provided for a regency government so complex that it probably could not have managed the kingdom, but neither the Prince of Condé nor the Duke of Orléans was willing or able to insist that this testament be carried out. Mazarin, who had quietly stepped into Richelieu's vacant place, was then able to assure the queen that she would be regent without the crippling clauses of her husband's will. This, however, did not necessarily mean that France would have a strong government to carry on the work of Louis XIII; indeed regency governments in France were traditionally weak, traditionally the opportunity for the "great ones" of the land to insist upon their "liberties" and their "rights."

No one knew what sort of a regent Anne of Austria, the queen mother, would be, but the Parlement of Paris was only too happy to set aside the will of its old enemy, Louis XIII, and confer upon her the right to rule for her son. This was as much in conformity with the ancient traditions of the kingdom as it was agreeable to parlementarians who were hopeful that the new regent would recognize their special place in the kingdom. There were many others who hoped for favors from the regent. The doors of the prisons had opened a little when Richelieu died; when Louis XIII was no more they were flung wide open to allow the political prisoners to join the exiles who now flocked back to court demanding revenge against the creatures of the late Cardinal. Anne was expected to be sympathetic. Indeed, until her husband's death she could be counted as one of the enemies of the Cardinal. She had suffered indignities at his hands; her friends had been his enemies. But Anne was the mother of the young king and she also was a Spanish princess who understood her duty to God and to her *gloire*. She was determined to govern the kingdom so that she could give it to her son on his maturity with all the power and prestige that had come

---

[2] Had Louis XIII died without a son, his irresponsible brother Gaston d' Orleans would have become king, but Gaston, in turn, had only daughters, so according to the Salic Law the crown would have gone to the house of Condé as the eldest princes of the blood. It is probable that the crown would have become the prize of a civil war.

to it from his ancestors. In her mind the throne was an entailed inheritance; and God would hold her responsible for maintaining it for her son just as she had received it from her dead husband. The ex-prisoners and former exiles did not understand this; they expected her to place them in the positions of power lately occupied by Richelieu's relatives and friends.

There is a story of questionable truth, which should have happened even if it probably did not, in which Anne while passing a picture of her late enemy, Cardinal Richelieu, whispered softly: "You would be surprised, sir, if you were alive, at the powers that I would bestow upon you." In any case, Anne followed the Cardinal's policies. When she became regent she understood little of the complexities of French politics, but enough to know that there was one man in her entourage who did understand the problems and who probably was the only personally disinterested advisor in the court. This man was Cardinal Mazarin. He was destined to identify his life and his career with the interests of the Bourbon house, and to govern France for almost two decades, more completely than Richelieu had ever done.

His enemies have called Jules Mazarin a Sicilian or a Neapolitan on the assumption that a South Italian is necessarily a shady character, but as a matter of fact he was born and raised in Rome, a member of a respected family serving the papacy. His career led him to a university in Spain as the companion of a Colonna prince, and back to Italy in the service of the Pope. He met Richelieu in 1629 and so impressed the Cardinal that he invited Mazarin to enter the service of the French king. For more than a decade before Richelieu's death, Mazarin travelled about Europe on Richelieu's business. He received the cardinal's hat intended for Père Joseph when the capuchin's death ended Richelieu's plans to make him his successor. On Richelieu's death, without anyone saying anything about it, Mazarin took over the work that the late cardinal had done to help Louis XIII govern the kingdom; the dying king never officially made Mazarin his First Minister, but he did name him godfather of his son and president of the Regency Council provided for in his will. After Louis XIII was dead Mazarin had no commission from the queen regent, but he was the man who knew what was important and how to manage affairs. He assured the queen that he would retire as soon as she found someone to take his place. Anne, however, soon learned that he was indispensable to her.

There is another story in which Richelieu introduced Mazarin to the queen with the bantering, almost insulting, remark: "You will like him, Madame, he has the air of Buckingham about him."[3] To a woman who had been married to Louis XIII for almost thirty years, the "air of Buckingham" must have been a wonderful change. Where her late husband was surly, sickly, suspicious, and unresponsive—indeed almost everything that a woman would not want in a husband—Mazarin was gallant, handsome, kindly, and sage. He knew how to make a woman feel important. He was just Anne's age, he spoke Spanish, he understood the affairs of state, and he understood women. There is little doubt about it; she fell in love with him, and eventually married him.[4] Of course, this relationship did not develop overnight; Anne became dependent on Mazarin as a statesman who could manage the kingdom's business; out of this dependence came the intimate bonds that were to link Anne, the young king and the cardinal into a closely knit family.

The deaths of Richelieu and Louis XIII did not check the onrush of the war in Germany and the Netherlands, but a great French victory at Rocroi (May 19, 1643) that came just at the time of Louis XIII's death did drastically alter the course of that war. The battle of Rocroi introduced a new military personality to Europe, the Prince d'Enghien, who would soon be known as the Great Condé, and presented Europe with the fact that French military power would probably emerge from the conflict in first place among the kingdoms of the continent. Richelieu's new army, as much as the daring genius of the young commander, was in the process of shaping the future. The immediate impact of this victory on the frontier between France and the Spanish Netherlands was a subtle change in the policy of the United Netherlands. The Dutch had depended upon French aid and alliance against Spain almost from the first days of their rebellion against their Spanish rulers, but now

---

[3] When Buckingham visited France a decade before, this handsome Englishman made a strong impression on the Queen and her whole Court.

[4] This is the only conclusion that can be drawn from her letters if one will recognize that Anne's Catholicism would never allow her to live in disorder. Her letters are not those of a queen to a minister, but to a lover—Mazarin's are those of a husband who expects to be obeyed. Mazarin was not a priest so no problem of clerical vows could arise.

they had to ask themselves whether they preferred France or Spain as a neighbor. The answer that a declining Spain would be preferable to a rising France not only affected the course of the war because the Dutch softened their military pressure on the Spanish, but also determined the political decisions that excluded the Franco-Spanish conflict from the negotiations in Westphalia where men made the treaty of peace for Germany. This Dutch conviction that France was a good friend but would be a bad neighbor was an important factor in the high politics of western Europe for the next two generations.

The death of Prince Bernard von Saxe-Weimar freed Richelieu of this dangerous soldier whose personal ambition to become Margrave of Alsace conflicted with the French intention to annex that territory. It also allowed the appointment of a French soldier, the Viscount de Turenne, to command the Weimarian army in Germany. Turenne was a Huguenot and a member of one of the great noble families of the kingdom; he also became one of the great captains of his era. With him in command in Germany and the Prince d'Enghien (Condé) in the Netherlands, the French diplomats at Münster could depend upon the progress of their arms to support their politics. Nonetheless, the negotiations for peace were slow, difficult, and deeply involved. Without an armistice, the negotiations were drawn out for they depended in part upon the military situation both in Germany and in the Netherlands. The diplomats followed the fighting and relaxed or stiffened their demands as the military balances seemed to justify them.

This fact presented a problem: Turenne and Condé could command soldiers and win victories, but only as long as they had money with which to pay their troops; the Swedish armies too, as French allies, were dependent upon a French subsidy. Every statesman has learned that war is fought with money, that the skill and valor of soldiers and the wisdom of diplomats cannot be a substitute for the gold that pays troops and commands the materials of war.

It was this need for money that had upset the plans and programs of sixteenth century rulers, and it continued to be the major difficulty facing princes in the seventeenth century. The simple fact was that the economy of Europe was so primitive, and the amount of money available so small that princes could not depend upon taxes to support their projects. In the seventeenth century this problem was further aggravated by the weather. Any society dependent upon agriculture for its most important economic activity is in trouble when crop failures impoverish the kingdom, and seventeenth-century European men were confronted with more or less severe crop failures every decade from 1620 until well into the eighteenth century.

Nor was this the end of the trouble. Since the government could not, or at least did not, provide the king's subjects with information that would make them sympathetic to his wars, the wealthy as well as the poor who were asked to supply the money to support their prince's projects were often uninterested or even hostile to the involvement in foreign affairs; they could see no reason for raising new taxes for a war quite unrelated to their interests. In this they were probably right, for the policy of the king in the mid-seventeenth century was based more on dynastic interests than on the needs of the people ruled by the king's government. And yet the king's government had no alternate sources of revenue; the war required more taxes, and when the Parlement refused to register edicts raising them, the little Louis XIV had to be taken to Parlement in person to hold a *lit de justice,* that is, to force the Parlement to register the edicts. The first time there was a gentle protest, but with each succeeding imposition, the members of Parlement became bolder and bolder in their objections. The need for money also forced the government to do everything possible to be sure that taxes collected actually did flow into the king's chest. This meant that the collectors and receivers of taxes found themselves under the supervision of officers sent from the king's council into the provinces to supervise the king's business. These intendants of police, justice, and taxation had already aroused hostility among the provincial officials who held their offices as hereditary commissions, but under the duress of these last years of the war in Germany, they became more insistent. Soon there was a wave of protest from the tax officials who did not like to have their work so closely watched. In the seventeenth century the route to private wealth was often found in the collection of the king's taxes.

By 1647 the honeymoon between the regency government and the Parlement of Paris that had started when the latter set aside the late king's will, was definitely over. Equally ominous for the future was the fact that the regency government had also succeeded in alienating the sympathy of a considerable body of royal officials in all parts of the kingdom. This presented real problems, for these people owned their offices and could be removed only if the government were in a position to repurchase them. This, of course, was impossible.

Unhappily for Mazarin there were others who disliked the regency government. At the Cardinal's suggestion, Queen Anne had not taken reprisal against Richelieu's family and creatures, and had not reversed her husband's policies. The first reaction had been the "plot of the Important ones" when the Duc de Beaufort (a member of the bastard line descending from Henry IV) with a clique of noblemen, plotted to murder Mazarin. Unlike her husband, Anne was not cruel; the plotters went to jail rather than to the scaffold, but their fate did not end the hostility to Mazarin. In the eyes of so many important French noblemen it was a scandal that a foreigner, supported by a foreign-born queen, ruled Frenchmen, and became rich in the process. When a bevy of Mazarin's nieces arrived in Paris to share his fortune and to be married to Frenchmen who would serve his policies and support his interests, this hostility increased. These great noblemen were the descendents of the men who had forced Henry IV and later Marie de Medicis to buy their loyalty to the crown; they had seen Richelieu erode their positions and now, after the formidable Cardinal's death, they were in no mood to have his successor complete the task of humbling their order. By 1648, many of these men, like the venal royal officials, were spoiling for a fight with the regency government.

Nor did Mazarin's troubles end with the hostility of enemies of the late Cardinal Richelieu. He was also plagued with the domestic problems that had not been solved—perhaps could not have been solved during the reign of the late Louis XIII. Basically the most serious of these problems arose out of the conditions of French agriculture in the seventeenth century. As we have noted, the agriculture was so primitive that it could not provide any important surpluses beyond the needs of the people who farmed the lands, but equally important was the additional fact that the climate of western Europe during most of the seventeenth century created periodic years in which the harvests were far from normal. This meant that grain prices soared two to four times the "normal" level, and both the peasants whose own lands were not extensive enough to feed their families without outside opportunities and the artisans in the cities and towns who lived very near the margin of existence found themselves facing starvation. Recent studies have clearly shown that the real factor controlling the population was famine or the results of malnutrition during this century that saw the population remain stagnant or even decline. Given this situation when the government tried to increase its tax income after 1630, the tax collector added his bit to the problem created by bad harvests, and the inevitable result was rebellion. During the decades following 1630 peasant rebellions were endemic in the French countryside. It is not important for this study to know whether or not they were supported by the noble or bourgeoisie landowners who saw the king's tax collectors take revenue that should have been channeled into their pockets. The present state of research would indicate that the simple solution of class conflict does not really explain these rebellions, but it made little or no difference to the king's government whether the tax collections were interrupted simply by peasant reaction to the tax or by peasants inspired by their landlords. In either case the king's tax officials were murdered and the revenues badly needed for the army and to subsidize allies, failed to reach the king's treasury. The year 1648 was one of those years when famine stalked the land and made the poor ready for some violent course of action.

At Münster, the treaties of Westphalia were almost ready for final signature, but the government could not be sure of success without further sources of revenue to support its soldiers and allies: new taxes were necessary. But this (1648) was one of those years that came almost every decade during this century in which unfavorable weather and poor transportation drove the cost of bread up to approximately four times the normal price. The poor were destined to die of hunger or of illness resulting from malnutrition. In Paris, tensions mounted with every dispute at the bakeries or food markets; it would be easy to arouse a mob in the manner of past Parisian riots. The problems that led to the crisis of 1648 were more deeply rooted than a simple question of high prices for bread. The French involvement in the Thirty Years' War had been extremely expensive; before actually becoming a belligerent, Richelieu had given subsidies to the kings of Denmark and Sweden as well as to some of the German princes; and after 1636, the French kingdom supported an army in Germany and another in the Netherlands. All this cost money, and that money had to be squeezed from the French taxpayers. The rebellions of the 1630's and 1640's were often enough inspired by noblemen or even royal officials who resented the burdens of taxation that deprived them of income. In some cases the taxes were tripled within a decade; the peasants and townsmen who had to pay this tax could not understand the government's reasons; they saw only the impositions and exactions that threatened their existence. When bad harvests brought an additional problem, there was much material available for rebellion. Members of Parlement and noblemen alike understood how to use the discontent in the country and in the city for their own advantage.

The crisis of 1648 came to a head when the regency government arrested several members of the Parlement. The Parlement of Paris had undertaken on its own account to bring together representatives from the other Sovereign Courts in Paris to reform the government; the meetings in the Chambre Saint Louis were unquestionably revolutionary, but Mazarin and the Queen had to wait until Condé could win a striking victory in the Netherlands (the Battle of Mons) before they dared attempt to curb these revolutionary forces.

The arrests turned out differently than they had expected. The parlementarians posed as "Fathers of the country" as "Roman Senators"; they confused themselves with the Parliament in England that was at the moment in the act of taking over control of that kingdom.

When the Regency arrested leaders of the Parlement, it was easy to transfer the debate from the council chamber to the streets of Paris, and before the government could prevent it, the queen, the boy king, and the whole government found themselves under siege and virtually captive in the city. There was no help for it. Mazarin could not risk upsetting the balances in Europe that might prevent the ratifications of the Treaties of Westphalia, so he had to persuade the queen to pretend to give in to the Parlement and the city by restoring the arrested Parlementarians and accepting the charter being prepared by the Chambre Saint Louis.

This was only the beginning of four years of civil disorders called the *Frondes*[5] (slingshots). There actually were two *Frondes*, the one led by the Parlement, the second by the princes. The two

---

[5] The French like to give familiar names to events. The word *Fronde* comes from the name of a slingshot with which French boys sometimes broke windows.

movements could not actually merge their efforts because they were fighting for such different objectives, and the royal government's victory must be credited to the fact that its opponents were often muddle-headed, usually self-centered, and mutually hostile. Nonetheless, these were difficult years during which the disruptive forces that had played so large a part in the past again threatened to rob the royal authority of its power. The king's government had to lay siege to Paris, and at one time see the city occupied by troops supplied by Spain while the king's armies were shut out of the city. Noblemen, even princes of the blood, held treasonable correspondence with Spain and finally joined their forces with those of the Spanish king. Louis' own uncle and his first cousin were in rebellion, and when he was consecrated king with the holy oils in the great ceremony at Rheims, none of the princes of the blood were in attendance. Mazarin directed the policy of the king's government, but he was twice forced to go into exile—from which he continued to advise Queen Anne in terms that indicated that he expected her to obey him. These were indeed hectic times: years later Louis XIV wrote for his son's education that it was hard to find loyal men during these years; that there was even danger that he would be forced to partition the kingdom between himself and the Prince Condé. But the *Frondes* were defeated. They had no politician the equal of Cardinal Mazarin, and no soldier the equal of Turenne who, after a brief period on the side of the *Frondeurs*, returned to the king's service.

One of the real reasons for the defeat of the *Frondes* was the fact that the rebels lost the support of the majority of politically active Frenchmen. France was loyal to its king, especially to a boy king who could not be blamed for the troubles. But more importantly, the *Frondes* introduced into the kingdom of France the mercenary soldiers who had fought in the preceding Thirty Years War in Germany. They were masters of the art of pillage, robbery, and rape and soon earned for themselves the intense hatred of the French people who had any contact with them. Any government that could assure internal tranquility and freedom from these "pillagers" as they were quite properly called, could be sure of popular support. And lastly, as the *Fronde* played out its role, the slogans of "French Liberties" were revealed for what they really were. Like "German Liberties," "Hungarian Liberties," and other "liberties" of seventeenth century fame, "French Liberties" really meant the rights and privileges of a few great noblemen and hereditary office holders: the aspirations of the new feudal order that was striving to be born. When "French Liberties" also came to mean civil disorder, riots, pillage, arson, and public insecurity, the majority of the people were quite happy to allow the king to exercise power unchecked by these people. This is what was meant by *pouvoir absolu,* power unrestricted by the traditional feudal orders in society; this was the "absolute" power that Mazarin insisted was the prerogative of his king. It did not mean the right of the king to do whatever he wished to do—only the right to rule within the framework of French customs and laws without the interference of the ancient checks upon royal authority imposed by estates and corporations in the kingdom. Once the favorable harvests deprived the rebels of the urban and rural mobs that could be directed against any authority, most articulate Frenchmen were glad to allow the king this *pouvoir absolu.*

The *Frondes* left an indelible mark on both the young king Louis XIV and on France. Louis XIV had seen his mother insulted, his friend and trusted minister exiled, his government forced to roam the countryside while his enemy occupied the city of Paris; he was resolved never to allow such an uprising to occur again. He would curb the ambitions of the Parlement, limiting its action to its traditional functions as a court of law rather than the censor of the king's government. He would also curb the ambitions of those great nobles who wished to build a new feudal order.

The one thing that was absolutely necessary to guarantee the internal tranquility of the kingdom and to secure the victory over the Spanish empire was the development of the royal army. The mercenaries in Germany had proven their unreliability to both sides during the *Frondes;* only an army under the supervision of the king's secretary for war could assure the force needed to assure the authority of the king. The real architect of this royal army which emerged in the years immediately after the *Fronde* was Michel Le Tellier who followed de Noyers as secretary of state for war. He was an able administrator, but even more important, he was absolutely loyal to the king and Mazarin. In the letters that passed between Anne and Mazarin when the latter was in exile, their code name for Le Tellier was "the faithful one." His task was to transform the mercenary armies into forces dependent upon and loyal to the king and subservient to the orders from the king's minister of war. The war office kept its supervision over the soldiers through the extension of the functions of the intendants of the army —civilian officials who acted in many capacities both to inform the minister and to carry out his orders. Le Tellier himself had been such an official under Richelieu and de Noyers; when he became secretary for war he increased their numbers, extended their authority, and supported their impact on the military organization. It was not until later that the secretary for war would also be in a position to give orders to the actual commanders of the king's armies.

In the decade 1654–1664, Le Tellier's ordinances gave organizational form to the new army. These ordinances defined the duties of officers, the organization and regulations for the control of the soldiers in the line, the definition of the king's part in recruitment supply, and other services for the army. Like other effective administrators, Le Tellier would post an ordinance and then after two to four years of experience, he would redefine it and give it more exact form conforming to the actual practice. It is interesting to see how well he worked; for the next century and a half there were changes in the French military organization and in the regulations for the royal army, but the vast majority of them were simply modifications of Le Tellier's original ordinances. He set the pattern for the standing army that lasted until the French Revolution provided a new base for recruitment and organization of military force. This does not say that Le Tellier's army of 1660 was the fighting machine that began the war in 1672, or again in 1688; it was neither as large nor as well equipped and drilled, nor as well supplied and administered, but the characteristic form for these later armies had come into being by 1661, and this form was to influence the military evolution of all Europe before the century was over.

Turenne used this army to win victories over the Spanish even when their armies were commanded by the Prince of Condé, and when the war was over, in recognition for his services, Turenne was given a commission as generalissimo of the armies of the kingdom. This commission is of considerable interest to us for in it we find a concise statement of the *rationale* for the development of the new army:

"We find ourselves obliged, for the conservation of our state as much as for its glory and our reputation to maintain ... in peace as well as in war, a great number of troops, both infantry and cavalry, which will always be ready and in good condition to act to keep our people in the obedience and the respect that they owe us, to insure the peace and tranquillity that we have won . . . and to aid our allies."[6]

Mazarin's last important act was the conclusion of the peace with the Spanish empire. Philip IV was tricked into coming to the peace table by a threat to marry Louis XIV to the princess of Savoy; Philip IV, like his sister Anne, had always assumed that Louis would marry his daughter, Marie Thérèse; indeed almost from the time of their births these two young people had been intended for each other, and Philip was willing to swallow his pride rather than allow Louis to be married to another. While the union did bring peace in 1659, it proved to be an unhappy match, for Marie Thérèse was a dull woman, and in the long run it led to a great war ruinous to France. Nonetheless, in 1659 the Treaty of the Pyrenees was a signal triumph for Mazarin and the Bourbon dynasty. It rounded out the Pyrenees frontier by attaching Roussillon to the French kingdom, and extended the northern frontier of France a bit deeper into the Spanish Netherlands. Perhaps most important of all, the kingdom of France was recognized as the first power in Europe. Mazarin died two years later, having also had a hand in the pacification of the Baltic area by the Treaty of Oliva.

Thus, as we have already seen, the young Louis XIV took over the administration of his kingdom at a time when profound peace prevailed in Europe. The young king placed his confidence in a corps of advisors that he had inherited from Mazarin. Le Tellier was his minister of war; Lionne, who had written important parts of the Treaty of the Pyrenees, became his minister for foreign affairs, and after the king had dismissed Fouquet, who had hopes of taking Mazarin's place as first minister, Colbert, another of Mazarin's creatures, became superintendent of finances and virtually minister of the interior, of the navy, and of commerce. Disgruntled wags in the court who found themselves excluded from power made up wicked stories, wrote scurrilous poems, and told bad jokes about these three men whom Louis XIV used "as God uses secondary

---

[6] *Bib. Nationale,* Recuèil Conge, Salle des Res. 30 (21).

forces to accomplish His will," for, with the occasional exception of Turenne, only these three were invited to join the important deliberations on politics. They met with the king in high council; they kept no notes of their deliberations, they told no one—not even the king's mother—about their decisions.

Since the kingdom was at peace, the programs of the minister of finance and the interior were most important during these first years of the regime. Colbert found the kingdom wallowing in fiscal chaos. The tax collectors did not make complete returns, the taxes were woefully unbalanced in their impact on the people, tariffs were different from one port to another, and the royal debts were overwhelming. Colbert was not a financial innovator, but he was a careful administrator, and he strove to bring order out of the chaos. By a special court he forced tax collectors to disgorge some of their peculations, and to make fuller returns of the money that they collected; he reduced the interest on the royal debts, he introduced new taxes, excise taxes, for they would fall upon the privileged nobles who could avoid direct taxes. He also brought order into the tariff schedules of the kingdom. All this was necessary if the kingdom of France was to keep the momentum that Richelieu and Mazarin had imparted to its course, for without money and systematic administration, there could be no real power at the king's disposal. The bureaucratic state that Le Tellier was creating in the ministry of war had to be supplemented by a bureaucracy capable of gathering in money to support the army.

In another area too, Colbert's advice helped to prepare the kingdom for the role that it was to play in the course of the reign. He wanted his king to be Justinian as well as Augustus, and so he proposed reforms of the laws, the courts, and the police powers. The task of reforming the laws was too great for the resources available, but the writers of the Napoleonic Code almost two centuries later, found their task easier because of the groundwork laid by Louis XIV's commission. In the realm of police action, however, there was greater success. The *Grands Jours*, when itinerant judges backed by soldiers held hearings, were not always successful, for the malefactors often enough drifted out of the district before they could be apprehended, but the central government appointed more officers as intendants of justice, police, and taxation, who took a serious interest in crimes and forced delinquent officials to act.

The kingdom still had murders, kidnappings, robberies, and other acts of violence, but the incidence of these crimes was somewhat checked by police and judicial pressure.

Colbert's reform movements had a stimulating effect upon the kingdom and happy results for the king's treasury, and they greatly facilitated the development of a new *mystique* for the monarchy. Frenchmen had long been loyal to their king: even soldiers defending walled towns against the king's forces at the time of the *Fronde* had shouted "*Vive Le Roi!*" when they learned that the king was in the camp before their fortifications. The king of France was "father of the people"; he was the object of their admiration; he had a sacerdotal as well as a political image in the minds of his subjects. Omar Talon, in criticizing the policies of the regency government at a session of the Parlement, forcefully admitted that "God had given France the king" and that he should be obeyed; he qualified this by saying that the king of France ruled over free men, not over slaves, and that he also had to respect their rights and privileges.

Thus there had long been a *mystique* of royalty in the kingdom, a *mystique* that associated the king with divine intentions and made his person sacred. But in the past those kings who ruled by divine right had associated their family and the great nobles of the kingdom in the enterprise of government, and often enough had been forced to do the bidding of the "great ones" of the land by threats of violence or actual armed rebellion. Louis and his advisors were determined that this should not happen again. There were several measures to prevent it. First the king must have at his disposal a standing military force capable of overawing potential rebels, secondly the king must elevate his status high above those "great ones" or "people of quality" who had traditionally shared his power, and lastly he must impress both his own subjects and Europe with his magnificence. Louis set out to achieve these last two goals through several channels. He brought the great noblemen to court, persuaded them to accept positions of great honor but no power as his household officers, placed them in straitjackets of court etiquette, and reduced even the most important of their number to a common level. Primi Visconti, one of the most astute observers in the French court, could not understand how cardinals who were so important in Rome could find themselves elbowed and jostled in a crowd attempting to see the king. It was a way of bringing the "great ones" under control by placing the king far above all his subjects, even above his brother and cousins who also had Bourbon blood in their veins. It pleased Louis to appoint the heads of noble families descended from neighboring sovereign princely families like that of Lorraine or of Mantua, "first" officers in his household; they were thus given great honor and place in the ranks of "people of quality" but, in effect, reduced to servants of the king's table, stable, or wardrobe. The elaborate rituals regularizing the right of "people of quality" to sit on a folding stool or an armchair rather than to stand in the presence of the king and his immediate family had the same effect: by such measures the *mystique* was established that justified the king's assumption of powers and direction of policies. His *grandeur* underlined his power.

Colbert assured the king that a great king must build magnificent palaces to impress his own subjects as well as his fellow princes. It was the minister's idea that a great king glorifies his capital city, and so he encouraged the construction of a new section to the Louvre. This project caused talent to come from all Europe, particularly from Italy, to build on the scale of a "grand monarch." A few years later the construction of the Chateau at Versailles filled this same objective even more brilliantly and more to Louis' taste, for he hated Paris as the hotbed of erstwhile rebellions. Some writers have missed the point of these constructions: they were not the result of the king's egomania any more than the etiquette came from foolish pride: Louis knew that with the new Louvre, the imposing chateau at Versailles, and this display of wealth, he was setting the king and his government above the unruly forces in the kingdom.

This same *mystique* also set the king of France apart from his fellow monarchs, raising him to the first place in Europe. His elaborate court, his beautiful palaces, his subservient nobility, were a challenge to his neighbors. Louis insisted that his brother, the Duc d' Orléans outranked in importance all the princes in the Empire, but as the Duchesse d' Orléans wrote, her husband's greatness was a sham for he was simply a slave of his brother. This was true, but in being true, it set forth a hierarchy in Europe that seemed to justify the powers of the king of France.

Thus if we are to understand the impact of the regime of Louis XIV upon Europe we must start with the emergence of a new political force in France that came from the work of the two cardinal ministers. The eccentric and potentially rebellious forces in the kingdom were crippled, and the king came to command the soldiers, the finances, and the political machinery needed to govern his heretofore unruly kingdom. At the same time a *mystique* was developed based upon a doctrine of Divine Right and illustrated by the symbols of power that etiquette, architecture, and court life could provide. The France of Louis XIV had sprung into first place among the European powers, a place guaranteed by the treaties of Westphalia and the Pyrenees; there remained only the question: "What would her king do with this power and *grandeur?*"

# Chapter 2

# The Netherlands[7]

Louis XIV inherited from Richelieu and Mazarin a deep concern about his frontiers; in the parlance of the day, they were anxious to secure the "gates" of the kingdom to prevent the foreigner from using them for an invasion, and, also, perhaps, to have them as a point of departure in case the king should wish to invade the lands of a neighbor. Thus we find that no little part of Louis XIV's attention throughout the reign concerned the acquisition of territory that would allow him to bar invasion of the kingdom. In the first years of his personal rule, treaties with Charles II of England and Duke Charles IV of Lorraine secured Dunkirk and Lorraine for France in return for money payments, and, in the case of Lorraine, the integration of the ducal family into the French peerage. Dunkirk was duly transferred to the kingdom, but because of the uncertain character of Duke Charles IV and the opposition of his successor, the status of Lorraine remained in doubt for the next thirty odd years. These treaties closed "gates" that might open the kingdom to English or German invasion, but they were not the ones that caused

---

[7] The Netherlands was formally and legally separated by the treaty of Westphalia into two states: the Spanish Netherlands to the south and the United Provinces, or the Northern Netherlands, to the north. These latter provinces are also referred to as the Dutch Republic. In this account the terms are used interchangeably.

the most concern. The treaties of Westphalia had transferred the Hapsburg rights in Alsace to the king of France, but what were the rights of the Margrave of Alsace? The treaty was purposefully ambiguous, an invitation to a future conflict. There was a league of ten towns in Alsace that claimed to stand immediately under the Emperor; the status of the ecclesiastical holdings were also open to question, and the Free City of Strasbourg was clearly quite separate from the Margrave of Alsace. During his whole career one of the most pressing problems before Louis XIV was the validation of the Treaty of Westphalia through the French interpretation.[8]

Alsace was not all. To the south was Franche-Comté, a Spanish province on the shoulders of the Alps; it also was dangerous to France, or could be under government more effective than it enjoyed under the Spanish rule. This province had long been marked for annexation to the French crown, and the haphazard administration provided by its Spanish governors seemed to indicate that they, too, realized that Franche-Comté would someday become French. But in the 1660's the provinces of the Spanish Netherlands were much more important than Franche-Comté to the French king and his advisors. The Treaty of the Pyrenees had given Louis XIV enough of the border of these provinces to whet his appetite for more. The reason for wishing to acquire them was obvious: the whole French frontier to the north was weak as long as these lands were in foreign hands, and even the ineffectiveness of the Spanish regime after 1659 did not change the fact that this was an exposed frontier, dangerous to the kingdom of France. It was the ancient "invasion route," and it remained the "invasion route" down into the twentieth century. There were other advantages that might accrue to the kingdom by the annexation of these provinces; their potential wealth as an industrial and commercial prize made them doubly attractive.

As early as 1646, Mazarin hoped to negotiate a marriage treaty with the king of Spain by which his eldest daughter, Marie Thérèse, would bring the Spanish Netherlands to the young king of France as her dowry. It proved to be impossible: both Spanish pride and

---

[8] During his entire reign, Louis XIV was deeply concerned with this legacy of the treaties of Westphalia: its vagueness and ambiguities made Alsace a problem for the government of the kingdom. Louis, unlike Mazarin, was unwilling to allow that province to manage its own affairs under a vague overlordship of the king.

the fears of the Dutch Republic blocked the project. The attitude of the Dutch, however, had been the more important factor. The French were allies of the United Netherlands; one would think that they would have been happy to see the French armies annihilate the Spanish at Rocroi (1643), but they were not. That battle warned them that France might someday be their neighbor, and they suddenly realized that they would prefer a weak Spanish dependency on their frontier to a strong France. France could threaten them militarily; and even more important, France in control of these provinces would insist upon the reopening of the Scheldt river and the reentry of the city of Antwerp into the commerce of the high seas. After 1643 the Dutch relaxed their pressure on the Spanish in the Netherlands and even helped the Spanish governor to find the money and materials that he needed to sustain himself against the French. The Dutch were largely responsible for the fact that the Treaties of Westphalia did not end the Hapsburg-Bourbon war.

The attitude of the United Netherlands was understandable if not exactly acceptable to the French. The Netherlands undoubtedly was unhappy at the prospect of a strong military power situated on their southern frontiers, and with every new indication of the strength of France this attitude grew. The Problem of Antwerp was even more important to many Dutchmen. In the fifteenth and early sixteenth centuries Antwerp had been the great commercial center of the Netherlands;[9] its harbor on the Scheldt River and the rich industrial hinterland made it a natural site for a great commercial city. During the war for independence, however, the Dutch succeeded in closing the Scheldt to world commerce and transferred much of the business formerly centered at Antwerp to Amsterdam. Like most seventeenth century economists, the Dutch knew that the only way to improve a country's commercial position was to ruin a rival. Thus when the Treaties of Westphalia were written, the United Netherlands succeeded in maintaining the "happy situation" that allowed it to prevent Antwerp from trading freely with the world. Obviously if Antwerp became part of the kingdom of France, it would be unlikely that the king of France would tolerate such limitations, for Antwerp could become a great port for much

---

[9] Henry Pirenne remarks that in the fifteenth century the Netherlands could be equated with Antwerp; everything else was simply suburbs of Antwerp.

of northern France as well as for Flanders. Small wonder that the
Dutch decided that France was a "good friend," but would be a
"bad neighbor."

Mazarin tried several times to persuade the Dutch to abandon
this attitude. He proposed partition of the Spanish Netherlands between France and the United Provinces or the creation of an "independent canton state" like the Swiss confederation as possible solutions, but the Dutch backed away from any change in the status
quo. When Cromwell's England was punishing the Dutch in the
first Anglo-Dutch war, Mazarin stood aside even though Cromwell's navy gave France good reason for entering the war on the
side of the Dutch; he could see no reason for helping an erstwhile
ally that had become unreasonable. And later when he needed a
fleet to assure the conquest of Dunkirk he turned to the "regicide"
Cromwell who had been responsible for the death of Louis XIV's
own uncle, for he knew that the Dutch would not help his efforts
to conquer the Spanish Netherlands. Again in 1658, when Turenne
was sure that he could sweep the Spanish from these provinces,
Mazarin made peace and a marriage contract with Philip IV without demanding the cession of more than the borderlands between
France and the Spanish Netherlands. He understood that the Dutch
would somehow try to prevent any such event from coming to pass,
and he did not wish to bring the United Provinces to a war with
France. However, one of Mazarin's legacies to his young king was
the suggestion that these provinces should someday come under the
French crown; both Louis XIV and the men who surrounded him
in the first decades of the reign believed that this must somehow
come to pass even though the United Netherlands wished to prevent it.

Twentieth century men sometimes find it difficult to understand how the little United Netherlands could play so large a role
in a world that included the kingdoms of France, England, Spain,
and the Holy Roman Empire of the German nation, but the simple
fact is that these seven little provinces, banded together in a confederation with a cumbersome constitution that baffles the imagination, did play a great role in that world. This state made war on
equal terms with the greatest of kings of the era. The secret of
their greatness is to be found in their economy. Under Burgundian
and later Spanish rule of the fifteenth and the first half of the sixteenth centuries, the merchants of these provinces became impor-

tant, first in the fish trade of Europe, and then as carriers and middlemen in the commerce of the Baltic, the North Sea, the Rhine, and the Atlantic coasts. Dutch merchants went to Portugal and Spain to buy the products of the Orient, Africa, and the Americas, and traded cloth, hardware, leather goods, naval supplies and other items of northern Europe. Antwerp became the center for banking and insurance, as well as for the commerce of much of Europe. When the Dutch revolt broke out, the rebels early seized the islands and held control over the shallow waters of the estuaries of the Rhine, the Scheldt, and the Maas, and they transferred the commerce of Antwerp to the port of Amsterdam which they could keep free from the Spanish soldiers. When they were cut off from American and Oriental goods by orders of the Spanish king, they ranged south first as freebooters or privateers, but finally as merchants rounding the Cape of Good Hope and established themselves in the markets of the Orient. In the first half of the seventeenth century they further consolidated their position by taking over Brazil, territories on the north coast of South America (Guiana), islands of the Caribbean, and a post on the Hudson River (New Amsterdam), as well as extending their Oriental activities from Ceylon and the Indies as far north as Japan. The English and Portuguese were summarily elbowed out of most of the spice trade as well as much of the commerce of India, the Islands, and China.

But it was not simply this world commerce that brought wealth to the merchants of the United Netherlands. With ten to fifteen ships for every one that sailed under the flags of their rivals, the Dutch had control of the carrying trade of northern Europe and after 1648 they got mastery over much of the traffic on the Rhine and the Maas (Meuse). They guaranteed their hold upon these rivers by garrisoning the fortifications along their courses even though the cities were legally the property of other princes. These "intrusions" were necessary to control the flow of commerce and guarantee Dutch safety. Goods from all the markets of the world poured into their warehouses where they were graded, sometimes finished by simple manufacturing processes, and then resold. In this way the Dutch created a remarkable position for themselves. All the European world used them as the middlemen for commerce. England sent to Amsterdam tin, wool, coal, and cloth, often enough assembled for the market by Dutchmen who had migrated to England during the troubled times of the preceding half century;

England bought from Amsterdam wines from France, Portugal and Spain, German arms, Russian furs, Oriental goods, Baltic amber and naval supplies, Swedish iron, and a host of other products. Frenchmen at Bordeaux waited for the Dutch to buy their wine in exchange for goods from Germany, the Orient, and the Baltic; the merchants who arranged the transactions were often enough Dutchmen resident in French ports, and Dutch ships carried the wine back to the Netherlands, where it was cut and graded. As a result of this commercial monopoly, Europe had very little multilateral trade: that is to say Germans did not trade much with Frenchmen, Spaniards with Swedes, or Russians with Englishmen; the Dutch managed, for a nice profit, the trade between other nations. The story of the Russian merchants from Archangel who sent a ship with Russian furs and other goods to Europe only to find that they could not sell their cargo until they returned it to Archangel where the Dutch waited to buy, illustrates the Dutch monopoly; they were able to block the Russians from the market they considered to be their own. So complex a thing as commerce can never be quite as simple as this tale would make it, but the fact remains that the Dutch position as middlemen for the commerce of much of the European world (excluding the Mediterranean where they also traded, but not with the same sweeping effect) was a formidable source of wealth and power.

This commercial stance was further strengthened by the Bank of Amsterdam. In the mid-seventeenth century this bank was the most important financial institution of all Europe. Its paper passed everywhere; any merchant who hoped to do business on a European scale had to have deposits in this bank. A glance at the personnel that controlled its affairs will reveal a striking fact: the same people who sat on the boards that controlled the Dutch East India Company and the Dutch West India Company also ran the bank. A closer look will show that these men were also the "Regents" who controlled the affairs of the commercial towns, who sat in the provincial estates, and in the General Estates that spoke for the Confederation as a whole. These men were interrelated by marriage as well as by their business interests; they formed a commercial and financial oligarchy with great influence over the affairs of their own country as well as over those of Europe as a whole.

And yet these United Netherlands were not free from troubles. In the first place the constitution of the Confederation was a source of much difficulty for it was very hard to find the locus of sovereign power. There was no "Sovereign Prince" in the Netherlands to play the role that the king of France played in the confederation of provinces that made up the kingdom of France, and yet there was a dynasty that wanted to play that role and, in fact, tried to establish itself as hereditary ruler. The House of Orange, a princely family owning the principality of Orange in the Rhone Valley, possessing vast landed holdings in the seven provinces as well as in the German Rhineland, related by marriage to German sovereign princes and the English ruling house of Stuart, had taken an important part in the war for independence, and had been rewarded by hereditary offices in several of the provinces of the Confederation. During the war for independence, republican oligarchs who could not conceive of an army that was commanded by anyone but a prince or at least a very high nobleman, had given the princes of the House of Orange the offices of Captain-General and Stadtholder (governor), and the family had come to consider these positions as near hereditary rights. Moreover, the House of Orange had strong support among the population of the Netherlands. The landed nobility, especially those of the landward provinces, had long regarded service in the army under the House of Orange-Nassau as a normal outlet for the energy and talents of their men, and they tended to accept the princes of Orange as their natural leaders. The mass of the people also regarded the princes of Orange as their protectors. It was the old alliance between the prince and the poor against the class in the middle, in this case the wealthy bourgeoisie—the oligarchy that ruled the warehouses, the counting houses and the ships as well as the town governments. The short-lived Prince William II (1626–1650) well recognized the oligarchs as foes to his progress toward a sovereign status over the land, and gave the leaders of this class a battle cry and a title, the "Loevesteiners" by imprisoning six of them in a castle of that name. But untimely death removed Prince William II from the scene before he was able to establish securely his family's position, and his posthumous son could hardly be expected to take his father's place in the political arena of the 1650's.

The oligarchy made up of the patricians of the towns, merchants, bankers, ship owners, and professional people distrusted the monarchical ambitions of the House of Orange, and yet without a prince to assume executive direction and military control as Stadtholder, it was difficult for the United Provinces to act effectively. Their "High Mightinesses" who sat in the General Estates were simply representatives of the provincial estates, and there was no regularly constituted executive to administer their will. Even so, the regents were not sorry to see the House of Orange unable to act because of the death of William II who had shown a desire for executive power far beyond anything that they wished to grant. With a child as heir to the Orange tradition the oligarchy was in a position to seize control but only if it could find a suitable solution to the problem of organizing the will of the Republic. It had two decades after William's death to try to accomplish this. The "Loevesteiners" who had suffered under the "tyranny of the Prince of Orange" assumed the leadership for the regent class.

Actually the Orange faction was under a double handicap during the years that young William III grew to maturity. His mother was Mary Stuart, the daughter of Charles I of England whose loss of head and throne had resulted in the Commonwealth government in England. She regarded her brother, Charles, as "her king" and thereby made herself and her son objects of suspicion, perhaps even hate, in the eyes of the men who ruled England. Thus was added a powerful foreign enemy to the domestic ones who also disliked the House of Orange. Another fact complicated the situation. Young William's English-born mother and his Dutch grandmother were at odds over the care and education of the boy so that the family could not present a united front in any direction. Had there been an adult male member of the family with the courage to act, the Orangists might have salvaged something from the disaster, but none such existed.

Cromwell suggested that the whole problem could be solved if the two "Calvinist republics" could be merged into a single political unit, but the Dutch politicians were quite unwilling to accept his rule any more than that of the Prince of Orange. The idea was absurd anyway for the provinces of the United Netherlands were only incompletely "united"; it would have taken more political skill than existed in the seventeenth century to unite the Dutch Republic with the English Commonwealth.

There were also many Englishmen who wanted no union with the Dutch; they preferred to find a way to prey upon their commerce. Cromwell's response suited them completely. By the so-called "Navigation Acts" the English forbade the sale in English markets of fish caught by foreigners and denied ships under any but the English flag the right to carry goods between English ports, both metropolitan and colonial. Finally these acts denied foreign ships the right to carry goods originating in a third country into English harbors. These acts were leveled against the Dutch as middlemen, as carriers, as fishermen. They were tantamount to a declaration of war: it was to be the first wholly commercial war in modern times.

This war with England was a disaster for the Dutch. With thousands of ships at sea they were unable to check the predatory English raids nor could they retaliate effectively since the English commerce was so much smaller than their own. Defeat at sea meant that commerce, the lifeblood of the Republic, was choked off. Soon there was unemployment as well as great losses; it was easy to blame the ineffective government for the crisis, and inevitably there was agitation for the appointment of a "Leader" in the model of the erstwhile Princes of Orange, to head the government of the United Netherlands. The House of Orange, however, was in no position to take advantage of this situation, for even had there been an Orange prince to act as Regent for the little William III, the English would never have made peace with his government. The Orange and the Stuart interests were so closely bound together that the men who ruled the English Commonwealth could never have tolerated a prince of Orange as Stadtholder.

At this point the oligarchy found a new leader in the person of Jan de Witt, a young man, pensionary of Dort, who discovered a way to organize power and solve the crisis. As the son of a "Loevesteiner," he was a republican of the regent class with excellent credentials; he was also a very clever man who learned to manage the complex structure of the confederation. De Witt became Councillor-Pensionary of the Estates of Holland (Secretary-General) and permanent leader of the Holland delegation to the General States; in a short time he established his political hegemony over the complex structure, of which Holland was the most important factor, and became, in effect, a "first minister" of the United Netherlands. But he was first and foremost a Hollander, and his power rested on his position in Holland. As a Hollander he found a way to make peace with Cromwell. The Protector wanted guarantees against the Orange-Stuart family, and let it be known that the Dutch Republic could have peace only if it would exclude

the House of Orange from power. This could not be done in the
General States where the landward provinces, with their strong
aristocratic representation, would be able to block such a measure,
but De Witt acted through the Estates of Holland and secured an
Act of Exclusion by which all members of the House of Orange
were forever prevented from becoming Captain General in the
Netherlands. Although these offices were the gift of the General
States, without the consent of Holland, the largest province in the
United Netherlands, it would be impossible for anyone to hold
them. Thus Cromwell was satisfied when "Their Noble Great
Mightinesses," the members of the Estates of Holland, passed this
Act of Exclusion.

In the years following, De Witt made himself the real power
in the United Netherlands[10]; his personal ability and his prestige
among the regents allowed him to direct the policy of the state
in which there was no Stadtholder executive. But there were major
flaws in his position. He did not have a traditional office surrounded
by the aura of divine right; indeed he had no definite explicit constitutional basis for the power that he exercised. This made him
vulnerable to criticism, and opened his actions to charges of un-
constitutionality, especially when he usurped the duties and prerog-
atives that had belonged to the office of Stadtholder.

Even though the House of Orange might be at least temporarily
excluded from power, there were other serious problems that
plagued the United Netherlands during these years. Seventeenth
century men did not think of themselves as united by race, language, or ethnic culture; and even if they had, it would have been
difficult to find the common denominator for the Flemish, German,
and French dialects spoken by the people of these provinces.
Seventeenth century men did, however, regard religion as the
source of common loyalty, for as a French commentator remarked:
"Men who worship at common altars will fight under a common
flag." The Calvinist preachers agreed with this idea, but unhappily
the religious situation in the United Netherlands did not support
their conception of the society. When the war of independence
was fought, there had been a tendency for the Catholic city people
of the north to drift southward, and the Reformed city people of

---

[10] See the excellent article by H. H. Rowen, "John de Witt: The Makeshift
Executive in a *Ständes Staat.*" *Recueils de la société Jean Bodin pour l' historie
comparative des institutions,* XXIV, 439–451.

the southern provinces to move to the north; but no such exodus occurred in the rural villages, particularly not in the northern landward provinces. As a result the Catholic religion was still practiced in many small communities where it had a strong hold on the loyalties of the people. Furthermore, the Treaty of Westphalia had given to the United Netherlands a part of the province of Brabant as a common holding of the seven provinces. The people of this territory, many of them French-speaking Walloons, were strongly attached to the post-Catholic-Reformation church, and were quite unwilling to change. Thus when the Calvinist ministers demanded that all religious practices other than those of the Reformed Church should be banned from the land, they were asking the government to act against a considerable community, and any such action could easily have resulted in forcing the Catholics to look to their coreligionists abroad for support and assistance. Religious intolerance could make men into traitors against their rulers, as it had done in France, England, Hungary, and elsewhere.

Happily for the Catholics, the Reformed community also was not united. While the vociferous ministers probably represented a majority, for they had been able to convert the city artisans and workers, they were not able to check the spread of "heretical" opposition to Calvin's harsh predestinarian teachings, especially among the Regent class where wealth and culture created an atmosphere more or less unsusceptible to the orthodox Calvinism of the Synod of Dort. The result was that the Regents who governed the Netherlands were more tolerant than the preachers who filled its pulpits, and therefore the United Provinces tended to allow more religious freedom than was common elsewhere in Europe. Even a Spinoza could find some protection from both Jewish and Christian intolerance. However, because of the agitation of the preachers, the toleration given the Catholics was so niggardly that the ruling oligarchy could hardly expect much support from them against the Calvinist Orange faction.

There were other problems connected with the religious rigidity of the Calvinist preachers and theologians. Mid-seventeenth century Europe was astir with new ideas about the world and new teachings about epistemology; the earth had begun to spin around the sun, Aristotle's physics was giving way to novel ideas about motion, and the traditional philosophy was challenged by the Cartesians. Just as a Galileo got in trouble with the church conservatives in Italy, so the new science and the new philosophy came to blows with the orthodox Calvinists. In another era the disputes of professors and theologians would not become a problem for politics, but when religion was regarded as the cement for society, such wranglings could have political repercussions. Again the tolerance of the Regents cost them the support of the orthodox and the preachers who could reach the already pro-Orange crowds in the cities. The oligarchy was able to govern until a crisis occurred in 1672. Then the Orange faction took over, De Witt was murdered, and the Stadtholder regime again became the government of the Netherlands.

In 1660, however, the high politics that affected the United Netherlands centered on the triangle formed by Paris, London, and the Hague. Whatever happened in one of these capitals had almost immediate repercussions in the other two. As we have already seen, when the English navy punished the Dutch in the first Anglo-Dutch war, Mazarin did not lift a hand to aid his kingdom's ancient ally; apparently it was his way of repaying them for their refusal to allow France to annex the Spanish Netherlands. Indeed Mazarin even proceeded to ally France with Cromwell, the regicide responsible for the death of Charles I, Louis XIV's own uncle, in order to gain naval control over the Channel and assistance in reducing the Spanish garrisons at Dunkirk and Mardyck. Naturally this policy in no way reduced Dutch opposition; Marzarin had to content himself with the annexation of a string of provinces and counties along the Netherlands frontier, leaving the bulk of the Spanish Netherlands with the king of Spain. There seemed to be no way to persuade the Dutch that the kingdom of France would make a good neighbor.

The Stuart Restoration in England, in 1660, created a new situation. Charles II, restored to the throne in England without the aid of any outside power, called his sister, Mary, to join him in England where she almost immediately died of smallpox. This left her son, the young Prince of Orange, to be educated in the Netherlands, where his presence was a constant threat to the Regents even though the Act of Exclusion deprived him of political or military office. Charles II, however, obviously wanted to do nothing that might endanger his throne either domestically or in the area of foreign affairs, so he acted as if he did not know of Prince William's existence. This attitude encouraged De Witt to hope that he could neutralize any potential English support of the Orange faction by an agreement with England. In 1661, he proposed a triple alliance of England, France and the United Netherlands to assure the peace of Europe. The proposal was popular neither in England nor in the United Netherlands; at this point merchants of these two states were in fierce competition, and there were many in the Netherlands who could not forget that Prince William was Charles' nephew. The most that could be accomplished was a simple reaffirmation of the treaty that had ended the recent Anglo-Dutch war.

In the meantime the kingdoms of France and England established a number of subtle ties. Charles II, the son of a French princess and a long-time exile in the kingdom, was pro-French and pro-Catholic, but he was also a politician and realized that he must move cautiously. He married his sister to Phillippe d'Orleans, Louis XIV's brother, and he himself married a Portuguese princess who brought a handsome dowry to the kingdom. French diplomacy had much to do with this marriage, for Louis, forbidden by the Treaty of the Pyrenees from intervention in the Spanish-Portuguese war, wished to use England as a front for his assistance to the Portuguese in their struggle for independence. Furthermore, since Louis did not want England to drift into an alliance with either the Netherlands or Spain, this Portuguese involvement seemed to be just the thing to accomplish his objective.[11]

The more or less hostile Dutch relations with England seemed to be an assurance that France would not be confronted by an Anglo-Dutch alliance. The problem was simple enough: the merchant classes in England were bent upon undermining the Dutch commercial supremacy; like Colbert, they talked about waging a commercial war that would ruin their rivals; there were other Englishmen not adverse to the use of hot war for this purpose. Perhaps

---

[11] The Portuguese rebellion against Philip IV broke out at almost exactly the same time that the Catalan provinces of the Crown of Aragon also rose in revolt (1640). The Spanish, at war with France and the United Netherlands, and deeply involved in the war in Germany, were unable to act effectively against Portugal where a native dynasty mounted the throne and assumed control over the kingdom and its overseas empire. Naturally the French had a vital interest in the rebellion, for the separation of the crowns of Spain and Portugal assured the continued weakness of the Spanish crown. French money and diplomatic support continued to pour into Portugal even though this was expressly forbidden by the treaty of the Pyrenees. The king masked his assistance by having Turenne act for him.

inspired by Cromwell's wars and by the traditions of the Sea Dogs of the century before, they were spoiling for a fight that would allow their predatory ambitions to attack Dutch commerce directly. With their thousands of merchant ships on the seas, the Dutch were a likely candidate for the role played by Spain in Elizabeth's time. There were a number of points on the globe where Anglo-Dutch interests clashed: for more than fifty years Anglo-Dutch conflicts in the Far East had made for bad blood between merchants of the two states; in the Hudson River basin in North America the Dutch colony of New Amsterdam was a thorn in the side of the English, because it was the base for smugglers who made tatters of the Navigation Acts and because it had been founded in defiance of English claims to the whole coast. In Brazil where the Dutch had secured commercial equality with the English as a price of peace with Portugal in 1661, Anglo-Dutch merchants fought each other. Even more strained relations existed on the west African coast where English and Dutch slave traders competed at Gorée and Gambia for the commerce in human flesh. The Dutch could not miss the signs; the commercial war could easily change into another hot war with England.

Indeed, the Dutch decided that their safety demanded a defensive alliance with France. The French ambassador at The Hague suggested that there would be no trouble if they would only give up their absurd objections to French pretensions in the Spanish Netherlands. De Witt and his friends could not do this, but nonetheless they had hopes for an agreement with France since there was at the moment no question of French annexation of these provinces. The Dutch mission that arrived in Paris (1661) bubbled with expressions of friendship and assurance of Dutch goodwill; they were sure that the French would wish to renew the treaty of alliance and friendship that had been so profitable to both parties in the past. They would not, however, give any assurance of Dutch willingness to see any drastic change in the status of the Spanish Netherlands. The French had many second thoughts, but in the end Louis authorized Colbert, Lionne, and Le Tellier to negotiate a treaty of alliance that would mutually guarantee each other's possessions as well as the freedom to fish on the high seas. This treaty came in April of 1662; in October the French signed the treaty with England that transferred Dunkirk to France in return for a huge money payment. The Dutch were not pleased to see this channel port slip into the hands of the French king, but they did agree that the treaty of alliance would guarantee this port just as it did the rest of the kingdom of France.

Perhaps stimulated by French acquisition of Dunkirk, De Witt seems to have come to the conclusion that it would be almost impossible to halt the forward thrust of France, and so the better policy would be to come to an agreement with Louis XIV over the future of the Spanish Netherlands. He discussed the problem with the French ambassador, using the formulas that Mazarin had suggested a decade or so before: partition, cantonment on the Swiss model, and a Catholic Netherlands republic. But at every point he had trouble because his fellow Dutch statesmen really did not want France for a neighbor, and the Amsterdamers did not want Antwerp open to world commerce either as a French or as a Dutch port. For his part, Louis XIV had discovered a traditional law in several of the provinces under question that could be used to base a Bourbon claim to part of the Spanish Netherlands as soon as Marie Thérèse's father would die, and of course, if the sole surviving son of Philip IV, a sickly baby boy, should follow his father, then there would be a rightful claim upon the whole territory. He seems to have decided that it would be best for the kingdom to wait; thus in 1664 Louis broke off negotiations to "keep his freedom of action". In early 1664 it was clear that England and the United Provinces would probably soon be at war, thus providing Louis an even freer hand in the high policies of Europe.

The English acted first. In the early summer of 1664 Charles transferred to his brother, the Duke of York (the future James II), all the territory between the Connecticut and Delaware Rivers, and issued a royal writ against the Dutch interlopers who had "unlawfully and to the great damage and inconvenience of His Majesty's good subjects, taken possession of rivers and lands within our territory". Late in August an English fleet appeared before New Amsterdam and demanded the surrender of the settlement. An act of capitulation was signed on September 4. Before the end of the year, Anglo-Dutch squadrons also clashed off the coast of West Africa and in the Antilles. By the early months of 1665 the conflict reached the Channel and the North Sea when English vessels began raiding Dutch commerce. As in the preceding decade both countries were psychologically ready for war, but this time, with De Witt to direct the Dutch effort, the Republic's navy accounted for itself better than it had in the war against Cromwell when there had been no effective central organization.

The war was embarrassing to the French. Their Dutch allies immediately clamored for assistance against the English "tyrants", but since Charles II had as much as given Louis a free hand in the Spanish Netherlands, it was a little difficult to break with him to aid the Dutch whose hostility to France's "legitimate pretensions" was long known and deeply seated. Louis first sent his uncle to try to mediate; when the Bishop of Münster, allied to England, invaded the United Provinces from the east, Louis sent a small expedition to drive him out, but he hesitated to declare war. Then on September 17, 1665, Philip IV died leaving his sickly son as his universal heir, and his testament provided, in case of his death, that the children of his second daughter, Marguerite Theresa, were to inherit all of his crowns. Marie Thérèse, his eldest daughter and wife of Louis XIV, was explicitly disinherited. As for the Spanish Netherlands, the testament announced that they were henceforth inseparably bound to the crown of Spain. All this, of course, affected the king of France. As Louis wrote in his Mémoires for the education of his son, he now had the opportunity to fight two wars: one with the English in support of an ally, the other with the Spanish in defense of his wife's just pretensions to her inheritance. He explained that he decided to fight the former to validate his "pledged word", but the truth of the matter was that this war would be a perfect excuse to build the military forces necessary to support his wife's and his son's pretensions to the Spanish Netherlands.

Louis did declare war on his English cousin, but French military action in support of the Dutch was somewhat limited, even if it was not as little as the Dutch have claimed. Louis forced the bishop of Münster to withdraw, and he ordered his navy in the Mediterranean to the Atlantic to support the Dutch fleet. Although it got there too late to have a significant part in the fighting, the French did lose a few ships. The really important actions, however, were the preparations that the French made to build a fine army, and to assemble masses of supplies for the invasion of the Spanish Netherlands.

Since Charles II, the child king of Spain, still lived, it was not a question of the entire Spanish inheritance, but the French lawyers had discovered that in certain provinces of the Spanish Netherlands, the eldest girl from the first bed had the right to part of her father's inheritance even though there was a son from a second marriage. On the basis of this Law of Devolution, the French drew up an elaborate statement of the rights of Marie Thérèse to certain territories in these provinces, and, translated into several languages, they presented it to Europe as well as Spain. The regency government in Madrid refused to listen to any such arguments.

In the meantime, the Anglo-Dutch war was a costly enterprise for both belligerents; the Dutch with larger commercial stakes suffered the most, but in England two disasters unconnected with the war caused enormous suffering that distracted the war effort. There was a terrible visitation of the bubonic plague, the worst in the century, that heavily struck the city of London. Thousands were dead, and many more were demoralized. Then in the summer of 1666 as the Plague burned itself out, a fire near the London Bridge got out of hand and strong winds drove it through the city. For four days Londoners saw their homes, their warehouses, their shops, their churches become a roaring inferno of flames. More than 13,000 houses were destroyed; their value ran into the millions. Tens of thousands were homeless; no one had insurance. Superstitious men claimed that God was punishing England for the crimes of the recent revolutionary government; as Huxley explained two centuries later, only a few understood that control of rats and better firefighting equipment could have prevented these two tragic catastrophies.

The course of the war, as well as these disasters, made the English willing to talk peace. This war had not gone like the earlier one. With De Witt directing the Dutch effort, and the Dutch navies better prepared to protect commerce, there had not been the rich prizes, the booty, that would make up for the losses that English commerce suffered from Dutch privateers and the Dutch navies.[12] The Dutch, whose commerce also was adversely affected by the war, were also anxious for peace.

---

[12] The Dutch navy was not all under one central navy office; each of the seaside provinces had its own: they did cooperate with each other, but not always.

Early in 1667, peace conversations started at Breda, but since neither side was willing to call for an end of military action, this peace move was halting and slow.

In the meantime French preparations for intervention on behalf of the Queen's rights were being completed, and early in the spring of 1667 Louis was ready to act. On May 10th Turenne took command of the army on the Netherlands frontier; ten days later Louis XIV arrived to join his marshal as an "apprentice in the art of war", and the next day the French forces crossed the frontier to assure the "just rights" of the queen. It was not a war: Turenne had a splendid army of some 50,000 men; the Spanish may have had 20,000, but their quality was poor, their supplies lacking, and their morale bad. The only thing that slowed up the French advance was the problem of bringing up siege materials and supplies. Spanish governors would not surrender until the French were in a position to begin the siege; this took time, for the roads were poor and it was difficult to bring up the heavy equipment. But as soon as the besieging army was ready to open its fire, the fortifications usually surrendered without further delay. It is small wonder that the young apprentice Louis XIV got a wrong idea about war.

There was a wave of emotion in the Netherlands as news arrived of the progress of the French army. The war with England was dragging on in spite of the peace negotiations at Breda, and thus prevented any move to check the French advance. In a desperate effort to end the war, the Dutch navy appeared off the Thames estuary (June 1667), broke through the boom that guarded the harbor, and burned docks and warehouses on the river and four English warships that were tied up to the docks; they towed away two others including the *Royal Charles*. It was a great victory that could have caused the English to break off negotiations, but did not: on July 31, 1667, the English and Dutch plenipotentiaries signed the treaty of Breda that brought peace by mutual disengagement. The English decision to end the war rather than to seek revenge for the Dutch attack on London came in part because there were men in England who were more apprehensive of the French king than of the Dutch.

As his armies advanced into the Spanish Netherlands, Louis XIV sought to allay the fears of his neighbors by the calm announcement that his objectives were strictly limited to the "just pretensions" of his wife, the queen. He sought not the whole of the Spanish Netherlands, but only that part that rightfully belonged to his family. He was even more reasonable: he would be willing to accept the territories in the north that rightfully belonged to Marie Thérèse or equivalent territories elsewhere, perhaps Luxembourg or Franche-Comté.

The Spanish governor at Brussels could refuse to consider any such proposals, but he also could do little or nothing to check the march of the French armies. Obviously if France were to be stopped, the force would have to come from England or the Netherlands or both. De Witt's first impulse was to accept the French assurance of limited objectives at face value, and seek to secure an immediate solution to the war that would leave the Spanish in control of most of the lands that the Dutch were beginning to call a "barrier" between themselves and France. Charles II had mixed responses. His ego was still chafed raw by his loss of face in the recent war, and he hoped to get something out of the troubled waters. Should he join France against the Spanish and demand Ostend as his share, or would it be better to join Spain against France and ask for Ostend as compensation for his war services? As the rising tide of anti-French feeling in England became more and more articulate, he came to agree with those of his advisors who counseled cooperation with the Dutch to check the progress of France. Thus after the Treaty of Breda ended the Anglo-Dutch conflict, Sir William Temple approached De Witt with the suggestion of an alliance. The Dutchman, anxious not to lose the advantages of his alliance with France, was at first cautious, but then he realized that, under proper conditions, he could both check Louis XIV and retain him as an ally.

The agreement that ensued should be seen as the first of a series of anti-French coalitions that plagued the ambitions of the "Sun King". Sir William Temple and De Witt carefully cloaked this agreement as an offer to mediate rather than as an alliance aimed at balking the French "pretensions". They accepted Louis' candid offer at face value, and persuaded the regency government in Sweden (by bribes) to join them in tendering mediation on Louis' terms between France and Spain. But secretly the three powers formed a Triple Alliance by which they agreed to limit Louis to those gains by force of arms if necessary. When the French learned of this part of the agreement a little later, they were furious at what seemed to be pure treachery on the part of their Dutch allies. However, the proposed mediation and the treaty were negotiated in such secrecy that the French were actually unaware that anything was happening before the allies offered to put pressure upon Spain to force acceptance of the French king's demands.

The Spanish still hesitated. What should be the French reply? Mazarin had often warned against allowing the formation of a coalition against the kingdom; so, in spite of the opinion of soldiers that the whole of the Spanish Netherlands could easily be overrun before any aid could be assembled, the king decided upon another gambit. In the mid-winter of 1668, the Prince of Condé, "commanding under the orders of the king", invaded Franche-Comté and quickly subdued the whole province. Louis then agreed to negotiate with Spain as soon as the Triple Alliance could force the regency government in Madrid to accept his conditions. Was this a brilliant coup for De Witt in that he had persuaded the king of France to restrict his ambitions to his stated objectives, or was it a coup for Louis, for by occupying Franche-Comté, the French were in an excellent position to negotiate? The future would answer this question. At the moment, however, there were too many men in the Netherlands who hailed the act as a Dutch victory over France. It was a victory that they came to regret.

The Treaty of Aix-La-Chapelle (1668) that followed is instructive and important. The Spanish decided not to give up Franche-Comté because they thought it better to let Louis' conquests bring the French frontier nearer to the United Netherlands. Thus they surrendered Bergues, Courtrai, Oudenarde, Tournai, Charleroi, Ath, and Lille to satisfy the "just pretensions of the French queen". The French armies were in fact in possession of all these territories and more, but they in no way constituted a "frontier" in the modern sense of the term. Several of them were enclaves in the Spanish territory; a number of Spanish fortresses became near enclaves in the French lands. By no stretch of the imagination could this settlement become a permanent one in a world that was beginning to think in terms of states' interest rather than dynastic inheritance. De Witt, however, celebrated the treaty as a great diplomatic triumph; the United Netherlands had "reconciled kings", brought about a "glorious peace", and "established order in Europe." Unhappily by this same act, he convinced the court of the king of France that only by the destruction of the wealth and power of the

United Netherlands could the French king hope to achieve his "legitimate pretensions" in the Spanish Netherlands. Even before the peace was signed, French diplomacy began the process of isolating "the ungrateful Republic of herring merchants".

The political grievance against the Dutch was only one of the reasons for French antagonism. In one of his memos for the king, Colbert wrote that the commerce of the world was carried in about 20,000 ships of which some 15,000 to 16,000 were Dutch and only 500 to 600 French. He urged that the king employ all means possible "to get a bit closer to the natural number of ships that his subjects should have". In another note he remarks that Louis XIV "has undertaken a war of money against the states of Europe. He has already conquered Spain, Italy, Germany, England, and some of the others, in which he has caused great misery and want. . . . Only Holland is left, and it fights with great resources. . . ." Colbert's attitude and his measures to find relief were of a kind with Cromwell's war and the "Navigation Acts". The Dutch wealth aroused envy and predatory ambitions in the hearts of neighbors. The young king as well as his minister understood that a "war of money" might be a slow way to reduce an enemy; a hot war could accomplish the same results much more quickly. As Louis considered the ingratitude of his late allies, his anger grew and other good reasons for hating them came to the fore. They were republicans whose regime was based upon a rebellion against a legitimate sovereign who, by the way, had been Louis' great-grandfather; they were heretics who interfered with the practice of the Roman Catholic religion in their lands while Calvinists in France were allowed to worship God as they wished; they were people whose forefathers had been ruled by Louis' own ancestors; they were grubby merchants and bankers with no idea of honor. All this, added to the problems of the Spanish Netherlands and perhaps joined by the vision of a successful war led by himself, encouraged the French king to prepare for war against the Dutch.

At the time French diplomacy seemed to be successful. The treaty with the Emperor was indeed a triumph. By agreeing to a partition of the Spanish inheritance should Charles II die without heirs, Leopold tacitly recognized that both the renunciation clause in the Treaty of the Pyrenees and Philip IV's testament disinheriting Marie Thérèse were invalid. Leopold also agreed not to give any assistance to the Dutch "heretics" in case the king of France might find it necessary to go to war against them. While the Emperor could be bought by an agreement for peaceable division of the Spanish inheritance, the more important German princes required only money to assure their neutrality or, in several cases, their active assistance in the coming war. The French position in Germany had deteriorated considerably since the days of Mazarin's League of the Rhine, but impecunious princes could not resist French subsidies. Some of them, like the Elector of Cologne, even had reasons of their own to wish ill for the United Netherlands. The Dutch were heretics, but worse than that they had "intruded" into many of the cities of the Rhine by establishing garrisons to defend their interests. The city of Maestricht was an excellent example of this; it belonged to the Elector of Cologne, but the Dutch had intruded a garrison and created of the city one of the strongest fortifications of Europe to assure their control over the Maas. The Elector of Cologne was willing for the French to store war supplies in his lands and to use his territory, the Archbishopric of Liège, as a highway; he was not so happy the next year to hear that the French would rid his territory of the Dutch but only to establish themselves at Maestricht. However in 1672 he was pleased to be a partner in an enterprise that would humble the United Netherlands.

The most important *coup* for French diplomacy was the detachment of England from the Triple Alliance. Charles II was never entirely satisfied to be the ally of the Dutch against his cousin; he, like a goodly number of his subjects, disliked the Dutch Regents who hampered English commerce and excluded Charles' own nephew from the traditional offices controlled by the House of Orange. Unlike his brother and sister, Charles was not a devout Roman Catholic, but he did lean toward Catholicism; he employed Catholic ministers (until the Test Act prohibited it), and preferred his Catholic cousin to the Calvinist republicans in the United Netherlands. The Dutch Republic looked too much like Cromwell's regime to make it really popular in the Stuart family. Furthermore, Charles needed money; that is to say he had to find sources of money if he were not to go to his Parliament and exchange power for subsidies. All this played into Louis' hands. At this point in his career Louis XIV believed that he could buy anything with money: a German prince, the king of Poland, the Hungarian malcontents, the king of England—they were all the same in that they needed money and had a venal attitude toward their policy. Louis' belief is a fatuous idea shared by many politicians since his time, but in 1670–72 it actually *was* possible to buy the king of England, even if he was unable to stay *bought* as long as Louis wished.

The negotiations were kept secret from most of Charles' own ministers. Louis wanted England both to assist in a war against the Dutch and to restore public profession of the Catholic religion in the kingdom just as the Calvinists were allowed to practice their religion in France. For this the king of France was willing to pay a huge subsidy. The negotiations went slowly, but they were finally concluded when Louis sent his sister-in-law, the Duchess of Orleans, across the Channel to conclude the agreement with her brother. The Treaty of Dover provided for combined Anglo-French military action against the United Provinces and a secret clause by which Charles agreed to reinstate Catholic worship in England as soon as possible. Louis also promised a French subsidy that would free Charles from dependence upon his Parliament. The treaty was signed in June, 1670 and envisaged an immediate assault upon the Dutch; but the war could not get under way until the spring of 1672 because other French agreements could not be quickly concluded.

De Witt and his colleagues saw the French preparations for war and yet they seemed to be unable to defend themselves. Unaware that French money had corrupted the other two members of the recent Triple Alliance, they still believed that somehow a diplomatic agreement between themselves and France could be reached. On the other hand they could not miss the fact that the French king was assembling an army more numerous and better trained than any Europe had seen since Roman times. De Witt did everything that he could to try to turn aside the approaching avalanche, but there was no hope for it. The French ambassador at The Hague, fully in the King's confidence, blandly met De Witt's arguments, allowed him to protest the Dutch desire for peace, and quietly prepared for war. When it came, the Dutch were quite unready to meet the onrush of the French army.

The first campaign of the so-called Dutch War is interesting from several angles. In the first place, this was the "return of the Roman legions" to the soil of Europe; for this was an army well-drilled, well-equipped, and well-commanded under the direction of the king and his ministry of war. The army that invaded the Rhineland was the masterpiece of the Le Telliers; Louvois and his father had prepared a formidable, apparently invincible, military machine. It was commanded by the king, but Marshal Turenne and the Prince of Condé "commanded under Louis XIV's orders", and the rest of the marshals of France were required to obey Turenne's orders. When three of them refused on the grounds that a marshal of France obeyed only the king, they were summarily relieved of their commands. This was the first indication that the Ministry of War intended to end the anarchic military practices of the preceding period in which soldiers acted more or less as free and independent agents. This army was also supplied more effectively than any army had been up to that time. Louvois had established depots of food and military supplies of all kinds, some purchased from the Dutch themselves, at points on the river from Philippsburg to Cologne. In his *Mémoires* Louis XIV remarks that a battle could be lost by the chances of the field without bringing dishonor to the commander, but if the battle were lost because the army lacked supplies, the commander was to blame. The Le Telliers, father and son, saw to it that this army was prepared.

On the other hand, its high command (Turenne and Condé) was still obsessed with the military practices of the preceding epoch. The marshals of France of 1672 were all men who had won their batons in the war against the Hapsburgs (1635–1658). In this war against the Dutch they were committed to an aggressive action that required what later generations would call a *blitzkrieg*, but they could not conceive of a campaign such as a Eugene, a Marlborough, or a Villars would later direct under such conditions. They *had* to subdue every little fortification on the line of their march, and even though Louis XIV seemed to "direct four sieges at a time," there were dozens of these fortifications to be captured, and the process considerably slowed up the army's progress. Even more important than this, Louis' great marshals overlooked both the psychological aspects of the war and the possible physical defenses at the disposal of the enemy. They assumed that the Dutch were "reasonable men," and reasonable men, defeated as the Dutch were, would surely surrender. But the terms that the French offered were so harsh, so brutal, that they could be accepted only by a people utterly defeated and occupied. Unhappily for the French and luckily for the Dutch, this last condition could not prevail, for the French commanders overlooked the possibility that the Dutch would flood the land and isolate most of Holland, including Am-

sterdam, behind a water barrier. French troops had actually been
in position to control the sluices that let in the sea, but, ignorant of
their importance, they had failed to guard them. Later generations,
looking at the victories that Turenne and the Grand Condé had
won in the 1640s and 1650s in their early careers, too often have
assumed that these great soldiers served Louis XIV as effectively
in their last years as they undoubtedly did earlier.

It must be admitted that by the early summer of 1672 the Dutch
position was desperate. French soldiers were overrunning the land,
and the Anglo-French naval forces controlled the North Sea and the
Channel. It almost seemed that Louis was right when he assumed
that reasonable men, under such conditions, would surrender. Indeed they were ready to make great concessions for peace. They
would have ceded the lands of Brabant held in common by the
seven provinces, the fortifications into which they had "intruded"
on the Rhine and the Maas, including Maestricht, paid a huge war
indemnity, and surrendered considerable commercial advantages
in the French markets. Had Louis accepted these terms, the Spanish Netherlands would have been a ripe plum with no power able
to prevent his plucking it. But the French were bent upon destroying the very basis for Dutch wealth and power. Their terms were
so harsh that they could be accepted only as a last possible alternative to complete annihilation. When the French failed to prevent
the flooding of the land, these terms and, indeed, the terms that
the Dutch were willing to offer, were no longer possible. However
small it might be, the Dutch had a breathing space; they could
wait to see if their neighbors and France's neighbors would be willing to see the United Republic destroyed and the kingdom of
France so enormously enlarged.

There was a revolution in the unoccupied part of the Netherlands
that placed Prince William III in power. The De Witt brothers
were brutally murdered, and the regents in the several Estates
shifted about so that the Orange faction could control the government both in Holland and in the General Estates. The new government then sent up signals for help to the Germanies, Spain, and
even England, where they hoped that William's Stuart blood would
be able to counteract French influence. When an English embassy
passed through The Hague on its way to discuss possible peace, it
was hailed on the streets as an ally rather than as the enemy that
it, in fact, still was.

The Dutch resistance was further stiffened when the French con-temptuously released the prisoners of war that they had captured because they no longer feared their enemies and did not want to feed them. These soldiers were soon rearmed and enrolled under the banner of the young Stadtholder-Captain General. Then the governor of the Spanish Netherlands, who well understood that his lands were the real target of the French armies, sent Prince William several detachments of troops asserting that he owed them as the result of an earlier treaty of mutual assistance. In Germany both the Emperor and the Elector of Brandenberg made movements that seemed about to bring relief, and in England where part of the political establishment still wished to destroy the Netherlands as a commercial competitor, another part began to reconsider its attitude toward France. William III was quite unable to drive the foes from the land nor was he able to mount an offensive to threaten their communications, but conversely the French could not pass the water barrier and everyday their position, far from the French frontier, became more and more uncomfortable. Louis XIV, recognizing that the war would not end as quickly as he had hoped, returned to France leaving his army to await the frost that would allow it to cross the water barrier. But in the winter of 1672–73 the water did not freeze, and the French were as far away from Am-sterdam as ever. They had to find some response. The unhappy one made by the French army was to devastate large areas of the Netherlands, to destroy whole towns and burn villages so that they not only stiffened Dutch resistance to these "barbarians," but also created a legacy of hatred for things French that long outlasted the reign of Louis XIV.

In the spring of 1673 the changed military situation required a regrouping of the French armies. One army under Turenne con-tinued to occupy the Netherlands, but it also had to present a de-fensive stance toward Germany where the Elector of Brandenburg and other north German princes were making threatening move-ments. Another large detachment was established in the Spanish Netherlands to watch the Spanish armies and prevent any invasion of the frontiers of France from the north. This left a third force of about 30,000 men for an adventurous project, and yet it was only strong enough to undertake a limited objective. The target selected was Maestricht, the most important Dutch controlled fortress on the Maas (Meuse) River and one of the strongest fortified places in all Europe. As we have noted, the city legally belonged to the Elector of Cologne, but the Dutch had "intruded" to establish a control over the traffic on the river, and defense for their exposed southeastern frontier.

Louis XIV announced that he would command the army in person. This meant, in effect, that Vauban commanded the organization of the siege. By 1673 this young engineer, who had been recruited into the Le Tellier–Louvois service, had attracted the attention of the king both for his defensive plans and his ability to organize a siege. Vauban at this time was only an engineer; he had not yet become even a lieutenant-general, and his marshal's baton was far in the future. The "great soldiers" of the period did not consider an engineer even to be a soldier, and, were one of the marshals of France in command of the siege, Vauban would not have been able to direct the action. But with the king in command, Vauban's orders became the king's orders and they were obeyed.[13] Louis' confidence was well placed. Maestricht may have been the most powerful fortification in Europe, but it took only thirteen days after he drew his lines for Vauban to conquer it. There was no possibility that the Prince of Orange could get effective help from Germany or from Spain even to check the progress of the siege, let alone to raise it. The very effectiveness of Vauban's assault, however, probably determined the fate of the French army in the Netherlands; for the rapid reduction of this fortification was almost as striking a proclamation of French power as the invasion of the Netherlands had been the previous year; and European princes had now to ask themselves whether or not they wished to live under the aegis of the French king. If not, there was no alternative to the formation of a strong coalition to resist. If the so-called Triple Alliance of 1668 was the "first coalition," the year 1673 saw the beginnings of the second; for Europe could not otherwise meet the threat of a French hegemony. Prince William was right in hoping that Europe would rally to the defense of the Dutch.

Thus the fall and early winter of 1673 saw great diplomatic ac-

---

[13] There are two documents in the Archives of the Ministry of War that give us great insight into Vauban's influence on the king. The one is an autographed letter from Louis XIV to the Duke of Burgundy, his grandson, in which he tells the young man how he should treat Vauban (who was about to capture Brisack for the prince); the other is a memo in the king's handwriting in which he explains what is necessary for a successful siege of Maestricht. Both show that Louis learned his lesson well.

tivity that resulted in the founding of a "Grand Alliance" against Louis XIV. The Emperor, many of the German princes, and the king of Spain joined the United Netherlands, and there was strong pressure on Charles II to withdraw from the war. The formidable alliance structure which Louis had built by 1672 was beginning to crumble; in 1674 Cologne, Münster, and England had withdrawn leaving Sweden as Louis' sole reliable ally; and Sweden soon proved to be much less useful than the French had hoped. The coalition against France, however, was also relatively weak. The United Netherlands was still occupied (1673–74) by French soldiers, and Spain had long been revealed as a hollow giant, gradually losing all its real strength. Emperor Leopold had not yet developed either the imperial power of the Holy Roman Empire of the German nation, nor his own strength as ruler of the provinces and kingdoms that were to become the Danubian Monarchy. He was still obsessed with the idea that God no longer protected the Hapsburgs, and was harassed in his Hungarian realm by malcontents who received aid from both France and the Ottoman Empire. Of the German princes who joined him in the alliance, only the Elector of Brandenburg had yet created an army worthy of much respect. Nonetheless as this coalition began to assemble, men in the know well understood that the French would have to abandon the whole of the lower Rhine; early in 1674 the betting in Amsterdam was not whether the French would retreat, but rather on what day that retreat would begin.

The political situation in 1674 left Louis little choice. When England made peace with the Dutch, Louis' cousin, Charles II, assured him of his benevolent neutrality, which meant that English merchants would take advantage of the Franco-Dutch war to extend their commerce. The defection of the German princes meant that the army on the lower Rhine was far from France and greatly exposed. The only wise decision that could be taken in France was to retreat and to establish a defensive position that would permit the kingdom to face its gathering foes. With Emperor Leopold about to join against France, the province of Alsace presented a critical situation, for not only Strasbourg but also most of the walled towns in the province were loyal to the Empire rather than to the king of France. After the fall of Maestricht, Louis spent the rest of the summer in that province preparing for its defense, and events were to prove that his precautions were actually not enough to prevent invasion. The other critical frontier was that joining the Spanish Netherlands. Louis sent Vauban on an inspection trip to see what should be done to assure its defense. The soldier-engineer was shocked by the irrationality of the defensive position that permitted French and Spanish fortresses to occupy "pell-mell" enclaves that made no sense. He wrote the king, "What your majesty needs is a 'dueling field' for a frontier." There was no doubt about the strength of the French army, and yet the kingdom of France was in considerable danger by the year 1674. The French military position had to be consolidated to prevent defeat. Thus in that year, one French army pulled back from the lower Rhine leaving Cologne and Münster to their own devices at the same time that another invaded Franche-Comté and seized that province. Soon afterwards a rebellion on the island of Sicily offered the French an opportunity to extend their naval frontier in the Mediterranean basin by establishing themselves there as allies of the rebels.

The coalition was unable to prevent the consolidation of the French defense system. There had been very little experience with coalition warfare, and Prince William III, who assumed that he must be the leader, was still only in his mid-twenties and not entirely trusted by his German allies. He wanted to carry on an aggressive war that would bring the fight into the kingdom of France, but he found that the French fortification system along the Spanish Netherlands' frontier was formidable, and that the French army could not be discounted. He was unable to invade France, but he did turn what might have been a defeat into a bloody, but indecisive battle (Seneffé, 1674) when Condé forced a general engagement. Prince William was never destined to become a great general; stubborn tenacity rather than military brilliance was his greatest asset.

While William's progress in 1674–75 was less than brilliant, Elector Frederick William of Brandenburg won a decisive victory over France's only remaining ally, Sweden. The Battle of Fehrbellin (June 28, 1675) was striking evidence of the rising Brandenburg military power. The battle gave the Elector control over all Swedish Pomerania, and clearly marked him as the most important prince in north Germany. Western historians, following Prussian accounts, have somewhat overvalued the importance of this prince whose grandson and great-grandson in the next century were to make the Brandenburg-Prussian state into a great power. Nonetheless Frederick William, surnamed the Great Elector, was the prince that started this Brandenburg-Prussian complex on its revolutionary career; his victory at Fehrbellin was a defeat for the French cause.

In Alsace the Imperials under the aging general Montecuccoli gave both Turenne and the king a bad time when Strasbourg opened the bridgehead to the imperial army (1674), and the pro-imperial loyalties of the population aided the imperial campaign. The next year (1675) Turenne hoped to return the visit by an invasion of Germany, but when he was killed by a chance cannonball, the French army retreated across the Rhine in considerable disorder. The disgraceful behavior of several French officers contesting for power was responsible for a drastic sharpening of the orders from the war ministry regulating the right to command. Nor were the difficulties of the French armies in Germany over; a short time later, Créqui's army on the Moselle front was defeated under conditions that cast dishonor on both French officers and soldiers. The king ordered every twentieth man in one detachment hanged, and several officers were degraded and beheaded before their troops.

Only from Sicily did the French hear good news. The French navy established control over the waters around the island, and in 1676 defeated the famous Dutch admiral, de Ruyter, in an action that cost the latter his life. Unhappily for the men who won victories in this theater of the war, their successes were not destined to have any lasting results on the course of the war or the peace. Indeed, to the contrary, they caused English politicians to fear French competition and interference with England's Levant trade, and, in part, were responsible for England's actions in 1678.

It is difficult to speculate about the military situation of 1675–1676. The French kingdom was not really in great danger of invasion, and yet the war was going sharply against France. Had William of Orange or Emperor Leopold had more experience in fighting coalition warfare they might have better been able to take advantage of their strength. But as Louis explains in his military *mémoires*, the coalition did not have a common purpose or a common strategic idea, while the French were learning to take advantage of the fact that they could operate inside of the semicircle that gave them the superior position assured by internal lines. However, before a new strategy could emerge the old ideas born of the Thirty Years' War had to be discarded. It was a question whether the members of the coalition would be able to learn to organize a coalition war before the French developed a unified strategic plan for the defense of the kingdom.

In the years 1676 to 1678 Louis, freed from the advice of famous soldiers by the death of Turenne and the retirement of Condé, came to rely more and more on the strategic doctrines developed by his soldier-engineer Vauban. The task before him was the straightening and fortification of the frontiers, a problem that was to be the central axis for Louis' politics for the next decade or more. To rationalize the frontier meant to create a defensive or defensible line, buttressed at certain points by strong fortifications, but fixed so that troops could easily move from one position to another to prevent detachments of enemy armies from invading the kingdom. A river, a canal, or lacking this, a series of field fortifications between the larger fortified points, became important strategic considerations. This conception of the frontier was new. New also was the military thinking that developed to defend the frontier. Previously, armies had maneuvered as more or less independent units, from one fortified camp to another without reference to any defensive "line". The successful commander was the one who could force his opponent to attack against a fortified position. This was the kind of warfare that Turenne and Condé had known. By 1676 when these famous soldiers were no longer around to dominate military policy, the new strategy could develop rapidly. In 1676 and 1677 the war on the frontier between the Spanish Netherlands and France was primarily aimed at establishing a rational frontier line, and the war ministry detached troops from one army to another to maintain superior power over the enemy at every point that might be threatened. Thus by maneuvering detachments behind a fortified semicircle, the French could take advantage of their interior lines of communication. This system of interior defense reached a high stage of development in the two last and most serious wars of the reign.

Any war has to be fought on the political as well as the military level. The collapse of the alliance system that the French had so carefully created to assure their victory over the United Netherlands was almost complete when Frederick William defeated the Swedish army in 1675; but a new grave danger was the possibility that the Francophobe faction in England that had forced Charles to withdraw from his alliance with France might also compel that prince to join the coalition against Louis XIV. Domestic problems in England were important in the formation of policy; the Anglican clergy and both the Tory and Whig politicians were concerned for the future of the throne. Charles II failed to produce a legitimate heir, and his brother James, a staunch Roman Catholic, refused to take the sacraments in the Church of England as was required by the Test Act. The Test Act prevented him from serving in the Admiralty, but it would not prevent him from becoming king of England; and it proved impossible to pass a law that would exclude him from the throne. There was, however, one saving fact; James had two daughters by a previous marriage, who were loyal Protestants. There was now great pressure to marry them to Protestant princes to assure a Protestant succession. The eldest, Mary, was suggested as a wife for Prince William of Orange whose mother had also been a Stuart princess. This marriage, consummated in 1677, made a new tie between England and the United Netherlands.

Even more important for the emerging political picture was the fact that a considerable body of English opinion became frightened by the rise of French naval power. The successful expedition to Sicily was symptomatic of the fact that Colbert's efforts to create a formidable navy were beginning to pay off: by 1677 the French had more than a hundred ships of the line as well as a formidable fleet of smaller vessels. The French ambassador noted that a hatred and fear of France was growing in England, and that even though Charles II might wish to be friendly and neutral, there was pressure to bring England into the war on the side of France's enemies, as concern for the throne, the church, and for commerce all seemed to make Louis XIV a threat to the island kingdom.

Fortunately for France this rising tide of English opinion came exactly at the time when the Dutch were becoming more and more war weary and more and more concerned about their commercial position. Prince William had not really changed the constitution of the United Netherlands when he took over the reins in 1672. His friends were more important in the government, but anti-Orange regents still had considerable potential power, and as the Stadtholder's war record failed to give him a glamorous reputation as a soldier, their influence continued to grow. In 1676 after a long and costly siege, he was forced to give up his hold on Maestricht; the next year he was decisively defeated at Casal. In 1678 he was unable to prevent the fall of Ghent. William, however, insisted that he could win victory, and urged his fellow countrymen to stand firmly with the other members of the alliance to force France to accept terms; he had the hope that England would soon join the coalition and thus assure victory. The war, however, was costly to the merchant class in the Netherlands, and by 1677–78 there was a considerable group in the General Estates that wished peace, and in spite of the objections of the Prince of Orange, the Regents finally agreed to send a delegation to a proposed peace conference at Nymwegen. This conference got nowhere: first, because the Germans were quite unwilling to talk peace except on their own terms; and second, all the delegates watched the progress of the war for indications of the terms that might be militarily possible. This, however, was Louis' opportunity to talk secretly to the Dutch, and the French forthwith concentrated all their attention on the problem of separating the Regents from William of Orange and the Dutch Republic from its German allies.

By the end of 1677 these French peace feelers became more and more necessary because the Francophobe party in the English Parliament finally forced the king to conclude a new treaty with the Dutch. Like the Anglo-Dutch alliance of 1667–68, this one seemed to be an agreement to persuade France and Spain to accept terms of peace; but since it provided for joint Anglo-Dutch military action to make war upon the power that refused to come to an agreement, it obviously was an alliance directed against France. No one supposed that the Spanish could refuse any terms that the Dutch allies might agree upon.

In 1678 the French had to reach a settlement quickly or face the danger of a much prolonged war that could easily end in bitter defeat. They reacted on two levels: a rapid and highly successful military campaign reduced the city of Ghent and brought the French army very near the Dutch frontiers, while French diplomats assured the Dutch Regents of their willingness to accept a "reasonable" peace. The French terms were designed to satisfy the Dutch. They were willing to surrender the enclaves in the Spanish Netherlands that had been awarded to them by the treaty of 1668 and create a frontier that would be more rational, that would correspond to the lineal conception that had emerged in the war. This would assure the Dutch of a "barrier" between themselves and the kingdom of France. The French also agreed to withdraw the more objectionable clauses of Colbert's tariff of 1668. In return for these concessions, they demanded that Spain cede Franche-Comté to the kingdom of France. This province was far from the Dutch frontiers, it also could not be defended by the Spanish, and finally it, too, was important in the new conception of lineal frontiers emerging in French thought.

With the French armies in control of Ghent and camped so close to the frontiers of their state, the Dutch Regents decided that these terms were all that they could hope to obtain. In spite of William's protests, they sent a delegation to the French camp and quickly ironed out the terms for a final settlement. This action ignored the landing of an English expeditionary force at Ostend without any declaration of war, as well as the protests of Emperor Leopold, and the objections of the Prince of Orange who believed that better terms could be secured. William was so dissatisfied with the agreement that he attacked the French army under Marshal Luxembourg after the peace had been signed at Nymwegen. This attack, however, was a failure both as a military effort and as a political objection: the Regents were ready to make peace.

The Treaty of Nymwegen provided for rectification of the frontier between France and the Spanish Netherlands by which the French gave up several enclaves that had been assigned to the kingdom in 1668 in return for a more defensive lineal frontier. It was not quite the *"pré carré"* that Vauban had demanded, but much closer to it than had ever existed before. By this settlement, Louis seemed to give up hopes of obtaining the entire Spanish Netherlands in return for a defensible boundary. The Spanish retained most of their Netherlands provinces as a barrier between France and the United Republic. The cession of Franche-Comté to France could not have been a great shock to the men at Madrid, for they had done nothing to protect that province for over a generation; but it was important for the new strategic doctrines of the French kingdom. With Franche-Comté the French grip on Alsace could finally be made secure, and the eastern frontier of the kingdom could be properly defined. The Swiss, however, were almost as reluctant to see the province of Franche-Comté pass into French hands as the Dutch were to allow the French in Flanders, but the Swiss were in no position to do anything about it. When it became evident that the Dutch were going to sign this treaty, both the Germans and the Spanish had to follow suit, for neither of them was able to wage war without Dutch subsidies and Dutch military support.

The treaty did not take care of German interests, but without the Dutch as allies, Emperor Leopold and the German princes were unable to continue the war. Leopold did manage to retain possession of Philippsburg which Charles of Lorraine had captured the year before, but Frederick William of Brandenburg-Prussia was not so lucky. Louis would not agree that Sweden, the only state that had remained true to its alliance with France, should suffer the loss of Pomerania, and when Frederick William refused to surrender his conquest, a French army started to assemble for an invasion of the lower Rhineland. Since the war had returned to his control a number of fortifications in the lower Rhineland that the Dutch had usurped or "intruded" after the Thirty Years' War, Frederick William was vulnerable to this French pressure, and finally agreed to return the province of Pomerania to Charles XI. Frederick William did not give up hope of annexing Pomerania, but he now realized that he could achieve his goals only in cooperation with the French king, for Germany did not have the military power necessary to underwrite his aims. Years later, after an imperial army reappeared on the scene and the French king outraged his Protestant sensibilities by the revocation of the Edict of Nantes, Frederick William changed his mind and again was willing to defy the French power.

In 1678, however, after the Dutch Regents, satisfied with their own safety and advantages, withdrew the United Netherlands from the coalition, Germany could not hope to oppose the king of France. Nonetheless neither the Emperor nor the king of Spain really recognized the Treaties of Nymwegen[14] as a final statement of the frontiers between their lands and those of the French king. Had the French been ready to accept this treaty with all the ambiguities built in it both by reaffirmation of the Treaties of Westphalia and the document itself, it is improbable that the German and Spanish empires would have done so without more clarification. The French, however, had no intention of allowing

---

[14] The "Peace of Nymwegen" was, in fact, a bundle of treaties. The first one, made with the Dutch, was not ratified until a second with Spain was signed; after that it was easy to "roll up" the rest of the alliance against France, for each successive treaty made it more and more impossible for the remaining states to continue the war.

the treaty law of 1648 (Westphalia) and 1678 (Nymwegen) to stand without their own interpretations; these treaties established the frontiers of the kingdom of France to the north and the east, frontiers that had always been vulnerable to invasion, and the men around Louis XIV were anxious to seal off the kingdom from such a danger. Thus, the problem after 1679 was that of the frontiers of France.

# Chapter 3

# The French Frontiers
# and
# the Turkish Threat

The so-called Dutch War was started brilliantly in 1672 when
the French army, seemingly invincible, rolled up fortification after
fortification in the lower Rhineland; but by 1674–75, as a coalition
emerged to meet this advance, the kingdom of France was obviously in trouble and its king's bad dreams and cries in the night
suggest that Louis was suffering from feelings of insecurity. What
had begun as a military parade threatened to become a disaster.
In the next three years, with much limited objectives for French
policy, the situation improved somewhat, but at the moment of
signing the Treaty of Nymwegen, the king and his ministers well
understood that they had succeeded in separating their enemies
just in time; for if England had joined the coalition against them,
there might have been no satisfactory way to disengage from
the war. His courtiers called him Louis, the Great, but he understood that the treaties of 1678–79 in no way reflected the ambitious
war aims of 1672. The plan to destroy the economic and military
power of the Dutch Netherlands, to allow easy annexation of the
Spanish Netherlands, and to improve France's commercial position

in the European market, had been jettisoned by the facts of the war. The Treaty of Nymwegen did provide for an "adjustment" of the frontier between France and the Spanish Netherlands, but it was clear that both the United Netherlands and the Spanish Netherlands were to be free from French domination.

The Dutch had gained more than the assurance of their independence; for only by rescinding objectionable clauses of Colbert's tariff of 1668 did the French persuade the Dutch Regents to agree to peace over the protest of the Prince of Orange who wanted to be sure to defend the Emperor's "rights" as well as his own. In return for these concessions, the kingdom of France had been allowed to annex Franche-Comté, a province of doubtful value that had been a "ripe plum" ever since 1648. But at the same time the loss of Phillippsburg on the middle Rhine left the northern frontiers of Alsace vulnerable to an attack from Germany. The Treaty of Nymwegen might have appeared to be a French victory to men who did not understand or remember the ambitious projects of 1672, but Louis XIV and his ministers could not have had many illusions about it. The only bright spot was the fact that in making peace they had broken up the coalition and created some bad blood between the Dutch regent class and both the Prince of Orange and the Germans.

The war had not achieved the ambitious aims of 1672, but it had created new aims for French policy. Once it was over, Louis XIV was determined to seal off his frontiers so that never again would the kingdom of France be confronted by the desperate situation of 1674–1675. The war had posited the problem as well as provided the solution. The French army that gobbled one fortification after another (1672) showed how ineffective it was to garrison towns with inadequate fortifications; even Maestricht had fallen much more easily than anyone would have believed. Obviously money spent on weak fortifications was largely wasted. The lesson: demolish fortifications that could not be held and concentrate the money, soldiers, and material in the important ones that could be a real barrier to an invader. Both Vauban and the Prince of Condé reached this conclusion early in 1673–74, and prepared lists of French forts to be demolished. The actual destruction of many of the fortifications in Alsace had another motive: many of the towns could not be trusted to remain loyal to the king, and during the summer of 1673 when Louis spent a long time in

Alsace, a number of these towns had their walls breached to prevent their becoming useful to the foe. Other fortifications were blown up because they were considered to be a waste of manpower and money that could be better used elsewhere. When the war was over, the king decided to survey every fortification on his frontiers to determine which should be strengthened and which destroyed.

A second thing that had become painfully apparent during the course of the war was the fact that in the past French kings had not established the frontiers with a rational plan. Territories had been acquired by occupation or conquest or inheritance; some of these were cities or counties that were, in fact, enclaves surrounded by the territory of another prince. Along the frontier there were lands and towns belonging to foreigners that were enclaves surrounded or nearly surrounded by French territory. When Vauban made an inspection trip of the Franco-Netherland frontier, he sadly reported that the French and Spanish fortifications were stuck along the frontier "pell-mell" without rhyme or reason and surely without any plan for defense. His suggestion was that the king should "rationalize" the frontier so that he could have a well-marked dueling field (*pré carré*) between himself and his potential foes. The entire French strategy of the last three years of the war in Flanders and Brabant, after the death of Turenne and the retirement of Condé, was based upon Vauban's doctrine of the need for a "*pré carré*" on the frontier. The "adjustment" of the Franco-Netherland frontier at the Treaty of Nymwegen completely reflected this new concern for a lineal frontier that could be defended. When the French realized that they had failed in their effort to break the power of the United Netherlands and therefore must give up hopes for the annexation of the Spanish Netherlands, Vauban's doctrine made sense.

The third great lesson of the war had been taught by the Imperial invasions of Alsace. The Treaties of Westphalia had been intentionally vague about the transfer of Hapsburg rights in Alsace to the French crown. Neither Mazarin nor the Austrian statesmen wanted a clear cut definition of those "rights," and in fact, it was probably impossible to establish them for no one really knew what the Hapsburgs could transfer in that province. The French did retain their hold on Phillippsburg (1648), and with this fortification that had works on both sides of the Rhine, they were then in position to control the traffic on the middle Rhine and to

defend Alsace from the north; this position also gave them a "gate"
into Germany.

After 1679 this fortification was in the hands of the Emperor.
Moreover, the fact that Strasbourg was an independent imperial
city meant that it could, as it in fact did, become a "gate" for
the Germans into France. The pretensions of the so-called Ten
Alsatian Towns to a position immediately under the Emperor
without any relation to the "rights" acquired by the king of France
at Westphalia, also made the whole question of the eastern
frontier a thorny one. The invasions of Alsace during the war
clearly indicated that no time should be lost correcting this
situation.

Another problem grew out of the peace in view of the fact
that the province of Franche-Comté that was assigned to France
was separated from Alsace by the Comté of Montbélaird which also
was part of the so-called "Belfort Gap" that jointed the Rhine
Valley with the Rhone. During the war Condé, to Vauban's surprise, suggested the demolition of the fortifications of Belfort.
This was not done, but a glance at the map will show that Belfort
could not be secure with Montbélaird in enemy hands. It belonged
to the Duke of Baden, who, like the free city of Strasbourg, could
be depended upon to side with the Emperor against France in any
future conflict. Thus the ownership of this territory was as important a question as that of Strasbourg.

The French government was determined to give a rational solution to these frontier problems. A conference of delegates from
the signators of the Treaty of Nymwegen sat in Courtrai in the
late fall of 1679 to delineate the frontiers provided for in that
treaty, but neither Louis XIV nor his war minister, Louvois, had
any intention of submitting their needs to such a court. Louvois
instructed the French delegate, Le Peletier, "that it is in the king's
interest, without appearing to act so, not to press the business of
the conference with any diligence". Le Peletier probably needed
no such instructions to make him drag his feet until the army
could draw the frontier. Most men around the king in 1679 shared
Vauban's opinion that "cannons are the best advocates of the
king's interests", and the best arbiters for the solution of frontier
problems. Louis XIV was not the first ruler and surely not the
last one, who surveyed his frontiers with military force.

The king himself wished to make the grand tour of the frontier fortifications from Belfort to the English Channel as soon as the war was over, but the problem of forcing the Elector of Brandenburg to return Pomerania to Sweden prevented his making the trip. So Louvois and Vauban, under strict orders to report their findings in detail, made the survey without him. As a result, in Louvois' letters we have a mine of information about the problems of defending the realm in 1679, as well as a detailed picture of the fortifications, suggestions for changes, for new construction, and for demolition. By 1679 Vauban was no longer simply a "creature" of Louvois. He had become commissaire-general for fortifications, he was a great favorite of the king, his advice was sought by Colbert for the fortifications of coastal towns as well as by Louvois for those facing the land frontiers. Vauban's prestige had grown greatly, and his ideas about the defense of the kingdom were assured of a hearing. Louis XIV finally broke with the tradition that denied an engineer high military rank by making Vauban first a lieutenant-general and then a marshal of France, but in 1679 this bold and generous step was still far away.

The important result of the inspection was the decision to spend huge sums of money for the defense of the frontiers. This was the first time since the building of the Roman lines that any such elaborate, unified system of defense had been projected in Europe. There were two ways of interpreting such an outlay of money. It could be that the king of France had given up as no longer feasible the plans for expansion that had dominated the first two decades of his foreign policy. The recent war had clearly demonstrated the impossibility of acquiring the Spanish Netherlands in face of Dutch opposition, and therefore the kingdom of France was concentrating on a new defense program to assure its own security. Another conclusion could have been that the recent war demonstrated the fact that it would be impossible to achieve an ambitious foreign policy until the defenses of the kingdom were strong enough to hold off the enemy on one front while the king's armies invaded from another. This reasoning assumed that France was merely creating a defensive position from which to attack its neighbors. Neither in Germany nor in the Netherlands were men able or willing to lay out sums of money comparable to the expenditures needed for Vauban's fortified system, but in both lands men began to discuss the reorganization of military institutions on the model created by Le Tellier and Louvois.

It was not long before the policies necessary to give France a defensible frontier encroached upon the rights of its neighbors and further underlined the need for military reorganization to meet French aggression. The Treaty of Nymwegen allowed the French to iron out most of the ambiguities of the Flanders frontier and establish Vauban's *pré carré,* but further east, facing the Moselle and the Rhine, there was no rational plan possible. To secure a "dueling field" on this frontier, the helter-skelter, pell-mell organization of territorial rights resultant from treaties between France and the German neighbors since the mid-sixteenth century, needed to be clarified and rationalized. Perhaps an "interpretation" of the treaties could achieve this end. It was a simple problem as far as Louis XIV was concerned: he merely wanted to determine what the past treaties *really* transferred to his kingdom. With a pious air that seemed most hypocritical to the rest of Europe, Louis announced that he wanted only what was "rightfully his"; he was not "acting as an aggressor, only as a petitioner seeking justice and right". With this stance Louis ordered the "sovereign council" at Breisach, the Parlement at Besançon, and the Chamber of Reunions of the Parlement at Metz to examine the status of the "provinces and dependencies" that had been transferred to his kingdom. As we have noted, treaties of peace and cession did not draw lineal frontiers; they transferred provinces, *comtés,* towns, etc., "and their dependencies". Louis simply asked his judges to discover what actual territories were involved in the transfers.[16]

From the French point of view the need to fix the frontier was logical enough, but the rest of Europe, and particularly the Netherlands-Empire political complexes, could not be expected to share the French attitude. Every frontier was a jumble of rights and interests; a political swamp of obligations and rights and positions dating from both the recent treaties and the remote past. As we have seen, one of the interesting problems arose out of the fact that after the Treaties of Westphalia, the Dutch continued to occupy the fortifications of most of the towns along the lower Rhine and Maas even though these towns legally belonged to the Archbishops of Cologne, or Trier, or some other

---

[16] There is a considerable literature dealing with the so-called Courts of Reunion, and the aggressive program that they followed. Colbert de Croissy, brother of the great Colbert, seems to have been the central figure in the drama, but Louvois also played an important role.

prince. Maestricht, for example, belonged to the Elector of Cologne; the Dutch occupied the fortification, and when the French took Maestricht in 1673, they simply assumed the position held by their foes in spite of the requests by the Elector for the return of "his city." The French had occupied Phillippsburg in the same way until it was captured by the Imperials (1677). Throughout the Rhineland, indeed throughout all Germany, the holdings of princes, bishops, towns, and Imperial knights were jumbled together so that it was almost impossible to know exactly which was "a dependency" of the other; as long as these rulers were content to live together under a more or less anarchic confederation in which no one looked too closely at obligations and rights that had become either fossilized or forgotten, the problems of this situation could be ignored. Nonetheless, the mélange of fortifications, rights, obligations, and dependencies created a veritable political swamp; it is no wonder that Puffendorf exclaimed that the Holy Roman Empire of the German nation was a "political monster," an institution without prototype or predecessor in the political institutions of men. Nonetheless, this was the situation that the men governing this part of Europe regarded as normal and proper.

The French demand for order in this uncertain structure of overlapping jurisdictions, obligations and rights, inevitably caused a political crisis because the French naturally solved all problems in a way that suited their needs regardless of the presumed rights of others. The courts sitting at Besançon, Metz, and Breisach summoned noblemen and towns either to recognize the king of France as their overlord, or to expect military occupation of the villages and towns upon refusal to do so. This started an angry buzzing in the Rhineland; the king of France had stirred up a hornet's nest of major proportions.

If we look a little closely at the French "aggression," we can see what was involved. The first blow came when the Parlement of Besançon demanded that the Duke of Baden recognize the king of France as his overlord for most of the villages in the Comté of Montbéliard, and, a few months later, for the town of Montbéliard and the entire Comté. Naturally the Duke of Baden would do no such thing, and the French army proceeded to occupy the territory. This act closed the "gap" between Franche-Comté and Alsace, and allowed the French to prepare fortifications to defend the Belfort Gap. The Duke of Baden was not consulted. The next move came from the Sovereign Council at Breisach which proceeded to order one Alsatian town or nobleman after another to recognize the king as overlord, with no mention of the pretended relationship between the Ten Towns or, indeed any other relations between Alsatians and the Emperor. Within a matter of months the court "settled" the uncertain status of most of Alsace in a manner favorable to the interests of the king of France, and the French army in Alsace immediately occupied the contested cities and towns. The most active court of the three was the one seated at Metz. The king asked the bishops of Metz, Toul, and Verdun for a list of the vassals owing obligations to their sees, but not one of them could produce such a list. The frontier from the middle Rhine on the line with Landau through to Luxembourg, Sedan, and then on to Flanders was a tangled mass of conflicting juris-dictions. Some of the most complex of these arose out of the am-biguous status of Lorraine, others from the conflicting claims in Lower Alsace and the three bishoprics. The Chamber of Reunions in the Parlement of Metz had long been analyzing these claims; indeed Colbert de Croissy's knowledge of the situation probably stemmed from his earlier association with this court. When the government gave the signal to proceed, the Chamber of Reunions acted promptly and with astonishing boldness. In rapid suc-cession one place after another was pulled into the kingdom by its orders. The kings of Sweden and Spain, the Electors of Trier and the Palatinate, the Duke of Würtemburg, and a dozen other Ger-man princes saw lands that they believed to be theirs, swallowed up by French "aggression." The Chamber went so far beyond Louvois' own desires for speedy action that the war minister had to chide it for its haste: he did not want the princes of Europe to think that the king of France was an aggressor.

One has only to drive today through this territory from Weissem-bourg and Landau through the Saar basin on to Luxembourg to understand the strategic implications of these annexations. It was obviously a matter of providing suitable defenses for Lower Alsace and Lorraine. Since the Treaty of Nymwegen confirmed the Treaty of Westphalia and all previous treaties regulating that area, the French felt justified in exploiting their claims to the hilt. However, the rest of Europe was not convinced of French "rights," and when the French annexed the lands in the Saar that had long belonged to the king of Sweden's ancestors, as well as lands belonging to

German princes, a chorus of protests began to arise. It did not take long for the pamphleteers to point out that the king of France had annexed more territory since 1679 than he had gained by the Treaty of Nymwegen.

By the spring of 1681 there remained two important strong points that were still unoccupied; Alsace and Lorraine could not be secure as long as Strasbourg and Luxembourg remained in the hands of potential foes. No one in the king's entourage could forget that in 1674 and 1675 the Germans had crossed the river at Strasbourg and devastated Alsace, and every one knew that Luxembourg was a key point in the defense of lands between the Moselle and the Meuse (Maas) rivers. Strasbourg was first on the French list, and no one should have been really surprised when the blow fell on the city. What was astonishing was that Louvois arranged a *coup de théâtre* by annexing Strasbourg and Casale in northern Italy on the same day, an announcement to Europe that Louis XIV really was "Louis the Great."

The occupation of Strasbourg ran on schedule: the French army under Montclair took possession of the bridgehead on the Rhine, and then surrounded the city. Louvois summoned the city fathers to his camp and presented them with the terms of capitulation. They had no alternative for there was no German army to interfere with a French siege. On September 30, 1681, the French army entered the city; Vauban immediately set about to strengthen and modernize the fortifications; and at the same time in accordance with the capitulations, Franz Egon von Fürstenburg, the bishop of Strasbourg, reoccupied the ancient gothic cathedral and reconsecrated it for Roman Catholic services. When both the physical and the spiritual environment was safe, the whole French court appeared in Strasbourg for the king to receive the oaths of allegiance from his new subjects as well as the homage due to him from the noblemen of Alsace, and visits from German notables living on the other side of the Rhine, who for one reason or another wished to remain in the "good graces" of the French king. It was a brilliant display of wealth, beauty, and power, not lost on Germany. The voices of the pamphlets denouncing France and its king became a roar.

Not only the presses of Germany were protesting French action. Even before the annexation of Strasbourg there had been speeches at the Imperial Diet at Ratisbon demanding action. It was even proposed that the Empire should create an imperial army, perhaps modelled on the French army; up until this time, since none of the princes wished to surrender the command over his forces to an imperial war council, the problem of reforming the military constitution of the empire seemed hopeless. Nonetheless, something had to be done. In 1680 the princes on the Rhine immediately facing Alsace signed a defensive agreement, and then turned to their neighbors in hopes of enlarging it into a regular alliance. When Strasbourg was annexed there was no longer any question about the immediacy of the danger; in June, 1682, the so-called Laxenberg Alliances came into being, involving the Emperor and most of the princes of the Upper Rhineland and Franconia. These princes agreed to provide three armies with a total of 30,000 men for the defense of the Rhine frontier. In January, 1683, Max Emanuel of Bavaria, the Duke of Hanover and Celle, and the Emperor signed a defensive alliance, and a month later at the Hague the kings of Spain and Sweden and the United Provinces joined this treaty for mutual defense.

Behind this formal series of agreements buzzed the complex, often irrational political structure of Germany. Emperor Leopold hoped to detach Bavaria from its traditional alliance with France by the marriage of his daughter Maria Antonia to the young Max Emanuel. This princess was the granddaughter of Philip IV of Spain, but Emperor Leopold forced her to renounce her rights to the throne of Spain in favor of his sons who were grandchildren of Philip III. On the other hand, he held out to Max Emanuel the possibility of becoming governor, perhaps even sovereign, of the Spanish Netherlands. William of Orange also was deeply engaged in all these negotiations, but his action was limited because many of the patrician or regents faction in the General Estates of the United Netherlands had either been bought by Louis XIV's pensions, or frightened by his armies, and they wanted nothing to do with another war. Nonetheless William did succeed in detaching Sweden from the French system (October, 1681) and thereby breaking Louis' northern barrier. The king of Sweden who was also prince of Zweibrücken, had lost territory to Louis' Chamber of Reunions. On the other hand the Elector of Brandenburg, whose military support was needed if any move against France were to be successful, would have nothing to do with the anti-French coalition. His pockets were lined with French money, but even more important, he had come to the conclusion, after being forced to give up Pomerania in 1679, that nothing could be accomplished in Europe without French support. He hoped for French assistance for his Baltic aspirations. There was one other reason behind his coolness to the suggestions of the Prince of Orange. Frederick William was trying to establish a Brandenburg trading company on the West African coast to share the trade in slaves, gold, and ivory; but the Dutch, who owed him much for his aid in the last war, were unwilling to allow his subjects to share this trade. In 1681–82 these and many other petty things were obstructing any real development of a German coalition to confront the French aggression on the Rhine.

The Spanish government hopefully joined the embryo alliance system. Even though it had been impossible to prevent the annexation of Strasbourg, the Spanish hoped to find some way to save Luxembourg which obviously was next on the French list, for soon after the annexation of Strasbourg, the Chamber at Metz "discovered" that most of the villages of the Duchy of Luxembourg really were dependencies of the Archbishopric of Metz. Forthwith a French army proceeded to occupy them and to establish an informal blockade cutting off all traffic to and from the fortification. When the Spanish governor attempted to break through the ring, the French reacted viciously. Everywhere in Europe men held their breath, for a conflict seemed inevitable. Then, just before the blockade became a siege, the French army withdrew and the French king announced that he would accept the judgment of the king of England on his just demands. He did not, he announced, wish to prevent the German emperor and the Spanish king from doing their duty protecting Germany against the Turks. It was a piously hypocritical announcement that pointed to the greatest problem of 1683: the Turkish army was again hammering at the gates of Central Europe.

In the eras before secular "isms" separated societies, religious beliefs and cults were the important factors creating gulfs between men. By the end of the seventeenth century Islam and Christendom had faced each other for a thousand years, from the Crusades to the terrible pressures of the Ottoman Turks in the sixteenth century. The conflict had been endemic, a smoldering truce that would erupt into hot war at any occasion. Christians might hate each other, but Islam was the real enemy of all Christendom. In the Mediterranean Sea this conflict never ceased. The Christian knights of Malta (supported by the Christian princes) and the Barbary States on the North African coast (supported by the Sultan), waged continuous war on each others' commerce in that sea. Theologians and preachers often explained that Islam was the scourge of God, the punishment for Christian sins; the soldiers and sailors who confronted the Mohammedan (Islamic) power knew that it was a force that could exert pressure on Christendom from the Pillars of Hercules to the upper reaches of the Danube River. The mapmakers of the sixteenth century often represented Europe the reverse of the modern map: Africa was at the top of the page, so that anyone could see that a great crescent of Islamic power encircled Christendom.

In the mid-sixteenth century when Suleiman I, the Magnificent, was Sultan of the Ottoman Empire, this Islamic threat was a real danger. His armies reached the gates of Vienna, his navies prowled the Mediterranean, but after his death the throne fell to lesser men. Salim, surnamed the Sot (1566–74), was obviously not a highly respected successor to the great Sultan, nor were the men who followed him on the throne. The victory of Don Juan at Lepanto (1571) blocked the Ottoman navy from the western Mediterranean; the emperors at Vienna were able to stabilize the frontier that divided the ancient Hungarian kingdom into Hapsburg Hungary, Turkish Hungary, and Transylvania. Weakness in the central administration of the Ottoman Empire proved to be a great boon for Middle Europe. The Turks were unable to take advantage of the terrible German Civil War (Thirty Years War), and when that war was over the lessons in warfare that the central Europeans learned emphasized the gap between Ottoman and Christian power. It almost seemed that never again would Christian Europe tremble before the Turkish threat.

However, in the mid-seventeenth century, new life was injected into the Ottoman state by the rise of a vigorous family of Grand Viziers who substantially altered the traditional constitution of the Empire by making the Sultan merely a figurehead while the

Grand Vizier exercised the real power. Mohammed Kiupruili (1656–1661) purged both the court and the Janissary corps of much of the corruption that neglect and incompetence had allowed to develop; he and his son who followed him (1661–1678) gave the Empire a new lease on life by reintroduction of the basic principle upon which it had been founded, namely that the Turkish state must expand at the expense of its neighbors. This Ottoman Empire was not a state in the western sense of the word; it had no real organic unity or organization. Indeed it resembled nothing so much as an army of occupation in a conquered land, and if such an army ceases to be a real fighting force, it quickly decays. The Turks had rolled their conquests over the lands of neighboring peoples, but they had not attempted to incorporate their conquest into an Ottoman state. Tolerantly they allowed the vanquished to practice their religion and they left the control of justice, collection of taxes, and general administration in the hands of the noblemen or the towns' governments that had traditionally been responsible for these things. The subject peoples were expected to pay taxes, keep the peace, and respect their conquerors. If a state organized on these principles does not continue to inspire the martial virtues of its own people, it can easily become venal, corrupt, and ineffective.

The Kiupruili viziers understood this fact. They also seem to have realized that it was unlikely that the Ottoman Empire would ever again be as relatively powerful as it had been in the days of the great Suleiman. Their military adventures were less pretentious than those of the heroic period, and whenever they encountered really serious resistance, they backed off and probed in another direction. Thus when the Christian armies mauled the Janissaries at St. Gotthardt in 1664, the Turks quickly made a twenty-year truce with the Emperor, and turned their attention to the island of Crete where they fought a long war with Venice, or to the frontiers of Persia or the Polish Ukraine. The war with Venice considerably weakened the Republic; the war with the Poles gave Jan Sobieski a glamorous reputation that led to his election as king of Poland. None of these adventures had any really strikingly successful results. In 1681 there was a new Grand Vizier at the head of the state, Kara Mustapha, a man with great ambition and much confidence in his own ability; but he seemed not to have understood how great was the striking force of the new European armies nor how great would be the problems of logistics for a Turkish army far from the center of Turkish power.

The political situation in the three Hungarian territories gave Kara Mustapha reason to hope for success. When the sixteenth century push up the Danube was stopped, the Ottoman Empire was able to hold the greater part of the old Hungarian kingdom, including the ancient capital at Ofen (now Budapest). The Transylvanian noblemen retained a quasi-independence in return for recognizing the Sultan as their overlord. A crescent of Hungarian territory to the north remained independent of the Turks only by throwing itself under the protection of the German Hapsburgs ruling at Vienna. The Diet seated at Pressburg retained the ancient crown of Saint Stephen, but henceforth it was bestowed upon the Hapsburg prince whose control over Bohemia and the southern Alpine and middle Danubian German lands made his government a natural barrier against Turkish aggression. Hapsburg Hungary was ruled by a Palatine who acted as viceroy for the Hapsburg king and a spokesman for the Hungarian magnates. We should note in passing that both Hapsburg Hungary and Transylvanian Hungary were mountainous, relatively poor lands, while Turkish Hungary was a broad plain where wheat, fodder, horses, and cattle provided the base for power. The Turkish government, however, did not understand how to mobilize this potential force for its own advantage.

In all three Hungaries the great noblemen who controlled most of the land were the counterpart of the grandees in Spain, the great ones in France, the magnates in Poland, the princes in Germany. They were not simple lords but rather magnates who owned fiefs often enough as large as Connecticut or New Hampshire. They had hundreds of retainers, vassals, and serfs who were dependent upon their bounty and recognized their leadership. These men, like their counterparts elsewhere who defended French, Castilian, German, or Polish "liberties" were sensitive to their right to manage their own affairs. They recognized rebellion against a duly elected king as a "constitutional right". Furthermore, since many of the important families were related by marriage, it was easy for them to combine in the defense of their "liberties". They were not all hostile to the German Hapsburg king, but most shared a xenophobia that made them distrust a foreign ruler; and many of them found the tolerant, sloppy overlord of the Turkish

Pasha at Ofen less onerous than the "modern" German rule insti-
tuted by Ferdinand II and his successors. The great lords did not
like to see the court at Vienna assume functions and powers that
had formerly been theirs, especially if the ruler were a foreigner.
There was much talk of liberation from foreign bondage—both
Turkish and German.

In the mid-seventeenth century there were several plans for the
unification of Hungary. George II Rakoczi (1648–1661), as Prince
of Transylvania, proposed bold plans, but they came to nothing.
In the meantime in Hapsburg Hungary there arose a party hostile
to the emperor at Vienna; its core were men who had become
Calvinist probably to underline their dislike of the German-Jesuit
court. These "Malcontents" raised the flag of rebellion, and made
contact with Louis XIV through the French ambassador at Warsaw,
and with the Ottoman Pasha at Ofen. Their rebellion criss-crossed
the frontier; during the Dutch War in the west, French money
poured into their treasury in hopes of forcing Emperor Leopold
to give up his attack on France. When peace was made at Nymwegen, the leader of these Malcontents, Prince Imre Tökölli, turned
to Constantinople for assistance. He was willing to become a vassal
of the Sultan if the Sultan would unite Turkish and Hapsburg
Hungary under his rule. At first, it seems, the Porte (the government of the Ottoman Empire) was unsympathetic, but in 1681
Kara Mustapha became convinced that, with the aid of the Tran-
sylvanians and the Hungarian Malcontents, he could overrun Vienna and perhaps even establish a new Islamic state on the Upper
Danube. Since this bold project for the invasion of Central Europe
came exactly at the time when the kingdom of France and the
Germanic and Netherlandic princes seemed about to fall on each
other Kara Mustapha's ambitions may not have been unrealistic.

Emperor Leopold did not realize his danger until early in 1682.
His ambassador had gone to Constantinople confidently expecting
to negotiate a renewal of the Twenty Year Truce only to be put off
by specious excuses and delaying action. Suddenly he realized that
the Ottoman Empire was preparing for war, and that the preparations were centered at Belgrade, the natural supply depot for any
serious action in the Danube Basin. As the evidence of Turkish intentions began to pile up, the Imperial court at Vienna hurriedly
sent out calls for help and began to brace itself for the coming
battle. No one knew how strong the Turkish army would be, but,

as in 1664, it probably would be too powerful to be stopped by the Emperor's forces unless he could find support in Christian Europe. In 1664 a strong, well-equipped and excellently commanded French army had borne the brunt of the Turkish charge and earned a brilliant reputation for its part in the victory. In 1682 the French king assured the Grand Vizier that no French soldiers would aid the Emperor, and when Leopold sought allies he found the French ambassador working everywhere to prevent anyone from sending troops to help defend Vienna.

These were the years when Louis XIV justly earned the title: "Most Christian Turk" at Versailles. Only a few months before Louis learned that Kara Mustapha planned to invade the Danube, the relations between France and the Ottoman Empire were almost at the breaking point. A French warship, chasing a Moslem corsair into Chios, bombarded the harbor; in retaliation, Kara Mustapha unceremoniously imprisoned the French ambassador, and Louis XIV ordered his fleet to converge on Constantinople. It seemed probable that that city would learn what it meant to insult the king of France. But at this moment, through his contacts with the Hungarian Malcontents, Louis learned of Kara Mustapha's projected assault on the Hapsburg Empire. The Hungarians had many nebulous, haphazard ideas including a partition of the Hapsburg Empire with Tökölli emerging as king of a united Hungary, and the Grand Dauphin, Louis' son, as king of Bohemia. There is no reason to believe that Louis took these Hungarian dreams seriously, but when the French realized that Kara Mustapha was about to join the Hungarian Malcontents with a powerful army, they did understand that this diversion in the east could have important implications for French policy. The French fleet that was about to attack Constantinople was recalled, and the French ambassador apologized for the bombardment of Chios. Louis did not actually join the Ottoman Empire with any formal treaty for reasons that will appear shortly, but he did order the French ambassador to tell Kara Mustapha that, in light of the evil that Emperor Leopold had done to France, he could be assured that no French detachments would stand in the way of the Turco-Hungarian invasion of the Danube. Louis urged his ambassador to encourage the Turks, but ordered him to put nothing in writing!

As we have seen, French foreign policy following the Treaty of Nymwegen was primarily concerned with the problems of the frontiers; the late war had dramatically demonstrated the necessity for defensible positions if the kingdom's security were to be maintained. The king as well as his ministers[17] understood that the defenses of the kingdom were their first concern. It is true that the treaties between France and the German electors (Bavaria, Brandenburg, Saxony, and the Rhine bishops) by which the French king exchanged money for support, usually had a clause in which the elector promised to vote for Louis or his son, the Dauphin, or a candidate of French choice in the next Imperial election; but so long as Emperor Leopold was alive, this merely meant that Louis could block any attempt to elect the Emperor's son as king of the Romans, that is heir to the Imperial Crown. This had been a traditional policy of the French kings. Mazarin tried to prevent a Hapsburg's election, even proposed Louis XIV for the crown, when Leopold was elected Emperor in 1658. Louis was simply following the same procedure when he tried to be sure that at the next election his interests would be served. Nonetheless, even after the marriage of a Bavarian princess to the Grand Dauphin, there was an air of unreality about the French candidacy to the Imperial throne. In any case it was not significant enough to slow down the program of fortification on the Rhine frontier.

In 1683, however, the possibility of a French emperor ceased to be a vague ambition; with Kara Mustapha's invasion of the Upper Danube the political structure of Europe assumed new contours. What would happen if the Ottoman armies should overwhelm the Emperor's forces? The Turkish armament counted about 200,000 men; Charles of Lorraine, commanding the much smaller Imperial army, was able only to fight a delaying action in hopes that the defenses of Vienna could be readied to withstand the Turkish assault. But what if Vienna should not hold back the Turkish horde? If the Imperial army were broken and the Janissaries and Spahis pressed on into Bavaria, Bohemia, Saxony, even Franconia, where would the Holy Roman Empire of the German Nation find a protector? Indeed where would Christian Europe find defense against Islam? Would not all Europe look to the king of

---

[17] After 1679 Louis' ministers were Colbert for finance, commerce, navy, *Batiments*, etc.; his brother, Colbert de Croissy, for foreign affairs; Louvois for war. Le Tellier became Chancellor in 1677, but he continued to work with his son so that in fact Louis had two war ministers. All four of these men were charged with the problems of frontiers.

France as the shield and sword of Christendom? His armies alone could drive back the Islamic hordes, and then would not Christian Germany accept him as emperor? A long memoranda written by Chamlay, one of Louvois' most trusted creatures, leaves us no doubt that this was the vision of 1683. The French pulled back their troops from the blockade of Luxembourg so that "those who should defend the Empire" would not be embarrassed by French action, but Louis remained absolutely deaf to all suggestions that French armies should aid the Emperor. Even more than that, his ambassadors tried to prevent other powers from giving aid. France would not be accused of being an accessory to the Ottoman invasion, but France also did nothing to prevent Ottoman victory. When Innocent XI urged a crusade to save Europe, Louis blandly informed His Holiness that no one went on Crusades any more, and that he did not want to take any action that would injure French trade in the Levant. Innocent XI and all those who feared the Ottoman advance ground their teeth in anger; some of them poured out anti-French propaganda from Europe's presses; but none of them could do anything until the God of battles had decided the issue at Vienna.

Kara Mustapha's march up the Danube was a formidable thing to watch. As Hungarian, Transylvanian, Cossack, and other irregular troops added their weight to the Janissaries and Spahis, and Turkish irregular infantry, the numbers did indeed swell to 200,000 men. Horses, camels, siege equipment, and many more cannon than the Emperor could assemble made it seem that this Turkish armament was invincible. Charles of Lorraine fell back, and a tough old soldier, Count Rüdiger von Starhemberg, prepared to defend Vienna while the Emperor went to Germany to rally the Empire for a showdown with the foe.

Wherever the Emperor went he was faced with Louis' conditions: Germany could not hope to fight the Turk unless the Emperor would be willing to recognize the French annexations, the rightful claims, of the preceding four years. But Germany did not listen to the French ambassadors, nor did the king of Poland. The Pope protested to Louis XIV directly; the French foreign minister blandly explained that the king of Spain and the Emperor were to blame for the difficulty Christendom faced in defending itself: they prevented the use of German troops against the Turk by their refusal to accommodate themselves to the "rightful claims" of the French king. However, central Europe made a real effort at this moment by assembling an army: some 60,000 Germans and 24,000 Poles swarmed out of the north and descended upon the Turkish camp like avenging angels. The siege of Vienna was broken, and the Turkish armies fell back down the Danube in great disorder. The victory came on September 12; it was almost as much a defeat for the king of France as for the Ottoman Empire.

When Vienna showed its toughness and the German-Polish forces began to assemble for a showdown with the Ottomans, men at Versailles seem to have realized that the Empire was not going to go down in defeat. They probably should have known this even sooner, for the Christian military tactics had developed well beyond those available to Islam. On August 30 the French presented the Spanish Governor of the Netherlands with an announcement that, since the Spanish court had not recognized the decisions of the Chamber of the Parlement of Metz, the king's army would invade his territory to secure that judgment. On September 1, twelve days before the Ottoman defeat at Vienna, a French army of 20,000 men marched into the Spanish Netherlands, bombarding cities and levying contributions while another French force reappeared before Luxembourg. Louis XIV explained that he merely wanted a treaty with the king of Spain and the Emperor guaranteeing him the just acquisitions that his courts had awarded him in the preceding four years. The Spanish replied by a declaration of war against France.

The decision, however, was in the hands of two men: Leopold, Emperor of the Holy Roman Empire of the German Nation, and William III of Orange, Stadtholder of the United Netherlands. William was embarrassed. He wanted a showdown with France, but at every turn he was confronted with the fact that many of the regents of the Netherlands did not want any such thing. Some of them had French money in their pockets, others were involved in commercial activity that could only suffer in case of a war with France. They were able to veto any action proposed by the Prince of Orange. Leopold's position was even more complex. He had to listen to both the important princes of Germany and to the advice of his council of Vienna. In Germany the potent voice was that of the Elector of Brandenburg, Frederick William von Hohenzollern. He had learned the hard way that even victory would not assure any success without the consent of the king of France: his victory over Sweden had been put aside by Louis' insistence that Pomerania be returned to France's ally. Since he saw no alternative Frederick William had accepted a French subsidy and had himself become a French ally; he announced to the world that he would be willing to have Brandenburg soldiers fight on the Danube, but not on the Rhine. Leopold's most articulate advisors were of the same advice. A pamphlet published in Vienna pointed out that Austria "had the trumps if she would play them." The time was ripe for the conquest of Hungary, a vast agricultural realm rich in wheat, fodder, cattle, and horses—these were the elements of military strength in the seventeenth century. If Hungary were reconquered and reorganized on the model of Bohemia and the hereditary German provinces, then the Danubian crown would be a power comparable to, perhaps even more formidable than that of France. After Hungary was reoccupied and reorganized with the aid of the Empire there would be no question about the Emperor's ability to cope with the French power. These advocates of peace with France and war with the Turks also recalled vividly that William III had been unable to prevent the regents from making peace in 1678–79; they urged that the Orange faction could not be counted upon. Leopold did not need to be told that he could not fight a war on two fronts; it was either peace with France or with the Turks. Under such duress, Leopold decided to fight in Hungary. In one way the war that followed was the last of the crusades; in another, it was the war for the creation of the Danubian monarchy. Peace did not come until 1699.

Making a treaty with France proved to be a difficult operation. The French wanted a definitive treaty of peace giving them the lands that had been annexed to the kingdom since 1679, including Luxembourg; the Emperor and the king of Spain were quite unwilling to make any such sacrifices. The treaty between France and the two Hapsburg empires was signed at Ratisbon, but the negotiations for the treaty were largely conducted at the Hague where the ambassadors of the several powers ironed out their problems with the assistance of the Dutch who also had an important interest in the success of the treaty. Agreement came when Louis XIV with-

drew his most extreme demands and agreed to write a truce rather
than a definitive treaty. The truce left France in possession of the
contested lands for twenty years. At the end of that time the question could be reopened and a treaty of peace written. Louis XIV
understood that for all intents and purposes this truce was as good
as a treaty; twenty years are a long time, long enough time to inte-
grate the territories into the kingdom of France and make impossible their alienation. In agreeing to a truce in place of a peace, the
king of France posed as a good Christian who made concessions so
that the Emperor would be able to fight his war in Hungary; but in
fact Louis XIV had taken good care of his own interests. From
Franche-Comté to Luxembourg he occupied a crescent of lands
that allowed his kingdom to create a defensible frontier on its eastern side. The crown of the Empire had, for the moment, escaped
him, but Louis XIV had won a great victory, indeed the only
clear-cut victory of his entire career.

Even so, there was further business to settle with those who offended the king of France. When the Spanish declared war on
Ocotber 26, 1683, the French ordered the city of Genoa not to give
Spain assistance of any kind. Genoa had been the port of entry for
men and supplies flowing between Spain and Milan (and thence to
the Rhineland or Austria) for generations; the relations between
the city and the Spanish crown were almost those of overlord-
vassal, for Genoa was dependent upon Spain for many, many things.
Louis' orders were ignored: Genoese galleys helped to protect the
Spanish communications, Genoese shipyards continued to build for
Spain, and Spanish supplies passed through the Port of Genoa. This
disobedience was summarily punished when a French squadron
arrived before the city and bombarded it so that about half of its
buildings were completely destroyed. This was even more brutal
treatment than Louis had meted out to the Barbary Pirates at Al-
giers when their depredations offended him. Nor was the bombardment enough. The French refused to include Genoa in the Truce of
Ratisbon, and insisted that the Doge of the city and several senators must journey to Versailles to beg forgiveness. When the
Genoese hesitated, Louvois prepared an overland expedition to
"destroy the ruins" of Genoa. Louis loudly asserted that he wanted
no territory from these people, but they must apologize. The Doge
and three senators did go to Versailles, they did ask for pardon, and
then the king of France admitted them to his court and expected

them to be happy with the progress of his fame and power. It was as once an exhibition of brutal callousness and a proclamation to France and the world that the king of France, that is to say the central authority in the kingdom, was a great power in the world, a power that must not be offended.

These were the days when the mask of Louis XIV often wore an ugly, brutal expression. At the same time that French artillery bombarded cities in the Spanish Netherlands and devastated Genoa, a considerable population of people in France itself, whose sin was the practice of a religion different from that of the majority of their fellow subjects, found themselves under terrible duress. French Catholic preachers and writers had long urged the king to end the "scandal" created by the existence of Huguenot churches, schools, charitable institutions, etc. "Those who worship at the same altars," they insisted, "will fight under the same banners". The suggestion was that the existence of the Huguenot church was not only a scandal; it was a danger to the kingdom. Ever since the days of Richelieu the king's government had followed policies that eroded both the Huguenot community and the rights of the "so-called Reformed religion" in the kingdom. There were many ways to accomplish this: the conversion of important members of the community (Turenne for example) either by persuasion or by bribes; the strict interpretation of the Edict of Nantes that might allow a church building to exist, but prevent its being repaired; the limitation of professions open to Huguenots; harassment of the Huguenot schools and teachers. On one side the government affronted Huguenots by edicts forbidding marriage between Huguenots and Catholics; on the other side it granted relief from taxation and even cash gifts to those who would renounce their "so-called Reformed" religion. These measures had already made a deep impact on the Huguenot community by 1679, and, indeed, serious students of the movement have suggested that Madame de Maintenon was right when (in 1680) she assumed that within another two decades there would be very few Huguenots left in the kingdom. There were, however, forces and important people in the kingdom that did not want to wait two decades to erase the "scandal"; and following 1679 a brutal policy of quartering dragoons on the Huguenot population forced conversions on a broad scale. The soldiers of 1680 were not boys drawn into the army by selective service; they were rough, tough men often shanghied into the army from the very bottom of the social ladder. When such men were thrust into a home, they created no end of disorder for the family. Whole towns suddenly became aware of the desire to be Roman Catholic when threatened by such a fate. It may be true that the policy was only a mask to the king, that his ministers did not tell him how they procured the mass conversions; it nonetheless *was* the face of Louis XIV to the Huguenot community.

The Edict of Nantes which had assured toleration of the Reformed religion was repealed in 1685 by the Edict of Fontainbleau; the migration of Huguenot intellectuals and some business and professional people began several years earlier, but after 1685 there was a considerable exodus. Historians, hoping to find justice in the world, have long asserted that Louis' France suffered severely from the economic consequences of the edict because of the migration of Huguenot merchants and artisans. The evidence now available will not support this conclusion, but it can be shown that the migration of intellectuals did rouse voices all over Europe to condemn the brutality of the French king, voices that joined those already aroused by the annexations of the French courts following 1679, and by the bombardments of Netherlands cities and Genoa. The Huguenot intellectuals were not of one mind about the future or the policy that they should adopt, but even in their squabbles with each other they added to the din that was rising all over Europe against the king of France.

Again, historians in their desire to secure justice from history have tried to show that these intellectuals were in fact responsible for the rise of the great coalition of 1689–92 against France. This sort of argument would credit the German Jews who fled Nazi tyranny with the rise of the coalition that brought the United States and the Union of Soviet Socialist Republics in alliance. It was not the pamphlets nor the sermons of the Jurieus, the Claudes, the Bayles that assembled the alliance;[18] as we shall see, the war in Hungary, the situation in England, the fears of the French court, and a dozen lesser factors were more decisive than the pamphlet and sermon campaign, but unquestionably those pamphlets and sermons did help prepare a climate of opinion that supported the

---

[18] These men did not present the same argument: Bayle firmly accepted the idea of divine right and hoped for an understanding with Louis XIV, while Jurieu fell back to the slogans and ideas of the sixteenth century polemicists who justified rebellion and sought aid from abroad.

war against France. In this way the dragonnades and the revocation of the Edict of Nantes helped to prepare Europe to accept the emerging balance of power as the governing mechanism for European society.

After the signing of the Truce of Ratisbon, the interest of Europe shifted to the east where great events were in the making. A solemn treaty placed under the guardianship of the Cardinal, protectors of the signator powers at Rome, Poland, Venice, and the Empire united in a "Holy Alliance" against the Ottoman Empire. A short time later the Regent Sophia at Moscow signed the first important treaty between the western states and Russia by joining this league against the common enemy.[19] It turned out that neither Poland nor Russia contributed much to this league, but both Venice and the Emperor, perhaps for reasons that were not really religious, successfully waged war against the Turks.

The real heart and soul of the League was Pope Innocent XI: he taxed the Roman Catholic Church all over Europe to supply soldiers and munitions for the allied effort in Hungary and, after the Venetian landing, in the Morea. This crusade had been his dream from the time he was elevated to the throne, and Christian victories owed much to his fervent support of the "holy cause." It was as much the exhortations of the old pope as the opportunity for adventure that sent noblemen with proud names as well as humble people seeking salvation through crusade, from all Europe to the battlefields of Hungary; even a prince with Bourbon blood joined the Emperor's forces in spite of his cousin's prohibition.

Warfare in Hungary, however, was no simple matter. Distances in the seventeenth century were greater than they are today; traffic on the Danube was confined to small sail-driven boats or rafts made

---

[19] Only a few years earlier the Russian Court first discovered that the Ottoman Empire was an obstruction to Russian southward advance. Tzar Alexis tried to enlist the west in an alliance against the Turks, but at that moment no one was interested; Russia was still a relatively unknown land as far as Europe was concerned, and there was no evidence that Russian military power would be of any use to the West. Pope Innocent XI, however, sought all aid possible for his crusade—even the aid of schismatics.

of logs with a tent or rough hut for shelter. Men and horses had to walk on roads that did not encourage wheeled traffic, and through territory where supplies of food and fodder were often scarce. Furthermore, as the Christian armies pushed south, their line of communications lengthened while those of their enemy contracted. In 1683–84 the first lines of Turkish defenses were broken, but Ofen (Buda) did not fall until 1686. However, when Ofen was again in Christian hands, most of Hungary to the east of the Danube as well as Transylvania were quickly overrun, and by 1688 the Imperial armies were hammering at the great fortress of Belgrade, the very heart of Turkish power in the lower Danube basin. While the Imperials conquered Hungary, the Venetians seized the Morea, and in 1687 captured Athens. It is small wonder that the French ambassador in Constantinople sent lurid letters to his king explaining that the Turks would be forced to make peace, that it was even possible that Leopold would appear in Constantinople and dictate a treaty.

The military victory was only part of the story. As the Imperial army moved down the Danube, its commanders learned much about the art of war. The musket gave way to the fusil or flint lock, and the pike disappeared from the infantry, supplanted by bayonets and racks placed in front of infantry companies to hold off the horsemen. New concepts of command gave the Imperial generals greater freedom of action and greater mobility than they had theretofore enjoyed. Wherever Christian met Turk on the battlefield, the new German art of war won victory. In France, men followed this closely; however Louvois would not allow the fusil to take the place of the musket, nor would he give up the pike: Vauban experimented with the bayonet but it was not adopted until later. The French, arrogantly relying upon drilled and disciplined troops, assumed that no German army would be a match for their forces; they were giving each soldier a uniform, the "king's coat," as standard issue; they counted upon their commissary service, their medical service, their supply trains, and their well drilled troops to assure them a measure of superiority. But many men in the French war office must have worried about the experience that the Imperial troops were piling up as well as about the morale that victory instills in an army.

The political consequences of the Christian victories were as important as the military ones. Since so many of the Hungarian Magnates had joined the Turks in hopes of establishing Tökölli as king of a new Hungary, the Imperial victories were conquests as much as liberation of territory from Islam. As the Hungarians submitted, they did so under conditions imposed upon them by the Emperor, and the familiar Hapsburg pattern, first seen in Bohemia after the Battle of White Mountain, came to be the "solution" for Hungary. The Hapsburgs were not revolutionaries: they "corrected" rather than "changed" the constitution of the lands they ruled. The Hungarian crown had been an elective one; it became hereditary in the house of Hapsburg. The Golden Bull of 1222 was corrected enough to make rebellion against the crown a treasonous act rather than a legal one. Perhaps equally important, a great number of estates changed hands; just as Emperor Ferdinand II had rewarded his followers in Bohemia, so Emperor Leopold II gave confiscated estates to his soldiers and supporters: this meant that he could count on their assistance in the future Hungarian Diets. And lastly a Hungarian Chancellory was established in Vienna where the administration of police, justice, and taxation could be supervised by the Emperor's bureaucrats, a new race of men anxious to establish the king's authority at the expense of the ancient traditional centers of power. Tax collectors from Vienna, and Jesuit missionaries in the lands that had had the "misfortune" to become Calvinist, were the harbingers of the fact that Hungary was soon to take a place in the political complex of Bohemian, German, and Hungarian crowns that were to become the Hapsburg Danubian Monarchy. On December 19, 1687, Leopold's eldest son Joseph was crowned hereditary king of Hungary; the coronation diploma was dictated by his father rather than by the Palatine and the Hungarian magnates. There was even talk of calling a *Generallandtag*, a Diet of all the Hapsburg lands; but Emperor Leopold finally contented himself with a declaration that henceforth the crowns of this Danubian state were inseparable. The politically wise, watching these events, recognized that a military power of the first magnitude was coming into existence in Central Europe.

The rise of a Danubian monarchy with potential power perhaps equal to that of France was not overlooked at Versailles. These were bad years for the king of France; his kingdom was disturbed by the problems created by the revocation of the Edict of Nantes and the subsequent difficulties contingent upon the fact that converted Huguenots had many privileges vis-à-vis the tax collector, and that many of them relapsed to their earlier heretical beliefs. In addition to that, Louis XIV suffered physically; his teeth were bad but pulling them did not always solve the problems. There developed a fistula between his mouth and nose that caused much pain and really was dangerous to his life. Then came an anal fistula that was only healed by an operation that was as painful as it was dangerous. In 1687 Louis was fifty years old; in the seventeenth century this was an advanced age; no one would have predicted that he would continue to live for two and a half decades more. The king's bad health made it difficult to make political decisions in a state where the king really was important in the decision-making process. Perhaps this may even be the reason why the men at Versailles followed events in the Danube basin with a self-deception characteristic of this regime. In the spring, Louis and his ministers were always sure that the Imperials would not be able to accomplish anything: the letters to and from Versailles were always filled with the belief that the Christian armies would not have enough money, men or supplies to achieve any considerable objective; by fall, especially after 1686, it was always a problem to find some excuse to cover previous optimism which obviously had been based upon wishful thinking. It was difficult for them to believe that the German troops, the caterpillars," could really become the equals of French soldiers, and yet these troops were about to conquer a great kingdom.

Thus, even though men at Versailles did not want to believe that Emperor Leopold might come to rule a powerful state complex that might threaten the frontiers of France, it was difficult to escape the fact that this was possible. During these years a well-informed news letter sent from Versailles rarely failed to include news from the war in Hungary, for this war was altering the balance of power in Europe.

Unhappily for the men at Versailles, Hungary was not the only problem of these years that affected the frontiers of France. As we have seen at the time of the war of the Devolution, the Anglo-Dutch alliance called a halt to French expansion; again in 1678 the threat that Charles II would be forced by his Parliament to join the enemies of France was an important factor in making the peace. Louis XIV could and did regard the English king much as he looked at the king of Poland, that is as a mendicant who could be bought by money, and yet the English king could not really deliver his kingdom unless the Parliament favored the program. Louis explained to his son that no greater evil could befall a monarch than this dependence upon an elected body; where such conditions existed it made impossible both a royal policy and any real faith in pledged word of the kingdom. The situation in England after 1685 became almost as much a source of French anxiety as that in Hungary.

Stated briefly, it was simply this: Charles II died in 1685 leaving no legitimate heirs of his body; thus his brother James II mounted the throne as the legitimate king. James had been forced to abandon his post as Lord Admiral because he would not subscribe to the Test Act which required all office holders to receive communion in the Anglican Church. He was a devout Roman Catholic. The Test Act, however, could not prevent him from becoming king; indeed, when his brother's illegitimate son, the Duke of Monmouth, tried to raise a rebellion against him, Parliament gave James II money to assemble a large army to suppress the movement. Even those most loyal to the Anglican Church were also loyal to the ideal of divine right of kings, and would do nothing to prevent James from taking his rightful place on the English throne. This was an interesting dilemma facing pious men who believed that history was God's work on earth and that thrones were given by Him rather than by men. Thus even though James did not subscribe to their Anglican Church, these conservatives and the Tory politicians supported his right to be their king. A few years before the Whigs had attempted to exclude James from the succession. The Whig politicians and others were not so happy to see him on the throne, but they took hope from the fact that his heirs were two Protestant princesses: Mary, the wife of William of Orange and Anne, wife of a Danish prince. If James did not sire a son with his young wife, Mary of Modena, all would be well, for his daughters could be counted upon to defend the Anglican Church. Hopes for good relations ran so high that James' first Parliament was much more generous with him than Parliaments had been with his brother.

The situation, however, did not remain so cordial: James was determined to restore Catholic worship in England and to give his Roman Catholic subjects a significant place in his government. The Test Act prevented a Roman Catholic from serving, for a pious Roman Catholic believed that it would endanger his soul if he took communion in a heretical service. James found a way to circumvent that act. He provided Roman Catholics with a Declaration of Indulgence which exempted them from the provisions of the Test Act. At first James made each case a separate one, but when he got a court ruling supporting his right to give this Indulgence, he issued a general declaration exempting both Roman Catholics and Protestant dissenters from the requirements of the Test Act. As more and more Roman Catholics entered his government, and Anglicans were informed that they should convert if they wished to retain their posts, many people in England greatly feared that James would soon be in a position to call for a new Parliament and, by pressure exerted by royal (Roman Catholic) officials, he could arrange to have a Catholic majority that would legalize the restoration of the Roman Catholic Church in England. When James introduced Catholic priests into Oxford University, and quietly allowed the public practice of Catholic services, this possibility became more and more serious.

The crisis broke when James brought charges of seditious libel against seven bishops who refused to have the General Declaration of Indulgence read from the pulpit. Anglican England went into shock to see the king attack such God-fearing men, most of whom as good Tories had warmly supported James' right to the throne. The jury unanimously pronounced them "not guilty." This scandalous trial was immediately followed by the birth of a male child to Mary of Modena. The Catholics called it a miracle; the Anglicans insisted that the child was an imposter introduced into the queen's bed in a warming pan. No matter which might be true, the crisis deepened, for now a Catholic dynasty could establish itself on the throne and by royal prerogative it probably could reintroduce the Roman Catholic Church in England.

For a long time leaders of the emerging Whig party had foreseen this possibility. They had attempted to prevent James from mounting the throne by proposing an Exclusion Act, but the consciences of men who believed in Divine Right had not permitted such revolutionary action. When James began to introduce Catholics into high office, Irishmen into his army, and Catholic priests into positions of influence, the Whig politicians made contact with William of Orange in the Netherlands as a possible defender of the faith against their Catholic king who happened to be his father-in-law. When the crisis became acute in 1688 this relationship between the English Whigs and William became a plot to force James to "obey the law," or be driven from the throne. Louis XIV learned about the cabal that threatened his cousin's crown, but somehow James either did not hear of it or refused to believe it. He would not take seriously Louis' warnings.

Louis XIV saw with astonishment the blindness of the English king. He did not want to see England fall into the hands of his old enemy, William of Orange, and yet he could not "save James" without the English king's consent. How blind James really was to the situation that confronted him can be seen by the fact that, when Louis XIV invaded the Rhineland in the late summer of 1688, James denounced the act as contrary to the Treaty of Nymwegen and proposed action against France. This only a few months before William's army landed on English soil! It is no wonder that the French did not know what to expect from England.

While the war in Hungary moved with fire and blood to create a new political structure on the Danube and a new organization of power in southeastern Europe, and the crisis in England marched toward a showdown between Anglican and Roman Catholic interests that might involve the fate of the Netherlands as well as England, two new crises emerged in the Rhineland. The one concerned the future of the Electorate of Cologne; the second involved the territories of the Rhine Palatinate. The French government was deeply involved in both.

The problem at Cologne was very complex. The electoral throne had so long been filled by princes from the Bavarian House of Wittelsbach that it had become a prerogative of the family to place one of its members on that throne. At the same time the Cologne Electors had for so long accepted French money and acted in French interests that the men at Versailles regarded Cologne as an extension of their own power. The occupant of the episcopal throne in the 1680's was old and sick; he owed the king of France a huge sum of money that worried him greatly, for he did not want to leave such a debt for his successor; indeed, if he died with it unpaid, his possessions might be confiscated.

His government, almost from the time that he had assumed the throne, had been managed by the Fürstenberg brothers: Franz Egon was succeeded as prime minister and as bishop of Strassbourg at his death in 1682 by his brother William Egon. The latter became a cardinal in 1686, and, as a French agent, exerted a strong influence in the Elector's government. The Fürstenbergs had been enlisted into the French service by Mazarin just as Richelieu had enlisted him, and throughout most of Louis XIV's reign they had been important in shaping the king's German policies. Louis had secured the cardinal's hat for William Egon at a time when the Elector of Cologne himself wished for this high honor; the French, hoping to use von Fürstenberg's services in Germany, planned to have him made Coadjutor Archbishop of Cologne so that upon the death of the current incumbent he might step into his shoes. While this suited Louis and von Fürstenberg, it did not satisfy either the Emperor or the House of Wittelsbach. The Emperor did not want a French agent to become an elector in the Empire; the Wittelsbach family felt that the younger brother of Max Emanuel, Josef Clemens, should be the next Elector of Cologne even though he was still a boy and not yet a priest. There were other complications, but von Fürstenberg succeeded in getting enough votes in the Cathedral chapter to have himself postulated for the office of Coadjutor—only to have the Elector die before any action was taken at Rome. Innocent XI was pleased not to act; it was fortunate for him that he could not "appoint a coadjutor to a dead man."

The conflict then turned to the postulation for the place of the dead Elector, and neither von Fürstenberg nor Prince Josef Clemens received the required number of votes for postulation, so the whole problem was thrown into the lap of the Pope. Pope Innocent was at war with Louis XIV over other problems, and he resented the French attitude toward his crusade in Hungary, and yet he had to listen to the most powerful king in Europe. There were, however, other problems: Prince Josef Clemens' brother, Max Emanuel, was the Imperial commander besieging Belgrade just when the decision had to be made, and the Emperor had rights at Rome at least equal to those of the king of France. By the late summer of 1688 it was painfully clear at Versailles that Innocent was going to decide in favor of the Bavarian Wittelsbach.

The issue concerning the Rhine Palatinate also came to a head at almost the same time. This problem was much less clear. When the Elector Karl of the Palatinate died, May 1685, without male heirs, the electoral throne fell to the Pfalz-Neuburg family. This seemed to be a victory for Catholicism, but it was also fortunate for the Emperor since his empress was a princess of that family, and the new Elector could be expected to support imperial policies. The inheritance of the late Elector, however, was not entirely clear. No one could question the fact that the lands of the Palatinate proper could be inherited only through the male heir, but there were serious questions about the Pfalz-Neuburg rights to other lands of the late Elector. Louis XIV decided to find out whether his sister-in-law, Elizabeth Charlotte, who was also the sister of the late Elector, did not have a right to part or all of these disputable claims. It would be handy to have his brother, the Duke of Orleans, in the German Diet and occupying territory so near to the frontiers of France. However, neither the Elector nor the Emperor were willing to recognize these claims, and in 1688 they also were before Pope Innocent XI for arbitration. Like the French pretensions in the Electorate of Cologne, the chances for a decision favorable to France were slender indeed.

Hungary, England, the Rhineland, the unfriendly attitude of Innocent XI and the possibility that a collapse of the Turkish Empire would free the Imperials for adventures in the west: these were the problems of 1688 that had to be considered by men at Versailles to be sure of the safety and the power of the kingdom of France. The fortification of the frontiers was not complete before these dangerous crises appeared on the horizon to show how drastically the balance of power had been altered since 1683. The government in Versailles had now to decide what must be done to assure the kingdom and the integrity of the frontiers that had been traced since the peace of Nymwegen.

# Chapter 4

# The First Worldwide War

The summer of 1688 was a difficult one for the men who governed France. Louis XIV was fifty years old; his health had been bad for several years, so bad that many men were looking to the Dauphin as the next king. At this point in its history the kingdom of France depended upon a strong king to direct the work of his ministers and give unity to the efforts of his government; without a strong king at the center of affairs, no policy could have much assurance of success. Louis' son, the Grand Dauphin, was not one to inspire much confidence: fat, fatuous, indolent—he inherited enough of his mother's character and intelligence to place the very future of the kingdom in jeopardy. With such a man as the next king, it would be most unwise to become involved in any prolonged affair. And yet the march of events in Europe would not slow up to accommodate the situation at Versailles. In this summer the Imperial armies that had always been discounted at Versailles, were pounding at the last Turkish outpost on the middle Danube, the great fortification of Belgrade, and every indication pointed to an imminent Christian victory. Indeed the French ambassador at the Sublime Porte even seemed to fear that Emperor Leopold would soon arrive at Constantinople itself and dictate peace. If Belgrade should fall, how could Pope Innocent XI refuse the request of its conqueror, Max Emanuel, that his brother be given the Electoral throne at Cologne? Indeed who could believe that the Pope would listen to French demands either about Cologne or the Palatinate at the moment when victory in Hungary and the coronation of Archduke Joseph at Budapest as hereditary king, pointed to the striking shift in the balance of power in the European world?

Nor did French troubles end there. Louis' relations with England were important for the French position in Europe; in 1668 and again in 1678 the possibility that England might join his enemies had been important factors in forcing the French government to accept peace terms. Thus the alliance with James II was important. But James was in trouble: he was moving very fast toward the restoration of Catholic worship in England and the establishment of Catholics in important positions in his government. The birth of a male heir to the Stuart throne added to the danger, for many Englishmen were now much concerned about the future. Louis had urged him to move more slowly in his program for the restoration of Catholicism in England. And after the birth of the prince, James Edward, he added the warning that the troops being assembled in the Netherlands by William of Orange were intended for use in inland kingdoms.[20] But James II did not want to be dependent on France; he refused to believe that his son-in-law was planning action against him. It was a dangerous thing; for Louis could not "save" James unless the English king wanted to be saved, and yet, if he allowed William to invade England, there was always the danger that England would be made into an enemy of France.

The problem was complex indeed. Louis knew that a considerable faction of the Regents in the Netherlands was quite hostile to any intervention in England that might leave the Netherlands exposed. He also believed that there was a hard core of men in England who were committed so strongly to the idea of the Divine Right of kings that they would fight rather than allow a Dutch prince to usurp the throne. A half century earlier civil war in England had been a long hard struggle that had removed English influence from continental affairs for almost a decade. Louvois convinced both himself and the king that this would happen again should William invade England. Indeed, not only Eng-

---

[20] In 1688, England and Scotland were still a dual monarchy.

land but also the United Netherlands could become so involved in the civil war that both would be removed from European affairs at least long enough to allow the king of France to settle his accounts with the German empire.

There were other problems at Versailles. Even though huge sums of money had already been spent on the palace of Versailles and the lines of frontier fortifications, neither was completed. The chapel at Versailles had not even been started, and many of the fortifications were still only half-finished. These expenses, however, added to the deficits caused by the so-called Dutch War, were most embarrassing for the treasury. France was the richest kingdom in Europe, but there were limits to its wealth. The great trouble was that the king had no simple way to mobilize the wealth of the kingdom for the projects of his government. The tax system was relatively rigid and there were no obvious areas still untapped for the finance minister to invade. Unlike England, the excise field in France had been exploited as the only way to force the privileged classes to pay a share toward the public expenses. The Dutch War and the expenditures for construction had been supported in part by "extraordinary" fiscal measures, and it was not clear where new sources of wealth could be found. Louis XIV, like Mazarin before him, never liked to think that such a thing as money could limit his needs or his projects, and yet his advisors had to remember that the treasury was not in flourishing condition.

On the other side of the ledger, both the army and the navy were in excellent shape. Louvois' enormous labors as war minister bore fruit. The soldiers were now uniformed in the king's coat, armed with the king's muskets, recruited, commanded, and drilled by officers who could largely be depended upon to obey the orders of the ministry of war. The magazines were well stocked with war materials and there were forges and workshops to back up the troops with powder, ball, cannons, and muskets. True, the French army was still equipped with the matchlock, even though the flintlock (fusil) had proved its usefulness in Hungary, because Louvois feared that the latter would fail to fire during wet weather; and the bayonet had not yet completely displaced the pike, for Louvois could not believe that the latter really was obsolete. Nonetheless, there was no army in Europe with the siege equipment, the arsenals, and the supplies available to the French, nor had any other army in Europe yet established the same degree of discipline and control directed from the ministry of war that had been achieved in France.

The navy, too, was in excellent condition. After Colbert's death his talented son Seignelay gave the navy an effective administration. The French ships were models of naval architecture; in contrast to the traditional methods employed in England and particularly in the Netherlands where war ships were still constructed under the direction of "master craftsmen," the French men-of-war were built with the advantages of the best scientific knowledge available at the time. As a result France's enemies in the two wars following 1688 were always anxious to capture French war ships intact for their own use. Seignelay was also responsible for the building of navel arsenals on both the Atlantic and Mediterranean with workshops for the manufacture of cannons, anchors, and rigging for the ships, as well as naval supplies to keep them at sea. The revocation of the Edict of Nantes had deprived the navy of one of its best commanders, but there were others who could take his place. There was no question about it, the French army and navy were ready for a *blitz* war, but there was not enough money in the treasury to maintain such a military force in a long war of attrition.

As the summer of 1688 wore on, the situation became more and more tense every day. The French knew that the Imperials were going to win at Belgrade; they also knew that William III earnestly discussed the "Protestant cause" when he talked to German princes about the projected invasion of England, and that he stressed the need for bringing England into the balance against France when he talked to Catholic princes. Nor could Louis turn the religious issue to his advantage for Pope Innocent XI himself as well as Emperor Leopold seemed to favor William's plans. It was not a religious issue. What was at stake was the balance of power in Europe. The Imperial victories, the crowning of Hapsburg prince Joseph as king of Hungary and king of the Romans, the leagues and alliances involving Spain, Sweden, the Netherlands, and the Empire had all tilted the balance sharply against France. The League of Augsburg undoubtedly was a "paper league" since the troops that were pledged by its signers were nearly all involved against the Turks on the lower Danube, but that League was indicative of the future when victory over the Ottoman Empire would release the German veterans for adventures in the Rhineland.

By the last of August, 1688 a decision had to be made. Louvois added up all the counters and "discovered" that it would be possible to launch a lightning war against the German Rhine princes that would force them to accommodate themselves to France's demands. These demands were to be "reasonable"; the French king only wanted recognition of the truce of Ratisbon by a permanent peace treaty that would legalize all the gains that France had made since the peace of Nymwegen. Prodded by Louvois, the men at Versailles convinced themselves that a strong show of force would accomplish this objective and perhaps a little more.

Once the decision was taken, the French action was quick and effective. Troops and supplies were rapidly and secretly moved into position; many of the commanding officers did not know where they were going until the last minute. Then the French army appeared in force before Phillippsburg, and French ambassadors in every court of Europe announced the "generous" intentions of the French king. They explained that the rise of the League of Augsburg as a threat to France was evidence that the Emperor and the German princes were ready to tear up the Truce of Ratisbon and to trample on French pretentions in Cologne and the Palatinate. The French explained that their armies in Germany would be withdrawn and both Phillippsburg and Freiburg restored to the Empire (after the destruction of the defensive works) if the Emperor and Empire would make the Truce of Ratisbon into a permanent peace. To emphasize the need for haste, the French note carried an ultimatum: the definite treaty of peace must be completed by January 1, 1689.

In the nineteenth century Clausewitz explained that a state cannot expect to accomplish political objectives without having the military power to achieve them. This lesson was soon to be brought home to the king of France and his advisors. The French army that appeared before Phillippsburg was a powerful force, commanded by a brilliant corps of officers, including the great engineer Vauban, who directed the operations under the titular command of the Dauphin. But Phillippsburg was surrounded on three sides by swampy ground that prevented any military operations; the fourth side was strongly defended. As luck would have it, heavy rains turned the ground before this fourth side into a sea of mud just after the French set up camp before the fortification. The mud and the skill of the German commander combined to delay the siege; from the 25th of September until the last of October, the fortification held out against the assault. Louis and Louvois, reading the reports, were much upset at the slowness of the operation, but their urgent letters demanding haste could not overcome the difficulties before Phillippsburg. The whole campaign, intended to sweep the Rhineland, was delayed: Mannheim and Heidelberg could not repeat the performance of Phillippsburg, but neither could the French keep up their time schedule. The siege of Phillippsburg had blunted the lightning war!

Then a second problem emerged. The French had planned on quartering the army in the Palatinate and Baden for the winter, thereby forcing the Germans to pay for its upkeep. This was expected to make the German princes more anxious to negotiate. But the plan was frustrated by the appearance on the middle Danube of Bavarian and Imperial cavalry that were supposed to be bottled up in Hungary, and of Prussian and Hanoverian troops on the lower Rhine. It soon became apparent that French troops could not be put in winter quarters, indeed that they probably could not stay in Germany at all. Furthermore there was no indication that the German princes were ready to "accommodate themselves" to the demands of the French king.

It was at this point that the French arrived at another fateful decision. The fortifications on the Rhine-Moselle frontier and on up to the Channel had, in fact, made France into a massive fortress. The military thought of the period generally believed it necessary to destroy all houses or buildings outside of the walls of a fortification that was about to be besieged to prevent the enemy from using these buildings as shelter for his attacking operations. Such destruction left free the field of fire for the fortress artillery. France had become a massive fortress; what could be more reasonable than the destruction of all installations opposite France that might be used by an enemy army? This idea had been used at least once before during the Dutch war when the French prevented the planting of crops in a wide area along the Moselle frontier to make it difficult, if not impossible, for an enemy army to feed its horses in that zone, and without horses no army could hope to mount an offensive. In any case, in December 1688 the plan to devastate the Rhineland crystalized at Versailles; it was probably inspired by Chamlay and Louvois, but it was supported by the king as well. In Germany, opposite the French frontier, a band of territory fifty or so miles deep was to be devastated: the king ordered his soldiers to destroy all chateaux, villages, towns and cities that could be used by an enemy army. This was the fateful decision that was to give the French a reputation as bad as one acquired by the Huns when they penetrated Europe centuries before, and German propagandists were quick to pin that name upon the French. This destruction aroused all Germany as Germany had not been moved in all its previous history.

The orders were clear: the German side of the Rhine opposite Alsace and the Palatinate were destined for destruction, and the population of these lands were to be driven away leaving only desolation. Here and there the king relented to save a church or a shrine, but never to prevent the demolition of houses of men. But it is one thing to order such destruction and quite another to accomplish it. It was easy enough to burn thatched roofs and wooden houses, but much of the building in the area was in stone. The village house had little furniture, and a new roof could easily be rebuilt. To level these buildings, especially in the towns and cities, was a formidable task that would require large quantities of powder and many men. Furthermore, the destruction was put in the hands of the army, and many of the officers were quite unwilling to carry out such brutal orders, or if they did so, they carried them out only half-heartedly. The officer who suggested that the city fathers should get their fire fighting equipment ready because he had to set fire to the city, was obviously unenthusiastic over his task. Many noblemen, officers in the army, had second thoughts about turning harmless people into a cold German winter with no shelter; this was not their code. Furthermore the Imperial and Bavarian cavalry interfered with the operations. Louvois' letters to his commanders from the end of December until Spring are filled with reiterated orders, expressions of astonishment over failure to comply, and threats of reprisals against disobedient soldiers. Had the officers wholeheartedly cooperated, the French reputation would have been much worse than it was.

Even so the destruction was considerable. Mannheim was almost completely demolished and its inhabitants driven away. Those who sought to return to the ruins were shot. Louvois even considered removing the very stones that had been the walls of Mannheim's houses to strengthen the fortifications of Phillippsburg. Spire, Worms, and Oppenheim were left in smoking ruins; Mainz was bombarded and partially destroyed; at Heidelberg the *Schloss* was largely demolished, leaving it in the condition that tourists see today, but the town was only partially burned. The most disastrous blows fell upon the villages and the country chateaux: French cavalry carried the torch with terrible rigor throughout large areas leaving smoking ruins and desolate people with no recourse save flight to lands beyond reach of the French horsemen. These were the people who carried the word to all Germany that the stories about the violence and tyranny of the French king told by the Huguenots were true.

The years since 1680 had seen a rising storm of pamphlets and books condemning French policies; most of them were published in the lower Rhineland or the United Netherlands; they protested French aggression by the Courts of Reunion, accused the French king of being an ally of the Turk, and derided his perfidy. After 1685 when the migration of Huguenot intellectuals reached flood tide, these articulate enemies of the French king added to the clamor. Louis XIV was "a tyrant" and "oppressor of truth," a ruler who abused the powers that God had entrusted to him; he and his ministers could not be trusted to keep their word. One segment of the emigré population developed the thesis that they could not return to their homeland until war broke the power of the tyrant king; they became propagandists damanding war against their fatherland. After the devastation of the Rhineland, the Germans added their voices with moral earnestness to this clamor. The "dragonnades" were being re-enacted in the Rhineland; the violence against the innocent Huguenots was now directed against innocent Germans. Hatred for France and the French king seemed about to unite Germany for the first time since the Reformation. The invasion of 1688 and the devastations of 1689 can be set as the dates for the first flare of German nationalism. The princes of Germany now had the support of the articulate public for a war that would punish the invaders.

The French invasion of the Palatinate released William of Orange for a descent on England. The timid Dutch politicians were unwilling to let his army sail until after the bulk of the French forces were safely committed in Germany and therefore no longer constituted a threat to the United Netherlands. James' reaction to the danger that faced his regime is most interesting. When Louis invaded the Palatinate, James II announced that the act was contrary to the treaty of Nymwegen, and proposed that England would assist the signatories of that treaty to force the French to withdraw. No one paid any attention to this suggestion. Then James suddenly realized that his son-in-law really did intend to invade England. Hastily he tried to make amends by withdrawing some of the objectionable measures that had aroused the Protestant English politicians against him, but again, no one paid any attention for all eyes were concentrated on the Netherlands where the Protestant army was preparing to sail. James must have known that many of the men around him were ready to desert to William, but he apparently did not understand how impossible his position had become. The fact that he had adamantly refused to accept the aid that Louis had offered earlier in the year must be taken as evidence of the blindness, or perhaps the treason, of the men who were advising him. When the crisis was upon England, Chamlay proposed to Louis XIV that France should intervene anyway (October, 1688), but the king both piqued at James' blindness and unwillingness to associate himself with France, and convinced that William's invasion would result in a long civil war, refused to consider any action.

William's invasion of England was well planned politically. The Whig chiefs who had invited him were reasonably sure that the Tory politicians whose tender consciences forced them to accept James as "the king given by God" would stand aside once a Protestant army was on English shores. The military plans, too, were well made, but at the last minute contrary winds forced a change in the place of landing that might have been a disaster had James' followers been able to act promptly. But the invading army was well commanded (by Marshal Schomberg who had left the French service after the Revocation of the Edict of Nantes) and the English population received it hospitably. For a few days there was much confusion for no one really knew what was going to happen, and many English noblemen and officials were anxious to come down on the "right," e.g., the winning side, but the confusion was greatest in James' court where some of his most trusted officers were preparing treason against him. To cap it all, James' own action was foolish and indecisive; his final flight to France was complete admission that he did not know how to save his throne. The story has been told so many times that it does not seem necessary to repeat it here; James sent his wife and infant son to France ahead of him and then followed rather than face his son-in-law and the victorious Whig politicians who had been his enemies for a very long time.

The English revolutionary settlement does concern this story, for the "Protestant" victory brought England into the war against France and the constitutional settlement of 1689 gave England a government that had the authority and the will to mobilize the wealth and military power of the island kingdom. A "Convention Parliament" that met early in 1689 ended the confusion and the misunderstandings by declaring the throne to be vacant and calling Prince William of Orange and his wife Mary Stuart to become king and queen of England.[21] William could not dictate to the Parliament what its actions would be, but he refused either to accept a post as "Regent" for his father-in-law or to be a "Prince Consort" to his wife. The English politicians were not too pleased to have him as king, but there was no other solution. The Whigs accepted him as king *de jure;* the Tories, who still believed in divine right, as king *de facto.* In both camps there were many men who, while serving William's government, tried to keep in contact with the exiled royal family in France as political insurance for the future. This situation continued as long as William lived; it became especially marked after the death of Mary (1694) for William's Dutch manners and friends were then even more markedly foreign to England and English ways.

As we shall see in a later chapter (Chapter 6), the revolutionary settlement of 1689 proved to be a decisive act in the development of England's status as a military power. The Revolution armed the island kingdom as it had never been armed before, and the fact that Louis XIV was supporting the dethroned James II made it

---

[21] William was the son of a Stuart princess, the daughter of Charles I; Mary was the daughter of James II. These relationships to the House of Stuart seemed to give a modicum of legitimacy to their position, and yet everyone knew that James II and after him the baby prince, James Edward, were the legitimate claimants to the throne. Thus the Parliament established a new principle of law: namely, that the succession to a throne was not necessarily the act of God; it could be established by an act of men. This principle seemed scandalous to a king like Louis XIV, but it proved to be a powerful argument in the hands of English politicians and statesmen.

possible for all England to unite against France, and to dedicate the kingdom's resources to the needs of the war. In doing this, England prepared itself for its great role in the power mechanisms of European society for the next two centuries.

The proclamation of William and Mary as king and queen of England did not automatically bring England into the coalition that was forming against France. Indeed there were many men in England who would have preferred to remain neutral and garner the economic advantages that might become available when the continent was at war. The march of events, however, was inexorable. After William embarked for England, Louis XIV, fulfilling his earlier threat, declared war on the United Netherlands (November, 1688). In December-January the Elector of Brandenburg and then the German Diet at Ratisbon declared war on France, and within a few months all the German princes whose power amounted to anything had joined the alliance against France. About the same time the French-born queen of Spain, Marie Louise, suddenly died under circumstances that suggested poison. With her influence ended, the German faction at Madrid soon gained the upper hand, and German troops were invited to garrison the fortifications in the Spanish Netherlands preparatory to using them as a base for action against France. Louis replied with another declaration of war (April, 1689) for a "neutral" Spain could be dangerous if the Spanish Netherlands became a base for the Imperial army. As the list of France's enemies grew, Louvois' "quick victory" was soon lost in the smoke of cannon and musket fire, and his arguments about the ease of forcing German princes to "accommodate themselves", drowned in the sound of marching feet. Louvois' war had joined the war in the Danube Basin, and now the whole world would feel its force.

The coalition, of course, had already started to assemble before the invasion of the Palatinate, but those early alliances were not precise enough to form the basis for fighting a war. Thus on May 16, 1689 Emperor Leopold and the United Netherlands signed a new treaty in which they agreed to pool their military resources against France, and conclude peace only when they would be able to force France to return to the territorial settlements of 1661, thereby wiping out all of the gains made by Louis XIV since he assumed personal direction of his government. In this same treaty the Dutch agreed to support the Austrian Hapsburg claims to the throne of

Spain in the event that Charles II should die without an heir of his body. All of the important German princes joined this alliance with the Emperor, and in 1690 the King of Spain and the Duke of Savoy (October) also entered the coalition. Thus Louis was confronted with the same enemies that had come so near to frustrating his plans in 1673–78; it only remained for England to join the alliance to make his position really dangerous.

Louis himself provided William with the needed argument for bringing England into the war by supporting James II's efforts to reconquer his throne by an invasion of Ireland. The Catholic Irish had almost immediately rallied to the support of the Catholic king by attacking the Protestant landlords and governors who exploited their country, and by establishing a provincial council to aid James II. In France this seemed to be the opportunity either to frustrate William's plans or develop the long civil war that the French had counted upon to neutralize both England and the Netherlands. Louis sent his warships with supplies and a small contingent of soldiers to assist the Irish rebels. A naval engagement at Bantry Bay (May 11, 1689) between the English and French fleets gave the French the advantage and allowed them to land both the supplies and the English king in Ireland. This, of course, was the challenge to William and the English revolution that could not be ignored in London; England could hardly avoid entering the war. Unfortunately for Louis, the Irish rebels were little more than an ill-armed mob, quite incapable of undertaking any serious military effort, and James II, more interested in returning to England than in building a government in Ireland, failed miserably to merge what powers there might have been at his disposal in Ireland into any effective force. The French were appalled to see French officers killed in senseless battles while the supplies that should have supported them rotted on the docks. James was not even able to force the surrender of the handful of Anglo-Scotch Protestants at Londonderry before William ferried over relief. At Versailles the only consolation was that William probably could have found another pretext to bring England into the war even if the French had not supported the invasion of Ireland.

The summer and fall of 1689 saw little fighting on the continent. William needed his army in England, where men feared a French descent upon their coasts, and in Ireland, to defeat the rebellion and drive James from the island. The Emperor also could not deploy his forces because the war on the Danube still required much of the attention of his soldiers, for when France invaded the Palatinate, the Turks broke off the negotiations for a treaty of peace; they could hope that the Emperor would be unable to maintain his pressure on their Empire. For their part, the French still expected to see the coalition break up and allow the writing of a treaty of peace. In the meantime French armies occupied parts of the Rhineland and the Spanish Netherlands, levying contributions on the population so that the costs of occupation were unwillingly borne largely by others than the king's subjects. The next year the war would start in earnest.

William would have preferred to fight in Flanders, but the presence of a Franco-Irish army in Ireland forced him to concentrate on that theatre. The French re-inforced James' army in the winter of 1690, and William managed to ferry another 20,000 or so troops to support von Schomberg's detachments, and a naval battle was shaping up since the French managed to bring the Toulon fleet around to the Atlantic to join the fleet at Brest. At the same time the contestants moved toward a battle in Flanders where Prince von Waldeck, a close friend of William III, commanding an army of Dutch and German troops prepared to invade France while Marshal Luxembourg organized a French army to resist him. The time of crisis came the last days of June and the first few days of July. Marshal von Schomberg's army defeated the Franco-Irish on the Boyne, but the old Marshal was killed, and the Franco-Irish were able to withdraw in reasonably good order toward the coast. Happily for James II, the French navy carried the victory at Beachy Head in an engagement that aroused acrimonious disputes between the English and Dutch, and blackened the reputation of an English admiral. In control of the sea, the French were able to convoy James and his army back to France; a maneuver that proved the military power of the French king, but left Ireland in the hands of William III. In Flanders the decisive battle came with a French victory at Fleurus where Marshal Luxembourg showed himself to be a soldier of the mold of the Great Condé. The proposed invasion of France was definitely postponed, and yet the French were not in a position to follow up their victory by the occupation of the Spanish Netherlands. A few days later at Staffarda, Italy, Marshal Catinat defeated the Spanish-Savoyard army and presumably opened the gate into the peninsula. The cathedrals of

France sent up *Te Deums* to thank God for the victories, but there was a wry note in the atmosphere, for none of the French king's enemies sued for peace; indeed defeat seemed only to harden their determination to continue the war.

Thus by the end of the summer of 1690 Louis XIV found himself engaged in a war with most of Europe, and a war from which there seemed little hope for finding a way to disengage. The Turkish recapture of Belgrade in October of 1690 may have provided some satisfaction in Versailles, but it did not change the situation: France was at war and there was no obvious way to bring it to an end. The attempted negotiations with Denmark, Sweden, and North German princes that tried to create a "neutral party" to act as mediator, failed to persuade either the Dutch or the Germans that the better part of valor indicated peace on terms satisfactory to France. There was nothing to do but gird for war in hopes of finding peace with the sword.

While this situation was serious for the French, it was by no means desperate. The French frontiers were as secure as modern military engineering could make them. In the decade 1679–1689 Vauban had labored almost without rest to plug up the routes that a foe might use for invasion, and his efforts had produced the first great "line" since the days of the Roman occupation of western Europe. The French army too, was excellent. Louvois not only had reduced the officer corps to obedience to the Ministry of War, but also had provided his king with soldiers who were drilled, uniformed, and supplied more effectively than any army since the days of the Caesars. There were arsenals filled with war supplies, and workshops to make more. The French were probably correct in assuming that their army was the best in Europe. The victories at Bantry Bay and Beachy Head were striking evidence of the power of the French navy, a tribute to the Marquis of Seignelay, who had followed his father's footsteps in the creation of a great naval force. This was in 1690; who could foresee that within a very short time both Louvois and Seignelay would be dead and that terrible economic problems would cripple the French war effort?

There has been a persistent myth to the effect that after the deaths of Turenne and Condé, Louis XIV's soldiers were commanded by inferior officers. The facts are somewhat at variance with this tradition. Marshal Luxembourg proved himself to be as effective a field commander as any that appeared in Europe since

the Thirty Years War, and he was backed up by marshals like
Catinat and Boufflers, and others who were excellent division commanders, and lieutenant generals like Villars, Vendôme and several
others, some of whom were killed before their full capacity became apparent. It may be true that commanders like Marshal
Lorges and his brother Duras earned their batons by being nephews
of Turenne or that Vivonne and Villeroy earned theirs as childhood
friends of the king or even through the king's mistress, but the
French army of 1690 was surely better commanded than those of
its foes, especially after the death of Charles of Lorraine. Louis
may have had reason to be angry at Louvois for misjudging the
possibility of winning a quick victory in 1688, but he could not
have been dissatisfied with the war minister who had provided
him with engineers and tacticians like Vauban and Chamlay and
soldiers like Luxembourg and Catinat to command his armies in
the field.

The fall of 1690 and the spring of 1691 was a period of crisis
for the enemies of France. The Dutch believed that the English
had let them down at Beachy Head; they were sure that the Emperor should have made peace with the Turks so that he could
fight on the Rhine. The alliance included so many dispersed interests that it was difficult to find any solid foundation upon which
to build plans for the war. They were all agreed in their hatred
for France and the French king: aggressions, incendiaries, enforced
contributions, bombardments, and the mask of terror worn by
French power; these were the things that held together the coalition.
But the English, the Dutch, the Emperor, the German princes, the
king of Spain and the duke of Savoy each had ambitions, interests,
aspirations, hopes and fears that were not shared by the other
members of the coalition. To make matters worse they had had
but little experience in managing a coalition war. The Dutch war
of 1672–78 ended with the Emperor and the king of Spain suspicious of their allies, with William of Orange at odds with the
Regents of his own country, with the English uncertain whether
the force that they had landed at Ostende was part of the war or
not. It was now a question whether William had enough prestige in
both the United Netherlands and England to hold these two
powers to their alliances with the Emperor and the German
princes. Nor was the political question alone a problem. When
Charles of Lorraine died (1690), the coalition lost its only good

commander. William was a stubborn soldier, but not an effective one; Waldeck lost his reputation as well as the battle on the field of Fleurus, and Max Emanuel, the conqueror of Belgrade, may have had a flair for fighting the Turks but he was too careless, too inattentive to details to hope for success against Marshal Luxembourg. Ludwig of Baden, a methodical uninspired commander whose best hours were those when he resolutely stood on the defense, was as good or better than anyone available to the Imperials. But until Eugene of Savoy emerged in the latter 1690's as the great soldier of the Imperial armies, there were no really first-rate commanders available to the coalition. This was not a military situation promising any great successes.

In the early spring of 1691, William III assembled his allies in a conference at the Hague to formulate a common plan for the war against France. In Versailles the men who had so long recommended policies of brutal force assumed that this would be the opportunity to break the alliance by a strike that would demonstrate its weakness. One French army marched on Mons in the Spanish Netherlands, another on Nice. The Savoyards had no way of relieving the Mediterranean city, and when William marched to break the siege of Mons, he found himself confronted by a strongly entrenched French army of observation under Marshal Luxembourg. The city of Mons fell. But the coalition did not break apart. The weaker members decided that their only hope for safety was to be found in the Anglo-Dutch-Imperial alliance, and they convinced themselves that this coalition could win even though it had not succeeded yet in organizing a unified plan for action against the enemy.

This summer of 1691 also produced a new situation in France. Toward the end of July, Louvois, leaving the chambers of the king early because he felt unwell, suddenly worsened and in a few hours was dead. The preceding year had seen the death of Seignelay; now with Louvois' passing from the scene, the men of violence no longer had the preponderant voice in the king's councils. Indeed a few days after the war minister's death, Louis recalled Pomponne, the soft-spoken advocate of a gentler policy, to join his council and assist in the formation of foreign policy. He offered Louvois' post to Chamlay, long a close advisor of Louvois and one of the authors of the policy that resulted in the devastation of the Rhineland, but Chamlay refused to deprive Louvois' twenty-three-year-old son of his inheritance. The compromise left the war ministry in the hands of the young man, and Chamlay agreed to remain near the king as his military advisor.

One of the immediate results of Louvois' death was a French effort to persuade the Baltic powers to attempt to mediate the war, but the removal of the war minister also encouraged the coalition to believe that their chances for ultimate success were thereby increased. They wanted to hear no proposals for peace on French terms; if France wanted peace the basis would have to be the treaties of Westphalia and the Pyrenees.

Thus the war had to go on, for neither side would agree to terms that would permit disengagement. During the next four years the correspondence of the French king, of his wife Madame de Maintenon, and of the ministry of foreign affairs is studded with hopes for "finding a just peace," for making a "good peace," indeed for "peace." But every effort was rebuffed. On the other hand neither William III nor Emperor Leopold could mount enough military power to back up their ambition to deprive Louis XIV of all his conquests since 1661. France was well fortified, the French armies were able to operate more or less at will in the Spanish Netherlands, and, although by 1694 the kingdom was suffering severely from economic disorders, there was no reason to believe that France's enemies would be able to impose their pretensions by force of arms. Thus both sides had political aims without the military force needed to implement them. These years provide an excellent object lesson in the study of war and politics, and the problems involved in disengagement.

Actually the war went badly for both sides. In 1692 the French planned a double thrust: the siege of Namur and a descent on England with James II in command. The siege of Namur was a success, and when William III tried to challenge the French control over the lines to the city, Marshal Luxembourg won a striking victory at Steenkerke that left no doubt about French superiority on the land. However, since William's army was not destroyed, this victory could not be used to impose peace on the Anglo-Dutch Imperials. At sea it was the coalition that achieved striking success. A naval battle at La Hougue went against the French, and within a few weeks the dispersal of the fleet proved to be a great disaster. With Seignelay's death the French Navy lost its energetic advocate in the council; neither Louis nor Chamlay sympathized with or understood the problems of the navy, and the new minister of the Marine, on his own admission, knew little or nothing about the navy. The results of the loss of naval superiority were soon apparent. The Anglo-Dutch fleets established a base at Cadiz from which they were able to operate either in the Mediterranean or the Atlantic, and the French soon discovered that they no longer could make headway against Catalonia in face of this sea power. Perhaps even more important, they also found it impossible to import grain from the Baltic when bad harvests brought famine to the kingdom. The warfare conducted by French privateers against the Anglo-Dutch commerce was small advantage even though it did seriously annoy the enemy.

In 1693 the French still hoped for a successful military adventure that would convince their enemies of the need for peace. A council of war in the spring decided to make a vigorous campaign in Germany where it was believed the princes were tiring of the war and might accommodate themselves to France if they saw the futility of further conflict.[22] The Grand Dauphin, with a cast of marshals and lieutenant generals suitable to be the companions of the heir to the throne, directed the army in Germany. But Ludwig of Baden knew how to defend himself. Every time that they came in contact with the Imperial army, they were faced with the task of digging the Germans out of their fortifications with bayonets, and this did not appeal to the French commanders who had orders to fight "when there was a good chance for victory." Then a strange illness struck both camps; with half of both armies on sick call, the stalemate on the Rhine continued. By fall Louis called his son to him at Fontainebleau, consoling him for his lack of success by saying that these things happened this way. In the meantime, Marshal Luxembourg, with orders to fight William if he attempted to move against Namur, again defeated the Anglo-Dutch forces at Neerwinden. However, the fact that the allies did not seek terms even after the subsequent capture of Charleroi further underlined the proposition that at this moment, at least, France was not going to be able to impose the king's terms upon Europe.

---

[22] Saint-Simon, who knew nothing about the council of war, accused Louis of cowardice because he did not take command of the army in Flanders and seek out the Anglo-Dutch army and destroy it in a battle. The fall of Heidelberg a few days before the Council seems to have been the thing that convinced the French that Germany rather than the Spanish Netherlands was the theatre in which to win the war.

But 1693 was the last year that the French could hope to secure peace on their terms; bad weather rather than the bayonets and cannons of their foes put a tight crimp on the war effort possible for the French. The years 1691 to 1693 were years of progressive economic disorder caused by deplorable weather that blighted the crops. An agricultural society is soon in trouble at every level of its activity when the harvest no longer provides enough food for the community. Famine followed by failures in tax collections stalked the land and plagued the government. In the month of January, 1694, Chamley and Louis still hoped to mount an offensive in Italy that might succeed in the occupation of Savoy, and in Flanders the two commanders who took over after Luxembourg's death, Marshals Boufflers and Villeroy, had hopes for a sweeping pincer movement to wipe out William's army. By the end of February, however, the hard facts were that the government did not have money enough to hire the carts and buy the fodder that an Italian offensive would require. Indeed it was clear that no adventure either in Italy or in Flanders could possibly be undertaken. Louis' orders, reluctantly given, bluntly stated that his armies must stand on the defensive and protect the frontiers of the kingdom, "foot by foot if necessary." He was not yet ready to accept the sort of terms that his enemies were demanding, but Louis XIV now realized that the terms would not be those that he had hoped to get only a year before.

The war in 1694 was a stalemate; the coalition powers also were suffering from the problems caused by the bad weather and the war. In England William's popularity, never very great, suffered further declines after his wife's death. Many English politicians anxiously looked across the Channel to Saint Germain where James II held his court; others, even though they realized that winning the war was important for England, wondered whether it was worth the costs. By 1694 nearly the full weight of the war was falling on England, for England alone of the allies had an economy and, more important, the credit necessary to raise the huge sums of money that the war was costing. With the drought and economic distress spreading everywhere more and more, there was talk of peace. At Versailles where men still remembered the coup of 1678 that temporarily separated William of Orange from the Regents and brought peace between France and the United Netherlands, hopes were centered on the clandestine negotiations in Amsterdam, the Hague and elsewhere. The French did not seem to realize that the

Prince William of 1678 had now become King William III of England and William III Stadtholder in the Netherlands who could largely control the General Estates and the government in the United Netherlands. Peace with France this time could only come when he was willing to have it, or forced, by the march of events elsewhere, to accept it.

The break in the front of the coalition came from its weakest link. The Duke of Savoy had joined the coalition in hopes of freeing himself from French control over his government and army and, perhaps, of revenging himself on France for the humiliations that Louis had piled upon him. There also was the chance that a coalition victory would strengthen his position in north Italy. The Emperor, at little or no cost to himself, could give Savoy considerable advantages if he only would. But in 1695, with the obvious weakening of French resistance, the Emperor planned to besiege and take Casale; Eugene of Savoy, a rising general in the Imperial armies, was to command the siege; its outcome was almost a foregone conclusion. This decision faced the Duke of Savoy with the disagreeable fact that. he would soon see Casale, which he had hoped to secure from the French, in the Emperor's hands, a situation that could be more dangerous to his lands than the French occupation had been. Added to the rumors of French peace feelers everywhere, the Duke of Savoy decided to act: after all, Savoy could only retain its independence by the most skillful diplomacy and guile.

There had been a number of peace feelers in Italy, but the first one to have any chance of success was a "cloak and dagger" affair in which a representative of the Duke disguised as a peasant contacted Marshal Tessé with the proposal that the French should, after a summons by the Savoyard drums, voluntarily surrender Casale on the condition that its walls should be destroyed and the city returned to the government of the Duke of Mantua. Naturally the French garrison would be allowed to return to France after the fortification had been razed.

At Versailles, where men were hoping to find a peace with the Dutch as a means of breaking the coalition, this suggestion did not seem to be much of a bargain. The surrender of Casale might serve the needs of the Duke of Savoy, but what about France? Louis was interested to learn that the Duke feared Imperial occupation of the city: this at least confirmed his impression that the allies were suspicious of each other. Tessé was instructed to continue to negotiate, but to offer no particular hopes for success. Then the Duke of Savoy introduced a new note into the discussion by sending a picture of his eldest daughter to Versailles. There had long been a tradition that members of the house of Savoy and the house of Bourbon could marry each other: Louis XIII's sister became duchess of Savoy; Gaston d'Orleans' daughter (Louis XIV's first cousin) became duchess of Savoy, and Louis XIV himself might have married a Savoyard princess had Philip IV of Spain not offered his daughter for the place. The Europe of the end of the seventeenth century was still one in which dynastic interests and states' interests contested for primacy in the councils of princes. The suggestion that Marie-Adélaide of Savoy might marry the Duke of Burgundy, the eldest grandson of the king and his probable successor, was one that interested Versailles as well as Turin. Furthermore it could be justified on the grounds of states' interest: a peace in Italy would release French soldiers for use in Flanders where the king's forces were hard pressed, while if Savoy would change sides, the Emperor would not be able to shift his forces from Italy to the north.

Thus began a series of discussions between Marshal Tessé and the agents of the Duke of Savoy. They were not easy to conclude for the Duke was a slippery, bizarre fellow who always feared that he might be losing more than he gained, who was never sure if he should deal with the Emperor and the king of Spain or with the king of France. The negotiations had to be secret. Finally the jam broke: the first act was the surrender of Casale under the terms suggested by the Duke of Savoy. This was the great blow to French prestige: the occupation of the city in 1681 had been a great triumph, its surrender in 1695 marked the beginning of the end of French power in Italy. The next year the treaty of Turin completed the surrender by giving the fortification of Pignerol that Richelieu had acquired to the Duke of Savoy in return for neutralization of the Italian frontier. The young Savoyard princess Marie-Adélaïde crossed the Alps and journeyed to Versailles to become the bride of the Duke of Burgundy. On her first meeting with her grandfather-in-law she so charmed the aging king that he quite forgave the loss that her presence proclaimed. She was the bright spot in the life of both Louis XIV and his wife from that moment until her tragic death a little over a decade later.

The Treaty of Turin was a signal for the beginning of further negotiations for peace. It is probably untrue that Louis' enemies were fearful that the French troops, released from Italy, would be able to turn the tide toward a French victory, but they did realize that the changed military situation would at least insure the continuation of the stalemate on the Flanders frontier. Thus when Louis indicated again that he would be reasonable in his terms, that is, that he would recognize the weight of power lined up against his kingdom by a willingness to surrender some of his pretensions, the Dutch and the English were ready to consider negotiations. William sent his most trusted friend, Bentnick (Lord Portland) to make contact with Marshal Boufflers to see if some secret agreement between France and the Anglo-Dutch governments would not be a possible means of giving an impetus to the negotiations that the Swedish Government was trying to bring about at Ryswick. Swedish "mediation" could not hope for success unless the principals could reach some agreement before the negotiations would start.

The Boufflers-Portland discussions quickly isolated the problems that stood in the way of peace. William of Orange insisted upon being recognized as King of England. He also wanted his father-in-law and the entire "English court" at Saint-Germain expelled from France. James II was a continuous threat to William's position in England. William had never been very popular with the English; furthermore, even his sister-in-law, Princess Anne, was not at all sure that her father and her step-brother, James Edward, should not be returned to the English throne to which Parliament had made her the next heir. This respect for divine right was widespread among the English clergy, nobility and gentry. The result was that during the entire war, William had been surrounded by men whom he regarded as potential traitors. There was only one way to end this situation: James must be driven from France to an exile far from England. Louis also had a problem that caused him much trouble. No peace would be possible without his returning the Principality of Orange to William, its rightful prince. But Orange, on the middle Rhone, was an enclave deep in the kingdom of France, and if it again were to be governed by Prince William's officers, it could become a Huguenot refuge, a source of continuous trouble to the king. Furthermore, it was a foregone conclusion that France would have to surrender some of the territories that had been occupied since the treaty of Nymwegen, but Louis wished to limit these "adjustments" as much as possible by driving a wedge between the Anglo-Dutch interests and the Emperor.

Thus he was willing to agree to give the Dutch important commercial advantages that would, in effect, end most of the remaining tariff discriminations that Colbert had raised against Dutch merchants (particularly concerning importation of salt and fish). Of equal importance to the Dutch was French willingness to allow their soldiers to garrison a series of fortified cities in the Spanish Netherlands; this "legal intrusion" of Dutch military power into the principal fortified towns opposite the French border was a "barrier" to guarantee the United Netherlands against a French attack. Louis XIV also now recognized "the Prince of Orange" as "King of England" and, in a private agreement, gave assurances that neither he nor any of his subjects would assist or support any Jacobist plot for an invasion of England to restore the exiled king. However, Louis adamantly refused to drive James II from France.

William III and Heinsius, the Grand Pensionnaire of Holland, were finally satisfied with these terms, and were willing to force their allies to accept a peace that did not quite fulfil either German or Spanish ambitions. The French gave up Luxembourg, Zweibrücken, and a number of other territories annexed by the Reunions; they returned Lorraine to its rightful duke, and the Emperor retained Phillippsburg, Kehl, Freibourg and Alt-Breisach which assured him of some control over the routes from Alsace into Germany. But the French retained Strasbourg, the Comté of Montébéliard and their interpretation of the treaties of Westphalia and Nymwegen concerning the status of Alsace. The secret agreements William III and Louis XIV included understandings about the principality of Orange, the status of the English court in France, the Dutch "barrier fortifications," and the agreements to ease obstacles to Dutch commerce.[23] The French may have taken some satisfaction from the clause in the treaty that placed a legal barrier in the way of any interference with the practice of the Roman Catholic religion in the territories that he returned to German Protestant princes, but this was poor return for the losses that the French had to accept.

When the French concessions on the Rhine-Moselle frontier are added to those in Italy (Treaty of Turin), it becomes clear that this treaty of Ryswick was a severe check upon French ambitions and pretensions. However, the full impact of the changes in the

---

[23] William agreed to assure the French king that Huguenots would not use Orange as a base for anti-French actions or propaganda. Louis agreed not to allow any French subject to assist the Stuart cause against William.

balance of power in Europe were not yet evident when the treaties of Ryswick were signed.

In 1696 Jan Sobieski, the hero king of Poland, died, leaving a contest for the throne. The French candidate was the Bourbon Prince of Conti; the Imperial candidate was Augustus, the electoral prince of Saxony, who at the moment was commander-in-chief of the Imperial armies in Hungary. Both money and political influence played a part in the election that placed Augustus I on the throne as consecrated king of Poland, and brought that kingdom into the Imperial orbit. The failure of Conti's candidacy was evidence of the declining French influence in the east.

This election removed August from command in Hungary where he had proved himself to be a relatively incompetent soldier, and allowed Leopold to place his army under Eugene of Savoy, who had risen fast in the Imperial service because of his genius as a commander. Eugene had fled from France in 1684 to join the Imperial army's crusade against the Turks in part because Louis had decided that he should become a priest and therefore had denied him a commission in the French army. This son of a prince from the French branch of Savoy and a niece of Cardinal Mazarin went on to become one of the greatest soldiers of his era, perhaps of all times. In August, 1697, Eugene caught the Turkish army at Zanta when the latter was trying a difficult crossing of the river; in a matter of hours he practically destroyed his enemy, capturing huge booty that included the Sultan's treasure chests, and definitely ended the possibility that the Ottoman Empire could continue the war. This victory consolidated Leopold's long efforts to create a powerful state on the middle Danube, a state that would unite the Bohemian conquests of Ferdinand II and his own achievements in Hungary with the hereditary German lands of the House of Austria.[24] The war in Hungary and the Morea ended with the treaty of Carlowitz, which, unlike the treaty of Ryswick, was dictated rather than negotiated. The whole of Morea went to Venice, Hungary and Transylvania to the Emperor, Podolia and part of the Ukraine

---

[24] The victory at Zanta assured the Hapsburg sovereignty over both Hungary and Transylvania; the relief of Vienna (1683), the capture of Budapest (1686), the victory at Mohacs (1687), and the coronation of Archduke Joseph as hereditary king were striking events proclaiming Leopold's march to power in Central Europe; with the destruction of the Sultan's army in 1697, the Turks were compelled to recognize that the Hapsburgs had, in fact, become the rulers of Hungary and Transylvania.

to Poland, and a separate agreement between the Russians and the Ottoman Empire left Rostov in Russian control. The French had to stand by with folded hands as they saw realized what they most feared in the organization of Eastern and Danubian Europe.

The war that ended with the treaties of Turin, Ryswick, and Carlowitz had prepared the basis for balance of power in Western and Central Europe by the founding of the Danubian Monarchy of German, Bohemian, and Hungarian estates under the Hapsburgs and the development of a constitution in England that could mobilize the military power of the island kingdom. The mechanics by which the peace was made indicated that Europe had not yet learned how to conduct a coalition war, and yet the terms of these treaties gave ample evidence of the new constitution of Europe that would not tolerate domination of the continent by one state, or even by a combination of states.

# Chapter 5

# The Spanish Inheritance

By the end of the seventeenth century many factors combined to give form to the idea that royal policy should be conditioned by states' interests rather than dynastic ones. The expansion of commerce and the rise of standing military institutions controlled by war ministries had created a situation in which the collection of taxes, the encouragement of commerce, the superintendence of expenditures for the supply and training of soldiers, the maintenance of navies, and the assurance of public tranquility became the paramount interests of the king's government. Along with this new emphasis on mundane affairs came a new kind of statesman to direct the king's business. These men were royal officials who operated the king's bureaucracy and commanded his armies; they were different from their predecessors in that they were not usually the sons of important noble families of the kingdom; many of them had grandfathers who had sold cloth or wine; very few of them had grandfathers with great names. Without family or position of their own, their careers and fortunes depended upon the king's appreciation of their merits in the service of his government. These new bureaucrats and soldiers had elbowed their way into the king's councils all over Europe, and they brought with them their concern for the administration and defense of the state; they were not so much concerned with the interests of the king's family or his dynasty. The rise of this class of political and military servants subtly changed the role of the king in society; he had formerly been the head of the royal family and leader of the military nobility, and had shared his government with both the princes of his blood and the great nobles who were the dukes and peers of the realm. By the opening years of the eighteenth century he was being transformed into the "first servant of the state." Indeed a Louis XIII or a young Louis XIV could speak of "my state," which was in effect an entailed personal inheritance more in the nature of a fief than a modern state, for the orders and estates of the realm shared its government with him, but the old Louis XIV spoke of "the state" which was a political entity transcending the king that had largely usurped the powers formerly exercised by the estates and the ancient quasi-independent corporations of the kingdom. On his death bed Louis urged his courtiers to "serve the state" which would continue no matter who was the king; Frederick the Great of Prussia three and a half decades later frankly referred to himself as the "state's first servant". Such a conception of the role of king inevitably made the interests of state paramount.

While it is undoubtedly true that the changing conception of the state and the emphases given to its practical problems by the new royal officials made states' interests a central focus for politics, we must not conclude that the opening years of the eighteenth century had broken with the past in which kings regarded their lands as a family inheritance. Men do not easily escape their history nor can they brush aside institutions, customs, and traditions inherited from the immediate or even the remote past. The political map of Europe and the assumptions men held concerning sovereignty, were both rooted in dynastic political ideas and politics. Every crown in Europe was the fabrication of previous dynastic combinations. The "Spanish crown," for example, was actually some twenty-odd crowns that had been joined together by the accidents of marriage and inheritance. The same was true for the crowns of the British Isles and the crowns of France, of Poland, Hungary, and the Brandenburg Hohenzollerns. The French crown had absorbed the quasi-independent dukes and peers of medieval France, added the crown of Navarre, and sovereignty over the border provinces that had been joined to the kingdom in the preceding hundred and fifty years at the expense of the empires of Germany and Spain. The English "crown" was in effect a dual monarchy after James I joined the crowns of the British Isles under one king. No less striking was the complex of titles assembled by the Brandenburg Hohenzollerns which eventually became the kingdom of Prussia. Sovereignty rested largely on inheritance, only seldom on the conquest of war. Puffendorf, writing in the mid-seventeenth century, insisted that a prince who took unlawfully lands from another, owed restitution.

The political theory supporting this system was simple enough: sovereignty was the gift of God. He installed kings on their thrones, endowed them with the power to rule, and held them responsible for their actions. He retained only the right or the authority inherent in his position as supreme lord. Thus the king ruled by divine right, but he could not interfere with the order of succession to a throne like that of France which God had given to him by virtue of his birth. French theory, like that of other hereditary monarchies, was that the king does not achieve his position by virtue of a document, a testament, or an order; when the king dies, the man or (in cases where the Salic law did not supply) woman who was next in line was king by virtue of that fact alone. No other conception of sovereignty was fully developed in continental Europe until the American and French Revolutions established the idea of popular sovereignty as the basis for a legitimate state. Thus in 1700 dynastic politics were still important in shaping the structure of the European state system; and even though statesmen might regard states' interests as most important, they could not ignore the fact that dynastic combinations could create entirely new political situations. This fact became painfully evident at the turn of the eighteenth century when the question of the succession to the thrones of Spain became the burning issue of high politics in Europe.

Mazarin and Queen Anne had understood the importance of dynastic combinations when they planned the marriage between her son Louis XIV, and his cousin Marie Thérèse, the Infanta of Spain. The peace of the Pyrenees, of which the marriage contract was an important part, was in fact more a dynastic or family agreement between the Spanish Hapsburgs and the French Bourbons, than a peace between Spain and France, and this treaty became the basis for the "just pretensions" of the queen of France and her descendants to the thrones in Madrid. It is true that in the marriage contract Marie Thérèse renounced her father's throne conditionally upon payment of a huge dowry, but the dowry was never paid, and even if it had been, there was a serious question whether she could, in fact, renounce the rights of her unborn children. Philip IV obviously was also worried about this point, for in his testament he disinherited his eldest daughter, Marie Thérèse, in favor of her sister Margaret Thérèse, who became the bride of Emperor Leopold. But, like the renunciation, it was a question whether a dead king's will could bind the living; in France this testament was never regarded as an obstacle to the "queen's legitimate pretensions."

Other potential heirs, however, were not willing to agree that Marie Thérèse's claim placed her next in the line of succession to Charles II's throne. The cadet daughter of Philip IV, Margaret Thérèse, married Leopold I; she was survived by only one child, a daughter, Marie Antonia, who married Max Emanuel of Bavaria. At the time of her marriage this princess also signed a renunciation of her rights to the throne in Spain in favor of her half brothers, Joseph and Charles. However, this renunciation was never recognized by any Spanish court, and when her son Joseph Ferdinand was born, it was quite unclear that his mother had been able to deprive him of his place in the line of succession to the thrones of Spain. None the less Leopold insisted that his son Charles was the next in line after the sickly king in Madrid. This claim went back to the eldest daughter of Philip III who married Emperor Ferdinand III; she was the mother of Emperor Leopold and the grandmother of the Archduke Charles.

Thus by 1697 there were three princes who could claim the right of succession: Louis, the Grand Dauphin of France, or one of his sons; the Archduke Charles whose elder brother Joseph had become king of Hungary and of the Romans,[25] and the little electoral prince Joseph Ferdinand of Bavaria. Everyone knew, however, that the actual choice would not be made solely upon the legal claims of these princes. In 1697 Emperor Leopold and his son the Archduke Charles seemed to be in the strongest political position. When the coalition was formed in 1689 the western sea powers formally agreed to support the Archduke's claims to the Spanish throne; the victory in the Danube basin, the rise of Leopold's personal power and prestige in Germany, and the veteran army flushed with victory over the Turks made this treaty assurance of support for Austrian pretensions very strong. Nor was that all; in 1688 the French-born

---

[25] Leopold wished each of his sons to have a throne; he also understood that Europe would not look kindly upon the unification of the Spanish and Austrian crowns.

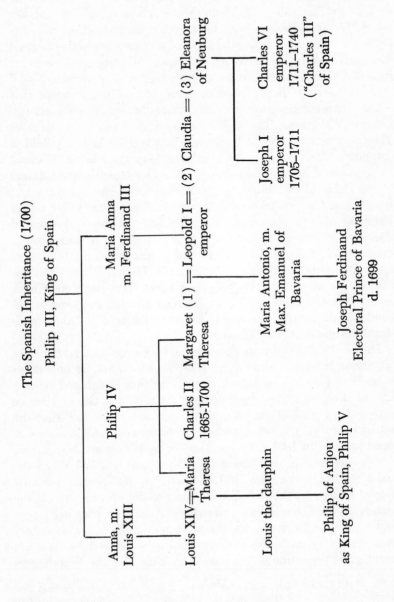

The Spanish Inheritance (1700)

Philip III, King of Spain

queen of Spain had suddenly died under conditions that suggest poison, and shortly afterward a German princess, the sister-in-law of Emperor Leopold, took her place in Madrid where there had always been a strong pro-German party. All this seemed to outweigh the fact that in many quarters in Spain the Germans had earned considerable hatred for themselves, hatred that might be turned to French advantage.

Had Charles II died at any time during the war of 1689–97, the Archduke undoubtedly would have mounted the throne in Madrid with the blessing of the members of the great coalition that was fighting Louis XIV. Had this happened, the peace that ended the war unquestionably would have contained either a recognition of the *fait accompli* or a compromise that Louis XIV would have been obliged to accept. But Charles II did not die. His whole life had been passed under the shadow of imminent death, and yet in spite of all the physical evils that beset him, he seemingly could not die. Thus when the Treaty of Ryswick was written, it was not necessary to raise the question of the Spanish succession, and in the compromises that Louis XIV and William III worked out as the basis for the peace, this troublesome problem was not mentioned. This suited Emperor Leopold for, while he felt secure in the treaty promises of his allies, he still had to disengage his forces from the Turkish war before he could be prepared to use his armies to support his son's pretensions. Apparently for the moment it also satisfied Louis XIV, for he could not hope to get any serious advantages for either his family or his kingdom in 1697. It is important to note, however, that the French army was not disbanded after the peace of Ryswick so when the problem arose Louis XIV, like his Hapsburg cousin, had the military force needed to sustain any pretensions that he might make.

The fact that Leopold obviously counted upon the treaty commitments made in 1689 to assure the support of the western sea powers for his son's candidacy underlines the importance of these two states in any final settlement of the succession to Charles II's throne. If the question were not to be simply a matter of law, then the political and military realities of Europe must become the key to its solution. At the end of the war in 1697, both England and the United Netherlands were ruled by William III of Orange whose whole life had been spent as an enemy, perhaps a personal enemy, of Louis XIV. He had rallied the Dutch to resist the invaders in

1672, and he and his friends had led the coalitions that emerged to fight the French in the following years. The treaty of Nymwegen had been written in spite of his objections, but in the next decade the French terror in Europe and the persecution of the Protestants had given the Orange party strength in the Netherlands. When Louis invaded the Rhineland in 1688, William's descent on England succeeded in uniting English power with that of the continental enemies of France, and William then played a most important role in the coalition that fought the war. Even though both in England and in the Netherlands tight-fisted members of Parliament and the General Estates forced him to disband most of his armies after the Peace of Ryswick, were William to throw prestige and influence of the sea powers on the scales in favor of the Archduke Charles' claim to the throne of Spain, it might be difficult to oppose him.

In France men well understood that neither the English nor the Dutch statesmen wanted to see the kingdom of France make any gains from a partition of the Spanish Empire, and that William could count upon considerable support in case he should decide to underwrite the Archduke's claims. Thus when the Treaty of Ryswick was finally written, the French had to make hard decisions about their interests and ambitions *vis-à-vis* the Spanish Empire. There were several possible types of solutions. A French or Austrian prince, or even the young Joseph Ferdinand, could mount the throne in Madrid and maintain the integrity of the Spanish Empire as it existed. Were this prince to be the grandson of Louis XIV, there undoubtedly would be objection from the Emperor, and probably also from the sea powers, for there would be no assurance that a French-born king in Spain might not be governed from Versailles. On the other hand, the French bureaucrats and soldiers who thought in terms of states' interest recognized that a French-born king in Spain would quickly become a Spaniard and conduct his policy in the interests of his kingdom; indeed such a solution would not only have no tangible advantages for France, but also might become a danger in case the French found it necessary to defend the ramshackle Spanish empire because of dynastic ties. On the other hand the members of the Bourbon family, particularly the Dauphin, welcomed such a solution for it would extend the family influence at the expense of their old enemies, the Hapsburgs. In case the successful candidate were the Archduke, the French

would regard his accession as disadvantageous to the kingdom
and the dynasty and would demand some sort of compensation
that would right the imbalance between the House of Austria and
of France. Considerations of states' interest made this idea of compensations attractive. The French kingdom would gain little if a
French prince became king in Madrid, but the French kingdom
would gain much if it could annex parts of the Spanish Empire to
France. If this could be done, perhaps it would not be important if
a Hapsburg prince ruled in Madrid; after all Charles II also was a
Hapsburg prince and his successor would soon be governed by
"Spanish manners." This line of reasoning, strengthened both by the
fact that the Archduke seemed to have a great advantage over the
Dauphin or his sons, and by the conviction that another war would
be a disaster to the kingdom, persuaded Louis and his advisors that
it would be wise to try to find a compromise solution to the question of succession.

Undoubtedly the conviction that Europe needed peace and an
opportunity to recover from the ravages of the late war over-
shadowed all considerations. The war had been a terrible burden,
but in addition to war, the other "horsemen"—famine, disease, and
death—rode roughshod over western Europe, and particularly over
France. The men at Versailles hoped that William III also understood how important it was that no new issue should cause a rekindling of the hostilities. This wish was so much father to the
thought that Louis and his advisors expected William's first ambassador to France after the peace to open the question directly. They
somehow failed to understand that William was more interested in
assuring himself against a Stuart restoration than in finding a solution for the Spanish thrones. In any case, Lord Portland had no
instructions to discuss the problem; he simply wanted to see James
II and the exiled English court at Saint Germain driven from
France. Finally, Pomponne and Torcy, who were directing French
foreign policy, had a long private talk with the new ambassador in
which they tried to impress him with the importance of finding
some solution for the impending question of the Spanish succession.
Privately both William and his ambassador were delighted to find
the French as willing to compromise as they seemed to be, but,
with all the good cards in his hands, William was quite unwilling
to move very fast. Portland continued to have no fixed instructions.

At last Louis decided to move the negotiations to London, where the French ambassador, Lieutenant General de Tallart, opened the discussion with William himself.

It was not easy to come to an understanding. William readily agreed that the throne in Spain should go to the prince of Bavaria. Joseph Ferdinand was the grandson of Emperor Leopold, he was also the nephew of the Dauphin and the first cousin to Louis' grandsons, but most important of all, he was a Wittelsbach rather than either a Bourbon or a Hapsburg. But Louis insisted that both the French Bourbons and the Austrian Hapsburgs should be given compensation. This raised difficulties, for there was no territory that the Anglo-Dutch politicians would willingly see joined to France. However, they finally agreed to a treaty by which Austria should receive Milan while France acquired Sicily, Naples and the Tuscan ports; Spain, the Spanish colonies, and the Spanish Netherlands were to go to Joseph Ferdinand (October, 1698).

Emperor Leopold, who at the moment was deeply involved in the negotiations for peace with the Ottoman Empire (Carlowitz, January 1699), refused to have anything to do with such a treaty; he was sure that his son the Archduke would become king of Spain. In Madrid this Anglo-French partition treaty was received with shocked surprise: it was regarded as presumptuous that Louis XIV and William III believed that they could so regulate the affairs of Spain. Charles II and the men around him, incensed at the idea that Italy could so summarily be detached from the Empire, drew up a testament in which Charles named Joseph Ferdinand as the sole heir to all of his crowns. It was Emperor Leopold's turn to be shocked and angry, for his sister-in-law, the queen of Spain, upon whom he had counted to assure the Archduke's candidacy, had joined in urging Charles II to name the Bavarian prince his successor. Perhaps the most satisfied of all was Elector Max Emanuel of Bavaria who had been named governor of the Spanish Netherlands by Charles II; if his son should actually mount the Spanish throne, it might be possible for Max Emanuel to secure the sovereignty of the Spanish Netherlands for himself, an ambition to which he clung for the next decade and a half. However, the ink was hardly dry on the treaty when the young Bavarian prince sickened and died. Some thought that he had been poisoned, but in light of the mortality figures of this era, it is more likely that he died of "natural" causes. Whatever it was, his death left the Bourbon and

Hapsburg heirs facing each other; if there were to be no war, a compromise had to be worked out quickly.

Louis and William again tried to find a workable solution. One thing was clear, namely that neither the English nor the Dutch wanted France or a French prince to control the Spanish Netherlands or the Spanish colonies; they were less adamant about French control of parts of Italy, but even this was unacceptable. Louis' advisors recognized the Anglo-Dutch objections, but hoped to find some solution that would be acceptable and at the same time advantageous to France. The terms of the second partition treaty can only be understood in light of these facts, for on the face of the treaty it seems that the French surrendered much to secure both peace and a share of the Spanish inheritance. The colonies, the kingdoms of Spain, and the Spanish Netherlands were assigned to Archduke Charles while the Spanish possessions in Italy and a few border countries on the Pyrenees frontier were the portion of the French prince on the condition that Milan, Sicily, and Naples would be given to the Dukes of Lorraine and Savoy in return for their territories adjacent to France. Surely the Archduke's share was much greater than that allowed to France, but were the treaty actually carried out, the kingdom of France would have emerged with firmer frontiers by the addition of Lorraine (which had been lost in 1697) and the territories of the Duke of Savoy (Savoy, Piedmont, Nice, etc.). These were acquisitions that would appeal to the soldiers and bureaucrats whose policies were based upon states' interests. On the other hand, the Austrian House of Hapsburg would retain in the family most of the possessions that had belonged to their Spanish cousins. But the word "most" was the problem word. Without control over Milan, the Tuscan ports, and Sicily, the link between Austria and Spain would be weak indeed, so weak that cooperation between the two branches of the family would be next to impossible. This fact also undoubtedly (though no evidence is available to prove it) influenced the French decision to allow the Archduke to mount the throne in Spain.

The second treaty of partition, however, could not be implemented until the Dukes of Savoy and Lorraine as well as the king of Portugal and the Emperor would be willing to agree to its provisions. This proved hard to accomplish. The Emperor adamantly refused to consider the treaty: his advisors argued that it was immoral to divide the lands of the king of Spain while he was still alive, that the Archduke as king of Spain without Milan would be "painted on canvass," a mere shadow, for he could not hope to hold the Empire together without contact with Germany. Perhaps the most telling argument in Vienna was the fact that the Turkish war had come to an end with a peace most advantageous to the Emperor (Carlowitz) thereby releasing his army of veteran troops to support his policy in Europe. Finally, Leopold still believed that his sister-in-law would be able to persuade her husband to leave all his crowns to the Archduke. Savoy and Lorraine also held back; both of these princes were closer to the Emperor than to the king of France, and both believed that they could get more by waiting than by signing a treaty. Only the king of Portugal subscribed to this second partition treaty, and his signature was accompanied by so many qualifications that its value was problematical. As these difficulties piled up, Louis XIV and his advisors reached the conclusion that neither the English nor the Dutch were honorably seconding French efforts to secure acceptance of the treaty; there was even some evidence that the Dutch ambassador at Vienna counselled against acceptance. It is small wonder that Louis XIV made ready his armies to be sure that he could occupy the territories that the treaty assigned to him.

The attitude of the Anglo-Dutch politicians provides interesting evidence about the nature of this treaty. In the years following the Peace of Ryswick, there was an extraordinary burst of commercial activity. It was almost as if the years of war had shored up a mighty stream of commerce that now was liberated. For the first time in years the new larger ships could ply the ocean without fear of capture by privateers, and the open frontiers allowed the goods from Asia and the Americas to flow into the markets everywhere. The "new" commodities of trade that were to play so important a place in eighteenth century commerce—sugar, coffee, tea, chocolate, and oriental art objects, porcelains, brasses, lacquered screens—now gave evidence that the European taste for the exotic would bring wealth to the merchants of England and the Netherlands who were ready to dominate this commerce. Any talk of war that would interrupt this flow of wealth was decidedly unpopular in London and Amsterdam. Even the idea that France might actually establish control over Naples and Sicily, while unpopular, was still acceptable so long as the flow of commerce were not interrupted. It is small wonder that William III upon being asked whether he would fight to force the Emperor to accept the treaty of partition replied that he had made the treaty to prevent war and had no intention of making war to impose the treaty.

Actually, William's problem was somewhat more complicated than this. After his wife Mary died (1694), William continued as king, but his cold personality, his preference for Dutchmen, his continental orientation, all combined to isolate him in his own court. Furthermore, there was always the question of the succession. He had been called to the throne of England, but there were many Englishmen who "knew in their hearts" that the "rightful" king was living in France. Even his sister-in-law, Princess Anne, who had been named as successor to the throne by an Act of Parliament, had serious reservations about the exclusion of her half-brother from his rightful place. Thus William's last years on the English throne were troubled by the possibility that a Stuart restoration might upset his crown. To add to his troubles, the Parliament in England showed itself to be quite unwilling to continue to support a strong military organization. While Louis XIV kept most of his army in being, William was forced to disband all but a palace guard; the navy suffered less severely, but it too was put on short rations. In other words, William did not have the military power to enforce the treaty even if he might wish to do so. His position on the Netherlands was somewhat stronger, but even there at the end of the war, the Regent politicians again emerged as important factors in Dutch politics, and their anti-Orange orientation, as well as their commercial interests, made them into a definite brake on any adventurous policy that the Stadtholder might wish to undertake.

The news of the second partition treaty was shocking to the court at Madrid. The idea that the Spanish Empire could be partitioned by an act of Europe could not be tolerated by men who had long regarded that empire as their own property, for as long as the king of Spain was king throughout the empire, appointments as soldiers and administrators were available for younger sons of the Grandees, and the markets of the Empire were open to Spanish traders and merchants. Partition would end all this, and with it the notions of *grandeur* that were associated with this first "Empire upon which the sun never set." But what should or could be done?

Seventeenth century Spanish politicians were not always willing

to face the realities of their situation: Spain had enormously de-
clined in wealth, population, and power since the death of Philip II.
By 1700 Spain was no longer even the "hollow giant" that it had
been in the mid-century; its navy was not prepared to put to sea,
its armies were weak to non-existent, its revenues were dilapidated,
and no immediate prospects could be seen for recovery. Obviously,
the kingdoms of Spain could not hope to prevent the partition of
the Empire ruled by their king. This fact finally forced a realistic
appraisal of the situation. If Spain could not defend the Empire,
who could? The possible candidates were the Danubian Monarchy
and the French kingdom. Emperor Leopold's complex of kingdoms
and principalities and suzerainties gave him considerable land
power, especially after the Turkish war had come to an end, but it
was difficult to see how his armies could defend Spain and the
colonies, perhaps even difficult to know how he could defend the
Spanish Netherlands. The Milanais, Sicily, and Naples were probably the only parts of the Empire that the Danubian Monarchy
would be able to reach. (It is no accident that this was the part *not*
assigned to the Austrian Archduke by the partition treaty.) On the
other hand, if France were obliged to defend the Spanish Empire,
its central position allowed easy access to the Iberian Peninsula, to
Italy and to the Spanish Netherlands, and the French fleet could
act effectively in the Mediterranean and provide some defense for
the colonies. Obviously if the Empire were to be held together,
France must have a reason for defending it.

This was the logic of the men who forced Charles II to sign a
will naming Philippe, Duke of Anjou, grandson of Louis XIV and
Marie Thérèse, universal heir to the Spanish Crowns. But it was
not easy to persuade Charles to sign such a testament. The king had
a strong feeling of family (Hapsburg) solidarity, and he had
experienced one act of violence after another from his French
brother-in-law. While he was still a baby, the War of the Devolution had stripped off territory from the Spanish Netherlands; by
the time that he had come of age, the treaty of Nymwegen had
despoiled him of Franche-Comté; a few years later at Ratisbonne
he lost Luxembourg and the lands of the "Reunions." It was true
that at Ryswick some of this lost territory was restored, but the
long war had cut deeply into any power that remained to the
Spanish throne. The only redeeming fact for Charles in French-
Spanish relations had been the marriage that Louis XIV arranged

between him and Marie Louise, the princess of Orleans, the lovely daughter of Henriette of England. This girl had been a bright spot in an otherwise unhappy life; the German princess who took her place after 1689 never quite established the same rapport with the poor king. But the German princess Marie Anne Von Pfalz-Neuburg, sister-in-law of Emperor Leopold, was the queen, and her mission in Madrid was to secure the throne for the Hapsburgs. Leopold, shocked that she had supported the Bavarian candidate, now expected her to be sure that his son the Archduke would be named heir; Louis XIV seems also to have expected her to succeed in this mission.

It took great pressure to make Charles II decide to give his crowns to a Bourbon prince. He consulted the Pope, he opened the grave of his long dead French wife, he listened to the harangues of churchmen and laymen. The queen was shunted aside as the politicians who hoped to save the integrity of the empire closed in upon the dim-witted king. Finally he agreed to sign a testament. The heart of this document provided for the succession; it made Philippe of Anjou, the second son of the Dauphin, universal heir to the crowns of Spain and its Empire, but, if for some reason Philippe should refuse the crown, it would then be offered to his younger brother, the Duc de Berry; should he refuse, the crown would go to the Archduke Charles in Vienna, and after him, to the duke of Savoy, and then the king of Portugal. The testament expressly forbade any partition of the empire. Charles signed this document only a few weeks before he died. The act was a badly kept secret that might have had repercussions if the poor king had lived long enough for Europe to react before his death. Louis XIV, who learned of the signature only a few days before Charles' death, refused to take it seriously because he suspected that the Spanish king would probably change his mind once he recovered from his current illness. Charles did not recover; he died on All Saints' Day, 1700.

The testament provided for a regency government to rule the kingdom until the heir should arrive. This government's first act was to send a special ambassador to France to offer the crowns to the son of the Dauphin. But when this ambassador arrived at the French court, his offer was met by Louis' traditional response to all requests: "We shall see." It was a reply that shocked the man who came with so handsome a gift, but Louis could not reply otherwise.

The problem for the French government was a difficult one. Almost up to the day that Charles II had died, French diplomats and ministers were assuring the world that Louis XIV intended to honor the treaty of partition. The whole French orientation assumed that Charles II would name the Archduke as universal heir, and that prompt military action would be necessary to assure the acquisition of the territories in Italy and on the Pyrenees frontier that were assigned to France in the partition treaty. Indeed the soldiers were poised, ready to move to prevent Emperor Leopold from creating a *fait accompli*. When the ambassador actually offered the thrones to Philippe, this situation was drastically changed. It was now a question for council. But the council was divided: the ministers who thought in terms of states' interest and treaty obligations insisted that the Partition Treaty must be implemented; the Dauphin and the Duke of Burgundy, his eldest son, spoke strongly in favor of the testament, the splendid gift that could not be refused.

As Torcy explains the decision, it becomes evident that other factors than mere family interest finally decided the king to accept the throne for his grandson. The problem revolved about the question of peace or war: If the thrones were refused, the Spanish ambassador had no choice other than to go immediately to Vienna to offer them to the Archduke, and no one in the French court believed that Emperor Leopold would turn them down in favor of a treaty that he had never signed. Therefore, Louis XIV would have to risk a war with the Danubian monarchy to secure the territories assigned to him by the treaty. This would be a war against the Danubian monarchy, perhaps the Empire, and Spain, for the Spanish would resist the partition. Louis and his son felt that it would be very ungrateful to make war on a state that had tried to give itself to the Bourbon family. One further consideration: how much help could be expected in this war from the Anglo-Dutch forces? The prospective was very little or none. What was the alternative? If the crowns were accepted, again war with Emperor Leopold was probably inevitable, but could Emperor Leopold expect aid from the Anglo-Dutch forces? The immediate response in many sectors of English political and economic life suggested that no such aid would be forthcoming. Many Englishmen preferred the testament to the treaty, for they were convinced that Philippe, as king of Spain, would be forced to rule in the interests of Spain, and they preferred to see Spanish rather than French military and political figures in control of Naples and Sicily. This sentiment was also reflected in the United Netherlands where no one wanted to see the outbreak of a new war. Louis' ambassadors in London and in The Hague both felt that the English and Dutch governments would end by recognizing Philippe as king of Spain. In this case, there would be war with the Danubian monarchy, but Spain would be an ally. The logic of the map of Europe also argued that the crowns could safely be accepted. Spain, France, Spanish Italy, and the Spanish Netherlands formed a block of contiguous territories that controlled most of western Europe and the western Mediterranean; in any war that might arise the advantage of interior lines that had proven so important in the wars of the preceding thirty-odd years would again be operative for the crowns of France and Spain. If there had to be a war with the Danubian monarchy anyway, and if the western sea powers would probably be neutral, then it would be best to fight the war as an ally of Spain rather than as a foe. This fact, plus the considerations of dynasty, brought the decision down on the side of acceptance.

"You may salute your king," Louis told the Spanish ambassador, and watched him go to his knees and make a speech in Spanish—a language which the young king did not understand. When the news of this scene reached London, William III thought of challenging the French ambassador to a duel on the grounds that he had deceived him. William knew that he had little or no support in London for a policy that would force Louis to reverse this decision. Englishmen, in the early winter of 1700, saw no good reason for going to war to make an Austrian archduke king in Spain, especially since there were two lives between the new king of Spain and his grandfather's throne at Versailles. Furthermore, it was probable that his brother the Duke of Burgundy would soon have sons to assure a succession to the French throne that would keep the thrones of Spain and France apart. Englishmen also knew that men in Spain were as reluctant to accept French domination as Englishmen were to see it. Similar arguments were urged in the Netherlands where William could not arouse any interest in forcing Louis to honor his treaty obligations. Thus when the little act was played out in the great hall of the mirrors at Versailles, only Emperor Leopold was prepared to use his military forces to oppose the decision, and Louis' armies under Marshall Catinat quickly occupied the Milanais and the Alpine passes so that the French ambassador at

Rome could boast that the Imperials would have to learn to fly if they were to send an army to undo the testament of Charles II.

For all the appearances of assurance, Louis XIV obviously had qualms of conscience for his failure to stand by his signature to the treaty of partition. One of its clauses now became important; it provided that Emperor Leopold would have ninety days after the death of Charles II to ratify the treaty of partition; if he failed to do so by that time, another prince could be given the throne. While Louis did not proclaim his intentions openly, he nonetheless kept his grandson in France until after this ninety-day period had passed. Philippe was recognized as king of Spain by the rulers of Portugal, Bavaria, Tuscany, Cologne, and a number of other potentates, but he did not sign himself "Philippe, yo el rey," (I the King) the customary signature of the Spanish rulers, nor did he make any changes in or suggestions to the Regency government in Madrid. When he finally crossed the frontier to assume his place as king, Emperor Leopold's period of grace for accepting the treaty had passed.

In the meantime, Louis prepared for the conflict with Leopold. A series of treaties brought Philippe's two uncles, the Electors of Bavaria and of Cologne, the Duke of Savoy, and the King of Portugal into alliances with France. The support of the two Wittelsbach princes was particularly important. The electoral Bishop of Cologne ruled the lands adjacent to the Netherlands and controlled the middle Rhine; access to this territory would be invaluable in case of war with either the princes of Germany or the United Netherlands. Max Emanuel of Bavaria was even more important: his German holdings cut the upper Danube and divided the Empire, while his recently acquired position as Governor of the Spanish Netherlands made his adherence to Philippe's cause doubly important. A secret agreement with him provided for the expulsion of the Dutch soldiers who occupied the "barrier fortifications" in the Spanish Netherlands. The Savoyard alliance was essential for communications between France and the Milanais. A by-product of this treaty was Philippe's marriage to Marie Louise, the second daughter of the Duke of Savoy. (His eldest daughter was Marie Adèlaïde, Duchess of Burgundy.) Louis hoped that the fact that his grandchildren would be heirs to the thrones of both Spain and France would keep the Duke loyal to his alliance—it did not. The Portuguese alliance presumably would guarantee Philippe's hold on

Spain by depriving any competing pretenders from having a land base from which to operate. These alliances completed the solid geographic basis of power that the thrones of France and Spain would have to check any objections to the Bourbon rule in Spain. With them, France and Spain were in firm possession of all the real estate under contest.

They might well have achieved general acceptance had Louis been willing to act tactfully toward the sea powers where strong parties were anxious to find a solution for the crisis, short of war. But Louis did not behave wisely or tactfully. Hardly had Philippe crossed the frontier into Spain when three acts mortally offended both England and the United Netherlands. The first was a proclamation registered in Parlement in which Louis announced that Philippe did not forfeit his place in the succession to the French throne by becoming king of Spain. The document, not softened by any assurance that the two thrones could not be united under one king, went out of its way to state the doctrine of divine right in a manner that could be interpreted as a challenge to the English succession. Neither William nor his declared successor, Princess Anne, could claim such right to the throne of the Stuarts. The second act was the occupation of the barrier fortifications by French troops; Marshal Boufflers, with the connivance of Max Emanuel, captured the Dutch garrisons, disarmed them, and sent them back to the United Netherlands while Louis blandly announced that his armies would also leave as soon as Philippe could assemble troops to take their place. The Dutch again were faced with the possibility that France would soon become their neighbor. The third act was to secure favored treatment for French merchants trading with the Spanish colonies. This trade was no longer so profitable as it had been when the mines were active, and yet neither the Dutch nor the English relished being excluded from the trade by favored French merchants. In one way or another these three acts struck at the interests of the very people who had hoped that England and the United Netherlands could remain neutral, that there would be no war. William III and his friends and the men around the Emperor were jubilant; the French had overreached themselves.

Negotiations for the reformation of the alliance that had fought the last war began almost immediately, but the conservatives in the Netherlands still insisted upon giving the French king a chance to back down. They prepared a formidable document in which they demanded that their merchants be given privileges equal to those granted the French, that the French immediately withdraw from the barrier fortifications and allow the Dutch to return (the English asked to be allowed to garrison Ostend), and finally that the French and Spanish would guarantee that the two crowns would forever be separated. The French reply was evasive, and plans for the reconstitution of the grand alliance against France proceeded.

Louis' last act of defiance thrown into the teeth of his enemies, came after the treaty of alliance had already been drawn up and signed. The aged James II was on his deathbed at Saint Germain; Louis visited him and was much moved by his wife's distress over the future of their son. When James II died, contrary to the advice of his ministers, but supported by his son and grandson, Louis decided (September 16, 1701) to recognize the young prince James Edward as king of England. If anything were needed to unite the business and political classes in England behind William's plans for war, this was it.

In March, 1702, William III died. For a moment the French believed that there would be no war, but William had associated John Churchill, Duke of Marlborough, in all his negotiations, and the duke and his wife Sarah were the confidants of Princess Anne who now became Queen. William's death only substituted a brilliant soldier for a mediocre one as the director of the coalition's efforts in the west. By the end of 1701, Prince Eugene of Savoy, the other soldier who was destined to give the French armies much distress, had already given evidence of his prowess. The two crowns were confronted by a powerful coalition directed by able and ruthless soldiers. The optimism that existed in Versailles was soon to be dissipated.

# Chapter 6

# England and
# the Balance of Power

Since the seventeenth century, Stuart kings of England had only slender resources at their disposal and the island kingdom could not play any important role in European affairs. When Elizabeth died, most of the monastic lands that her father had confiscated had been sold, so, when her successors mounted the throne they had to depend upon the subsidy granted them to support the needs of their government. If more money were required they had either to persuade Parliament to grant it or to seek extraordinary sources of income. The former was difficult because Parliament, assuming that the king should be able to get along with his own resources, would grant further subsidies only after considerable bickering and bargaining, and the latter aroused resistance in the kingdom because most "extraordinary" measures were regarded as illegal. Nor was the lack of money the only problem confronting these kings. Seventeenth century England, like the rest of Europe, still had many of the characteristics of a feudal monarchy: towns and cities as well as the authorities in the countryside more or less operated as quasi-independent entities, largely free from interference by the crown. While this political pluralism was common to all Europe, nowhere else did the representative assembly (Parlement, Estates,

*Landtäge, Cortes,* etc.) have the power and the prestige of the Parliament of England. The Tudor monarchs had encouraged this power because they had been able to use Parliament to strengthen their hold on the throne, and to accomplish many of their projects; the abler of the Tudor rulers had been superb parliamentarians who understood how to manipulate elections and to organize and manage majorities in both the houses of Lords and Commons. Their Stuart successors unfortunately lacked this skill, had greater needs for money, and often espoused unpopular policies.

The first two Stuarts attempted to get along without Parliament when their policies came under severe criticism and Parliament refused to grant needed funds. This led to much discussion of "English liberties," and finally to rebellion and civil war that cost Charles I both life and throne. Neither he nor his father was able to follow the footsteps of other seventeenth century princes who were in the act of strengthening the authority of the crown by encroachment upon the traditional centers of power represented in the pluralistic structures of feudal monarchies. In France, for example, Mazarin and Queen Anne were able to defeat the *Frondes* and force the Parlement of Paris to register royal edicts; while in England the rebellion created the Commonwealth.

When Charles II was restored to his father's throne in 1660 he had to accept a "settlement" that in fact assured the powers of Parliament to prevent the sort of action that prompted the rebellion, and created a new political situation in England in which the king and the Parliament were more or less co-equal powers in the kingdom. If king and Parliament agreed on policy, all might go well, but if they did not, the government of England would reach dead center, and could not act unless the king could find "extraordinary" sources of income that could not be called illegal.

Since mid-seventeenth century princes believed that their policies in general and particularly their relations with other princes were not subject to discussion by their subjects, Charles II found himself in an especially odious situation. His income was barely enough to cover the expenses of his government, but additional revenues could only be had by concessions to Parliament that the king wished to avoid. Thus the king of England, like the king of Poland or a German Elector, found himself obliged to seek a subsidy from the king of France. And even then he was not free from the constraints of his Parliament; as we have seen, in 1674–1678 Charles was forced by his subjects to withdraw from his alliance with Louis XIV, to make peace with the Dutch, and finally to threaten to join the coalition that had formed against France. But this process by which Parliament imposed its will on the king also was cumbersome and unwieldy for Parliament could not easily coerce the king any more than the king could coerce Parliament. The Restoration settlement simply did not provide political machinery for the mobilization of the power of the kingdom, and so England was condemned to play a secondary role in European high politics until after the "Glorious Revolution."

The men who made this Revolution of 1688–1689 thought that they were saving the church and establishing a regime in which the king would be obliged to obey the law. While the Revolution undoubtedly did accomplish these ends, it can be said that its most important outcome was the reorganization of the government of the kingdom in a way that permitted England to mobilize its potential power for action in the high politics of Europe. After 1689 the kings of England no longer sought "gratifications" or bribes from foreign potentates, for the Revolution created political machinery that allowed the government of England to play a significant role in European affairs with its own resources.

There were several aspects of this development. In the first place the act requiring new elections to Parliament every three years made the House of Commons more responsive to public opinion in the kingdom and prevented a king from acting as Charles II had, that is, to retain a Parliament that pleased him long after its members had any contact with the vital interests and intentions of the kingdom. This did not mean that elections to the House could not be influenced, but it did, at least, assure the kingdom that members of the House of Commons would have a fresh mandate for their action. A second measure was equally important. In the past, when a new king came to the throne, Parliament always granted him a subsidy to cover the expenses of his government for his reign. The practice after 1689 was to grant the king a small subsidy to cover his household expenses, the prototype of the modern "Civil List"; the expenses of his government and any "projects" that he might undertake were considered separately on an annual basis. This does not mean that the Revolution understood the importance of the "Annual Budget" that was later to become so important in English parliamentary practice, and yet the fact that the ministers of the king had to present money bills to Parliament to cover the government's expenses meant that they had to educate the members of the House in the intricacies of finance and high politics. In turn this meant that money granted to the king was lawfully his to use for the project, and when it was necessary to borrow money, the debts incurred were Parliament's debts rather than the king's. Perhaps as important as anything else was the fact that Parliament could raise money lawfully by any means that it might wish to employ.

In the war that followed the Revolution of 1689 and again in the terrible War of the Spanish Succession (War of the Two Crowns), Parliament's willingness to vote heavy taxes, and, even more important, its willingness to borrow against future income allowed William's government to build a powerful navy, to put a large army in the field under the English flag, and to subsidize allies. Out of this power emerged the Bank of England which became the financial institution that loaned money, transferred funds, created paper currency, and, as the ally of the king's treasury, helped to hold together the coalitions against France. Without this means of mobilizing the wealth of England, King William and later, Queen Anne, would have been unable to establish England's hegemony in the European world.

There was another Act of Parliament that facilitated the mobilization of power. Englishmen had long been suspicious of allowing their king to maintain an army; they believed soldiers could too easily be used to establish tyranny. The Revolution helped to cure this suspicion by the practice of having Parliament pass an annual Mutiny Act. The Mutiny Act gave the king the right to establish military courts and martial law over his troops; without it he would be at a loss to maintain discipline. The Parliament thus secured a measure of control over the royal army by requiring the king to come each year for the repassage of this important act. This meant in a way that the king's army, for which Parliament supplied the money, was placed under additional Parliamentary control, and thereby also became Parliament's army. These measures did not completely cure Englishmen of their mistrust of soldiers; as we will see, after the peace of Ryswick, Parliament forced the king to send his Dutch Guards back to the Netherlands and reduced the English army to a garrison force in Ireland and a pitifully small guard in

England, and nothing that William III could say would change this decision.

As might be expected this machinery did not function in a vacuum, nor did it work just as it appeared on paper. The Revolutionary settlement of 1689 did not really deprive the king of his powers, even though it forced him to adopt policies that could arouse support in the sections of the population that counted politically. When William became king, a surprisingly large number of bishops found it to be impossible to recognize him as their lawful monarch, for the doctrine of divine right was deeply ingrained in Anglican thought. Thus, William had the opportunity to appoint a number of new bishops in the House of Lords whose consciences were less tender, and whose politics could be depended upon by the king's government. Furthermore, the elections to the House of Commons could be influenced by the proper use of ministerial pressure. William's second Parliament had a Tory majority only because the ministry used its influence to elect Tories to the House. In other words, the king could, and did, act to secure the support that had become necessary for the operation of his government.

In practice this meant that the king had to act within the confines of the emerging party system. At first this created no problem for William since, even though the Whig politicians had been more important in bringing him to England, both parties welcomed his intervention, and both were anxious to defend him against James II backed by France. Unlike Charles II who started his reign after the Restoration as a "King of the Tories," William could act as King of England, and could call men from both parties to his service. As a matter of fact he disliked both parties almost equally; William was a seventeenth century prince with little love for the restraints of the Parliament or the General Estates with which he had to get along in England and in Holland. He would have preferred a more authoritarian role for himself. Furthermore, he did not understand the differences between Whig and Tory. These parties had come into existence as a result of past history of the Civil wars and the Restoration which he had not shared. Their party squabbles often seemed to him to be nonsense or at best quibbles, and yet their past did affect his regime. The Whigs tended to be the sons of "Roundheads" of the Civil wars; the Tories came from the "Cavaliers." Thus the Whigs insisted on Parliamentary power, and, in

William's eyes, verged painfully close to republicanism; the Tories supported the monarchy, but many of them also believed in divine right as the basis for sovereign power, and thus could recognize William as king *de facto* but not *de jure*. For this reason the Tories had wished to name William "prince consort" or "regent" with Mary as Queen, but the Whigs insisted on crowning them both as sovereign as a way of underlining Parliament's power to name the king. On the other hand, it had been a Tory politician who had arranged the marriage between William and this Protestant daughter of James II, but Tory Anglicanism made it difficult for the English government to cooperate fully with Calvinist Europe.

These ambiguities and conflicting interests, added to William's dislike of restraints on his power, account for his concealed contempt for both parties, and in turn, for the dislike that most English politicians had for this taciturn, difficult Dutchman, even more so after Mary's death removed her moderating influence and the link between the throne and the Anglican church. In the latter years of his reign, William had much difficulty with Parliament, especially after the treaty of Ryswick ended the war that both parties had supported since in their eyes it was a war over the English succession with England fighting France to prevent the establishment of a Catholic prince on England's throne.

Curiously enough, even though James was supported by the armies of France, it was hard for Englishmen to be sure what their attitude toward him and the exile court at St. Germain should be. They had seen one king beheaded and his son return to the throne; and they wanted to be sure not to be caught in a compromising situation in case James or his son should one day return to England as king. As a result there was a constant stream of intelligence and other communication between England and the exiled court in France. William was well aware of this quasi-treasonous activity and had to put up with it as a liability of his rule; English politicians wanted to be sure of the future, and so their support of William had always to have an afterthought that would prepare for another restoration. This same problem continued in the next reign; even Lord Marlborough at the time when his wife was Queen Anne's favorite and confidante, tried to keep some contact with the English exile court in France.

There were other centers of power in England that could act outside of the framework of Parliament and the political parties, and which had an important impact on the king's government. The City of London had only four representatives in Parliament, and yet its influence in some ways was greater than that of Parliament itself. Greater London had a little more than ten percent of the entire population and a much larger percentage of the fluid capital of the kingdom under its jurisdiction. London's governors regulated the most important financial and commercial activities of the country; its river front was the busy scene of world commerce and the obvious manifestation of England's part in that trade. It housed the élite of the business world, important commercial families, shipping magnates, manufacturing and refinishing shops, warehouses, and mercantile establishments. Here were the shopkeepers who traded with the great world, who sold spices, jewelry, luxury goods of all kinds; here were the goldsmiths, the drapers with cloth from distant lands as well as of domestic manufacturers on their shelves; here were the artisans who made everything from hammers and saws to trinkets suitable for exchange with redskins in America or to embellish my lady's gown. London's streets teemed with life, and the rich and powerful of the city, advised by lawyers as well as by bankers, were a most important element in the power structure of England. The overlapping and interlaced powers of the king and London's city government make an almost impenetrable maze of interdependent relationships. On several occasions the Stuart kings attempted to deprive the city of its chartered privileges, but each time the charters finally had to be returned.

The City of London was first of all interested in trade, and with the passing of every decade in the seventeenth century, this trade became more and more important. In 1600 England's commerce had been small compared with that of her rivals on the other side of the channel; indeed it had been the turbulent times in the Netherlands when rebellion and the "Spanish Terror" caused many men from the Lowlands to migrate to England, that had given England a significant place in world commerce. With each decade the seventeenth century saw a progressive growth of commercial activity. The India Company, which in 1600 had been tiny and weak compared to its Dutch counterpart, by 1700 had become a great power in the world. Other chartered companies carrying on trade with the Levant, Muscovy, Hudson's Bay, the Gold and the Ivory Coasts, New England and Virginia, with Spain and its colonies, in the Baltic as well as the North Seas, made the English merchant and the English flag a ubiquity all over the world. While English merchants traded in goods, English fishermen hunted the cod, the herring, the whale, and other marine creatures from the Banks off Newfoundland to the coasts of Norway.

English lawmakers pressed by London, tried to assure English-men a monopoly in all English markets, even at the cost of war with first the Dutch and later the French. By the end of the seventeenth century, the men in the City of London could speak and expect to be listened to by both king and Parliament; they were the men with money to loan the government, with the institutions and the know-how to manage transfers of money as well as purchases of supplies. Their interests had become the interests of England.

As long as the Dutch were the most important commercial and naval competitor, London could be counted upon to support either Cromwell or Charles II in a predatory attack upon the Netherlands and its commerce. Some of the depredations occurred in time of supposed peace, for English seamen, after having learned the game of "privateer-piracy" in the preceding century when Spain was the target, found it easy to revert to this primitive mode of assault, but at least three times these attacks were justified by a declaration of war. The first two Anglo-Dutch wars (under Cromwell and Charles II) were cold-blooded commercial ventures aimed at the rupture of Dutch market monopolies, while the third, which Charles II under-took in company with Louis XIV, had political as well as commer-cial overtones. However, after Louis XIV appeared on the scene as a threat to the "liberties of Europe," and the commerce of London, much of the hostility that had been reserved for the Dutch was turned upon the French.

The shift of opinion against France developed with the rise of French power. England was at war with the United Netherlands when it first became possible that the French king would establish himself as ruler of Antwerp and again open the Scheldt river to the commerce of the world. This was enough of a threat to bring the English commercial people to the support of the "Triple Alliance" that forced Louis XIV to make peace in 1668. In the years follow-ing Colbert's tariffs, his commercial companies, and the rapid rise of French commerce drew more unfavorable English attention to the "antics" of the French king. In 1672 Charles II joined Louis XIV in the effort to destroy the commercial position of the United Netherlands. The war may have been popular with the remaining segments of anti-Dutch opinion, but when Englishmen saw what Louis XIV really wanted, their fears were aroused. They forced Charles to make a separate treaty of peace with the Dutch.

At the time Frenchmen believed that English ambition to encroach upon both Dutch and French markets while their rivals destroyed each other had motivated the English merchants who persuaded their king to become neutral. This may even be true, but as soon as French conquests in the Spanish Netherlands again roused the specter of French control over Antwerp, the English began to make warlike noises and Charles wrote to Louis XIV that, in his opinion, France had all that she needed to protect her frontier with the Spanish Netherlands. It may also be that it was not only the French in the Spanish Netherlands, but also the French occupation of Sicily that brought the English around to the position that they assumed in 1677–78, for the English were unhappy to think that a French naval squadron might be able to cut their lines to the Levant. Perhaps the English would have learned to hate Louis XIV's regime for its religious intolerance that matched their own, or because of the large reservoir of anti-French feelings left over from earlier wars, but it was the threat to their pocketbooks that had the highest priority in the minds of the merchants and ship owners of London who watched the rise of French power with dismay.

In the years following Nymwegen when Colbert and his son created the powerful navy that could stand off the ships of both England and the United Netherlands at the same time, and French commercial companies in India, on the west African coast, and in the New World became serious competition to Englishmen, the hatred of France grew apace. The Colberts made France the enemy that the Netherlands had been in the mid-century. The City of London welcomed William and Mary as warmly as Parliament did, and when James threatened to return to his throne, backed by French military power, the City gave full support to the war. Without London's merchants, bankers, ship builders, and sea captains, William's war against France would have had rough going. But the war was popular in the commercial sections of the kingdom, so much so that a distinguished English historian who gave much thought to the problem has suggested that this war should be called the Anglo-Dutch war against French trade.

But when the war was over and peace was signed at Ryswick, neither Parliament nor the City of London could believe that their interests were still endangered by French power. The war and the treaty had set limits to French expansion: in the Spanish Netherlands the more important city fortifications were garrisoned by Dutch troops; in the Rhine Moselle area France had given back most of the lands that her king had taken "illegally" leaving her position weakened in the face of the German empire. Furthermore, the Emperor's power and authority and prestige were obviously going to grow greatly as a result of the victories in Hungary where a peace treaty would soon leave him in possession of vast lands that had been under Mohammedan rule for more than a century and a half. All this was added to the fact that in the years immediately following the treaty of Ryswick, the commercial communities of England and the United Netherlands experienced a prosperity beyond anyone's expectations; the rich grew richer and the burst of commerce promised even greater returns for the future. It is not surprising that in 1698–99 the City of London wanted no more talk of possible war that might dispel the prosperity.

The prosperity that came to England did not bring popularity for William III with it. English politicians disliked the favors that he bestowed upon Dutch favorites. They particularly resented the greed that Lord Portland (Bentinck) displayed in his efforts to get confiscated Irish estates. Indeed in 1698–99 Parliament cancelled William's Irish grants right and left. The English also disliked having foreign soldiers on their soil. This was difficult for William to understand since foreign soldiers were commonplace in the Netherlands. But it did him no good to scold; he was forced to send his Dutch guards back home. Even more serious from the king's point of view, was Parliament's insistence that he disband most of the English army as well. They were expensive, and could be used as a weapon of tyranny. The English were uninterested in his argument that Louis XIV had not disbanded the French armies. He was forced to reduce his forces to some twelve thousand troops for the occupation of Ireland and seven thousand for garrison duty in England. Since Louis XIV retained an army of about 200,000 men, William's diplomatic position was severely weakened by this parliamentary parsimony. Unhappily for the king, the General Estates in the Netherlands was only a little less unreasonable. There, too, the amount of money available for soldiers was sharply reduced after the treaty of peace.

Thus, when Louis approached William with the proposal for a treaty to prevent the outbreak of war over the succession to the Crowns of Spain, the disparity between the forces at his disposal and those of the French placed him at a position of diplomatic disadvantage. Nor was this the only problem. William knew that his subjects would be very critical of any treaty that might enlarge the power of France, and yet he was quite unwilling to take the Parliament into his confidence. Like other seventeenth century rulers, William regarded his negotiations with other princes as no affair of his subjects; high politics was the business of princes, and William, who had been at the center of European affairs for more than a quarter of a century, was in no mood to be "advised" by politicians in Parliament whose petty bickering had already caused him much distress. Thus William did not take Parliament into his confidence; he presented the partition treaties as a *fait accompli*.

This was unfortunate, for the second treaty which followed the untimely death of the young Bavarian prince did provide for a considerable increase in French power. This treaty had been difficult to make, since there was no other "third party" to whom the bulk of the Spanish inheritance could be awarded. Louis XIV felt that in giving the Archduke Spain, the Empire, and the Spanish Netherlands, he was surrendering much that rightfully belonged to his family: posterity, he wrote, would find it hard to understand how he could give up so much, but he insisted he was willing to make the sacrifice for the tranquillity of Europe. He did not, however, wish to see his kingdom weakened by the rise of the Hapsburg power. Louis was especially concerned that Leopold's treaty with the Ottoman Empire had already tilted the balance of power in favor of the German Hapsburgs; therefore he was sure that when they also got Spain, Europe would want French power to grow enough to act as a check on the Hapsburgs. The English Parliament and the shipping interests in London, however, felt that it had been William who had given up too much by allowing for the possibility that France might have naval bases in Sicily and Naples. William felt that these distant commitments would actually weaken France, but the men who sent ships to the Levant could only see French interference with their trade, and regarded the treaty as a monstrous blunder on the part of their king. When Charles II died, leaving the entire Empire to the Duke of Anjou, many Englishmen preferred this solution to the Partition Treaty, for, they argued, a French prince on the Spanish throne would soon become a Spaniard and his policies would be inspired by Spanish needs.

When the second Partition Treaty became public property, a hue and cry arose in the English Parliament. The procedure had not been illegal; nonetheless, the Tories in the House attempted to impeach Sommers, the king's minister, (probably partly because he was a Whig) for his acquiescence. The attempt failed, but William learned a lesson in post-1699 English political organization that he had not been forced to learn earlier because, between 1689 and the treaty of Ryswick, all parties supported the war. The lesson was simple enough: no king could henceforth govern England if his ministry and its programs did not have the support of Parliament. The support of Parliament was necessary to implement "England's secret weapon" that supplied the money for mobilizing power, as well as for the government to rule the kingdom. When William made the next important treaty, the alliance with the Emperor and the Dutch, he was careful to associate with his negotiations some of the men who were important in Parliament. This, however, was in the future.

In July, 1700, another crisis developed when the Duke of Gloucester, the last remaining child of Princess Anne, died, leaving the succession to the throne in question. When William and Mary became king and queen, Anne had been named to succeed them; she was the second daughter of James II and a staunch Anglican, so she was acceptable to the men who made the Revolution. She had had many children, but one after another they died, and with the demise of this last son, it was evident that Anne could not be succeeded by an heir of her body. The next prince in line, if James Edward the son of James II and Mary of Modena were to be excluded because he was a Roman Catholic, was the son of the Duke of Savoy who was a grandson of Charles I.[26] The Savoyard family was also Catholic, but Victor Amadeus was a man of few principles and would have been quite willing to send his son to England to become an Anglican. However, it was this same Victor Amadeus who had made a separate peace with Louis XIV in 1696 (Treaty of Turin), and William never forgave him that treachery. He did

---

[26] Victor Amadeus of Savoy married Marie d'Orleans, whose mother had been Henriette of England, daughter of Charles I.

not know that in 1703 Victor Amadeus would be equally willing to desert his alliance with Louis XIV when he saw that the war would probably go against France; but that, too, was in the future.

After the Savoyard family, the house of the Elector of Hanover was next in line for the throne in England. Princess Elizabeth, the daughter of James I, and her husband Elector Frederick of the Rheinpfalz,[27] left a daughter, Elizabeth-Sophia, who had married the Elector of Hanover; she and her son George were both descendants of James I and staunch Protestants, even though they had only slight connection with England. Electoress Elizabeth-Sophia had serious reservations about her rights since there was a legitimate son of James II who unquestionably had a right to the throne by grace of God and his birth, but she was finally persuaded to smother her conscience and her belief in divine right for the good of her family and the Protestant religion. In 1701 the Parliament of England passed the Act of Settlement which placed her and her son as next in line to the throne after Princess Anne. This Act reaffirmed the principle that Parliament had the right to fix the succession to the throne in England without regard for the traditional ideas about divine right. It is an interesting fact that Princess Anne, like Elizabeth-Sophia, suffered doubts about her right to take the place that God had intended for her half-brother; these doubts were shared by many people in England, but the prevailing public opinion would not tolerate the idea of another Catholic king on England's throne.

It is hard to know what England would have done had Louis XIV accepted the thrones of Charles II for his grandson without attempting to use this new honor that had fallen to the House of Bourbon to aggrandize France. There were many in England who wanted to hear nothing of a war that would disrupt the prosperity of the kingdom, there were others who suspected and disliked William too much to follow his personal policy. Many Englishmen preferred the testament of Charles II to the Partition Treaty that

---

[27] The Winter King was the sobriquet given Frederick who was king of Bohemia through the winter of 1619–20.

might leave France in control of all Italy and in any case would greatly increase French power. Unquestionably, had Louis assured Europe that the two crowns would forever be separated, and that his grandson would in fact rule Spain in the interests of Spain rather than those of France, there would have been a strong, perhaps preponderant, opinion in England that it would be to English advantage to accept the *fait accompli*. The same is probably true of the Netherlands, and it could be argued that Louis was right in assuming that he would get little help from the sea powers against the Emperor if he insisted upon the Partition Treaty, and little objection from them if he accepted the will of Charles II. That is, he would get little objection if he were wise in the use he made of this new position established for the Bourbon family.

However, as we have seen, Louis was not wise. He offended exactly those people in England and in the United Netherlands whose growing power was giving them a predominant voice in the development of foreign policy. The commercial interests that saw no reason for war simply because a French prince might become King of Spain, had a very different attitude when French soldiers occupied the Spanish Netherlands (including Antwerp) and French merchants seemed about to monopolize the commerce of the Spanish colonies. They may also have been much disturbed by Louis' affirmation of Philippe V's right to his place in the succession to the throne of France, even though he had become king of Spain. William took grim pleasure in the fact that now his subjects would support him in a policy that might lead to war.

William, however, had learned a lesson when Parliament tried to impeach Sommers after the Partition Treaty. This time when he negotiated with the Emperor as king in England and Stadtholder in the United Netherlands, he was careful to associate Lord Marlborough, who was both a close friend of Princess Anne and a powerful figure in the House of Lords, with his negotiations. Thus the treaty of alliance that became the basis for the Grand Alliance that fought the War of the Spanish Succession, was not simply his personal policy. A few weeks after it was signed, Louis XIV demonstrated to all England how "wise" king William III had been, for the French king, in spite of the provision in the Treaty of Ryswick to the contrary, recognized the son of James II as King of England. This action, however, only strengthened the determination of Englishmen both in London and in the countryside, to resist the enlarged powers that Louis XIV had procured for his kingdom.

Before an English army could depart for the continent, William III was thrown from his horse and never recovered from the injury, but his death did not weaken the will of the English crown to resist. In place of William, whose record as a soldier was something less than brilliant, Lord Marlborough emerged as the director of the war and commander of the Anglo-Dutch armies while Marlborough's friends and relatives, in control of Parliament, and his wife, as the favorite of the new Queen, assured the English armies and their allies that money and materials of war would be forthcoming to assure success. England was at last ready to play its role in the manipulation of the power structure of the western world.

# Chapter 7

# The War of the
# Spanish Succession

When Louis XIV introduced his grandson as Philippe V, king of
Spain, the uneasy balance of power established by the treaties of
Turin, Ryswick, and Carlowitz tipped strongly in favor of France;
indeed within a half year it became apparent that there could be no
balance of power in the west unless some readjustments were made
to weaken the French position. Within months after Philippe V
crossed the frontier into his new kingdom, French soldiers occupied
the "barrier fortifications" in the Spanish Netherlands as well as
northern Italy (the Milanais), and French warships patrolled the
Mediterranean sea from Naples to Messina to Barcelona to Cadiz,
while other French men-of-war joined the poorly equipped Spanish navy in the Caribbean where the treasure fleet was assembling.
Furthermore, Philippe's uncles, the Electors of Cologne and Bavaria, had become military allies of the Two Bourbon Crowns; his
father-in-law the Duke of Savoy had joined his army to the Franco-
Spanish forces in the Milanais, and the king of Portugal could see
no way to avoid honoring his signature to his alliance with France.
When we remember that the French army did not disband after
the last war, this array of power seems most formidable indeed.
The Two Bourbon Crowns were in full military possession of all the

real estate under contest; they held strong forward positions on the lower Rhine and the upper Danube from which to intimidate both the Dutch Republic and the German princes. Their control over the Mediterranean was greater than that enjoyed by Philip II a century and a half earlier and their hold upon Naples and Sicily, the islands of the western Mediterranean, and Spain seemed to guarantee the Two Crowns their continued possession of this naval advantage. In Flanders, on the Rhine, in Italy and throughout the Mediterranean basin, to assure victory the military forces of the Two Crowns needed only to stand on the defensive long enough to wear down their opponent's will to resist.

Furthermore, another political problem also favored the Two Crowns. A great war had broken out in northeastern Europe in 1700 that distracted both the sea powers and the Emperor. A plot by August I of Saxony, Peter I of Russia, and Frederick IV of Denmark to partition the realm of the young king Charles XII of Sweden had seemed to the three monarchs a cheap and easy way to acquire territory; unfortunately for them, the young Swedish king was destined to be one of the great captains of his era, and the war actually lasted twenty years. Charles XII hunted down his three enemies with the single-minded purpose of a man who must revenge himself for an injury; in the end it cost him his life, but not until after he had left a trail of blood and burning villages stretching from the Baltic to the Black Sea. This Great War of the North never actually became entwined with the war over the Spanish Succession, perhaps as much because both Charles XII and Peter I disliked Louis XIV and his France as because of the facts of geography of the era which made the Polish borderlands enormous distances from the Rhine and Italy; but the powers fighting in western Europe could never be sure that the two wars would not become one. Indeed, at one point, Charles XII appeared deep in the heart of the Holy Roman Empire of the German nation to punish the Saxon Elector, and for a moment all Europe held its breath to see which way the "Lion of the North" would turn. Charles did turn east toward Russia, the battle of Poltava, exile in Turkey, and the final story of his return to Sweden and death. Had he turned the other way, the story of the war involving the Two Bourbon Crowns would have been very different.

Nonetheless, this War of the North did have an effect upon the war effort of the Grand Alliance against Louis XIV. Saxony was involved in the war from the beginning and so could not be counted upon for help against France. Frederick I, Elector of Brandenburg and King in Prussia, could not be unmindful of a conflict that raged so close to his frontiers and, indeed, that might take a turn affecting his own territories. Furthermore, the Sea Powers were involved from the outset of the War in the North. Charles had called upon them to honor their treaty and assist his passage from Sweden to Denmark, and the warfare in the Baltic sea inevitably affected the commercial interests of both England and the United Netherlands. Since they, too, were at war, there was less controversy over the rights of neutral ships in the Baltic than there would have been under other conditions. Though Denmark was forced out of the War of the North only a few months after it started, the Danish government could not be unmindful of a war in the Baltic. Thus it was impossible for Louis to attempt to use Denmark as a "third force" as he had during the previous war, or for the allies to get more help from Denmark than the renting of a few thousand soldiers in return for an English subsidy. On the whole, this war in the Baltic and eastern Europe was more disadvantageous to the enemies of France than to the Two Crowns.

The Grand Alliance that was forming to challenge the arrogance of the king of France had other troubles as well. It enjoyed neither the political family unity that seemed to cement the treaties forming the block of the Two Crowns, nor the geographic advantages that so obviously bespoke strength for the ambitions of Louis XIV and his grandson. The Grand Alliance was a disappointment to the Emperor, for it did not agree to the dethronement of Philippe V who had already been recognized as king of Spain by both England and the United Netherlands. The treaty returned to the idea of partition, with Italy and the Spanish Netherlands as the portion of the Archduke, and Spain with the colonial empire the share of Philippe V, on the condition that the crowns of France and Spain must never be united. A closer look at the treaty would seem to indicate that the Anglo-Dutch politicians were primarily interested in three things: first, in keeping the mouth of the Scheldt closed so that Antwerp and the towns of the hinterland could not challenge the prosperity of London and Amsterdam; secondly, the maintenance of the military "buffer" between France and the United Netherlands by establishing Dutch soldiers in the "barrier fortifications"; and lastly, in preventing French merchants from acquiring any advantage over Englishmen and Dutchmen in the commerce of the Spanish empire. Beyond this, they were intent upon humbling Louis XIV and weakening his kingdom in any way possible.

There were, however, important points of conflict between the two sea powers, conflicts that sometimes threatened the alliance. The Dutch held fast to their tradition that even in war, trade with the enemy should be on the basis of "business as usual." In every Spanish port there were commercial houses whose Spanish names only thinly disguised the Dutch merchants who owned them, and in most French ports, Dutch merchants had "connections" to assure continuance of commerce even though the Republic might be at war with the kingdom of France. The English, with predatory traditions going back to piracy, to the Elizabethan sea dogs, to the pirate-privateers of the last century, insisted that all trade with the enemy must stop and that all enemy commerce was free game for privateer or naval vessel. No better illustration of the divergent attitudes can be found than the reception of the news that the Spanish treasure fleet had reached Vigo Bay in 1702. The merchants in Amsterdam hailed its arrival as a successful business venture; the British admiral, who had been somewhat lethargic in his action before Cadiz, stormed into Vigo Bay, captured the treasure and merchandise that was still on the ships, sank or towed away some fifteen French men–of–war, and generally wrecked the harbor. The Spanish treasure had already been removed; what remained both of goods and precious metals belonged largely to the Dutch merchants. The Dutch were appalled at the behavior of their ally. As the war progressed, Dutch hostility to English naval policy increased, as the Netherlanders became convinced that their allies were trying to establish themselves at strategic points in the Mediterranean and the West Indies to forward their future commercial interests at Dutch expense. Happily for the alliance, fears of France were shared by both powers, and as the war went on, Dutch dependence on English assistance helped to keep the two states together. But there was also enough mutual hatred in both countries to raise real concern over the future of the alliance.

The Emperor too had his troubles. At the death of Jan Sobieski, just about the time that the treaty of Ryswick was signed, the Imperial candidate for the Polish throne, August, Elector of Saxony, was elected king of Poland. He should have been a tower of strength for the Emperor, since Saxony was one of the richest states of the Empire and Poland could now be an ally, but, as we have seen, August I of Poland became involved in a dangerous war with Charles XII of Sweden; his electorate was as much a drain on the Empire as a pillar of strength. Another elector, Frederick III of Brandenburg, watched his fellow elector of Saxony become King of Poland, saw his relative, the Duke of Hanover, become heir to the crown of England, while the Elector of Bavaria became Governor of the Spanish Netherlands with a chance of emerging as its hereditary ruler. Naturally he wished similar honors for the house of Hohenzollern. Only a few months before the death of Charles II in Spain, Emperor Leopold and Frederick III signed a treaty of alliance in which the Emperor recognized the Elector as Frederick I, king in Prussia. But Frederick I did not supply the aid that the Emperor had hoped to have; he may have intended to be a loyal ally, but had allowed his father's fine army and effective administration to weaken, and he could not give his whole attention to the problems of the west as long as a great war raged in the east near his Prussia. Of the three German princes with considerable military forces, only George of Hanover, who was to become George I of England, brought the military aid that had been expected of him. This meant that the Emperor had to depend upon the scattered military forces of the Circles of the Rhine, Swabia and Franconia for soldiers to defend the Rhine; the Emperor's own forces were heavily engaged in Italy and Hungary.

Hungary had long been the Achilles heel of the Austrian Hapsburgs. The crown of Hungary had been awarded to them only because of Hungarian need for defense against the Ottomans, but Hungarian noblemen had never considered themselves bound to their oath of allegiance. They had been rebels and malcontents for over a century; Leopold's victories after 1686 had made the Hungarian crown hereditary and outlawed rebellion as illegal. But once the Emperor was involved in war on the Rhine and in Italy, there were Hungarian magnates ready to take French gold and again lead rebellion. These uprisings probably never had a chance of success, for the rebels could not match the Imperial soldiers in arms or military strategy; but they did occupy some of Leopold's best troops and generals. As soon as the war in the west turned against France, the Hungarian rebellion simmered out.

The most important Imperial efforts were spent on Italy. In Vienna, Italy loomed much larger and more important than either Spain or the Spanish Netherlands: Spain was far away and weak, the Spanish Netherlands were captive to the English and the Dutch, but Italy was contiguous to Austria and vital for Hapsburg entry to the Mediterranean. Thus from the first days of the war, we see the Imperial armies operating in Italy perhaps at the expense of the defense of the Empire. The men at Vienna were more anxious to seize Italy than to occupy Spain itself. This Imperial preoccupation with Italy perhaps explains why Bavaria was able to play so important a role in the first years of the war. Louis of Baden, who commanded the Imperial troops on the upper and middle Rhine, was never able to muster forces greater than those at the disposal of the Bavarian Elector, and have anything left over to face the French at Kehl or Landau.

Thus when the conflict over the succession to the thrones of Spain broke into a hot war, the Two Bourbon Crowns and their allies seemed to have considerable advantage. In the preceding war the kingdom of France had been forced to recognize limitations upon its ambitions; it had been opposed by the very combination of England, the United Netherlands, and the Emperor that now opposed the Two Crowns. In the last war Spain, Savoy, Portugal, Bavaria, and Cologne had been part of the coalition opposing the kingdom of France; this time they were France's allies. In the preceding war only the Ottoman Empire had vaguely assisted France. The Turks would have nothing to do with this war, but the Hungarians created a diversion in favor of France in the east.

However, all was not as well as it appeared. In the last war, the kingdom had been defended by a strong array of fortifications that defied the enemy and allowed the French army to maneuver behind shelter of these lines. This time the first lines of defense in the Spanish Netherlands and the lower Rhineland were not supported by fortifications created by Vauban; indeed, there were no lines or only hastily drawn ones, and the fortifications were weak and often poorly designed. The defense of these provinces was clearly dependent upon the valor of the French army and the skill of its officers. In Italy the situation was no better in spite of the boasts that the Austrians would have to learn to fly if they were to cross the Alps. The French did hold the Milanais and the more important passes into Italy, but they could not command the loyalty of the Italian people, who seemed always to help the enemy rather than their own ruler. Furthermore, Venice was at best sullenly neutral, at worst actively pro-Imperial; like the people of the Milanais, the Venetians were not pleased to have Philippe introduce French power into Italy. The problem of the defense of Bavaria had not yet been considered in Versailles in 1702; Louis still believed that the Elector would be able to cut the Empire in two and perhaps bring the German princes to accommodate themselves to the Two Crowns. However, the simple fact that the French fortifications were made to defend the Rhine rather than the Danube should have given pause to those whose imagination could soar a little. By 1703 the King became painfully aware of the problem and found it necessary to commit an army to the defense of his Bavarian ally.

Spain too presented a problem. In the last war Spain was the enemy, but it required more French troops to defend Spain than were needed to fight on the Spanish frontier. A century of political and economic decay had sapped the power of the Spanish Crowns to a point where the Spanish were unwilling or unable to defend themselves. Furthermore, the differences between Castile and Aragon created a situation dangerous to Philippe's reign; in Catalonia there was always support for rebellion against Madrid, and thus it was not hard to rouse a Carlist force to back the archduke against the Bourbon king. Moreover, the sea powers were soon to be able to land troops at many points on the Iberian peninsula. Indeed, it can be argued that only the scandalous behavior of the invading forces (loot, violence, and sacrilege) saved Spain for the Bourbons. In any case, during the first six or seven years of the war, Spain was a continuous drain on French resources of money and manpower.

Finally, in France itself there were serious problems. In 1685 the revocation of the Edict of Nantes had outlawed the huguenot cult but the king had not been able to rewin for the monarchy the hearts of a large number of huguenot Frenchmen, and, once France was involved in a dangerous war, a revolt broke out in the south of France that threatened dire things for the kingdom. Indeed, it was even believed that the enemy might be able to land troops and establish a front in France itself. No such thing happened, but in 1704 and 1705 troops that might have been used to punish the Duke of Savoy, and one of the ablest marshals in the French roster, were needed to suppress the revolt. On another level, the financial problems of the kingdom were even more serious than this huguenot rebellion. When the last war started, the French treasury was not in flourishing condition, but it was prepared for a short war. This time even though the harvests between 1701 and 1707 were good, the king's credit was overstrained, and his treasury in the red. The finance minister could keep afloat only through "extraordinary" measures. Even if the terrible winter of 1708–1709 had not brought famine and distress in its wake, the kingdom would have been on the verge of bankruptcy by that year. In 1701 the kingdom of France was in no condition to fight a war that would draw heavily upon its resources; by 1708 its financial plight was desperate.

The Imperials did not wait for the signature of their allies before opening the war. When Philippe V was proclaimed king, Emperor Leopold was incensed and angered; he could see no solution other than war. His problem, however, was a thorny one, for the Franco-Spanish forces occupied the more important passes between central Europe and Italy, and their commander Marshal Catinat was an experienced officer. Indeed, the French felt absolutely secure. The Imperial commander, however, was Eugene of Savoy, whose rise to important command in the Imperial armies had been rapid and brilliant. Eugene, with the considerable support of the Italian population in the southern slopes of the Alps, was able to pass an army into Italy. It was not as large as the one commanded by Catinat nor as well equipped with artillery, but Eugene understood how to use field fortifications to lessen the gap between the numbers of his army and those of his foe. Catinat soon found that imperial detachments swooped down upon his foraging parties and always in superior numbers while, whenever he attempted to join battle with his foe, he was confronted by earth works that made the issue of an assault problematical. His letters to the king at Versailles convinced Louis that Catinat had lost his nerve. At the French court there was still considerable contempt for the German soldiers (caterpillars) and their commander, who had been called the "little abbé" when he was a youth in France. Eugene was the son of one of Mazarin's nieces who married into the French branch of the house of Savoy. It would take a little time and harsh reverses before Versailles became aware of the new warfare that soldiers like Eugene had learned to fight.

Louis XIV called his friend Marshal Villeroy to Versailles and sent him off to Italy with orders to seek out and fight the Imperials. Any other course would threaten Philippe's rule in Italy. Unhappily Villeroy encountered the same problem that had faced Catinat: Eugene did not want to give him an easy victory because of superior forces, but Villeroy, armed with the king's orders, was bolder than Catinat; he vigorously followed the Imperial armies, found what he thought to be a rear guard holding a fortified position at Chiari, and fell upon it. The "rear guard" turned out to be the entire Imperial army. It was a battle like the one fought later in the century at Bunker Hill, except that when it was all over, the Imperials still sat behind their fortifications at Chiari. It took Villeroy and his king several weeks to realize that this battle tipped the balance of military power in northern Italy in favor of Eugene. Louis was very right when he ruefully wrote that it was true that he had "ordered a battle" but that such orders should be "executed with prudence." Before the winter of 1701–1702 was over, Eugene had actually invaded Villeroy's winter quarters at Cremona and captured the French marshal. Both Versailles and Madrid realized that this was an inauspicious opening for the war. Louis dispatched one of his best officers, Marshal Vendôme, to command the armies of Italy: to send a lesser man to contest with Eugene would have been folly.

During the winter of 1701–1702 both sides prepared for the coming campaigns. Then, without warning, a tragedy occurred that could have changed the course of events. King William III fell from his horse and did not recover from his fall; his death gave rise to hopes in France that a crisis would arise over the succession in England that would prevent the island kingdom from joining the war. When the political atmosphere cleared, however, Queen Anne sat serenely on the throne, and Lord Marlborough, supported by the father-in-law of one of his daughters, Lord Godolphin, and the husband of another, the Earl of Sutherland, had firm control over the queen's government; and, since his wife Sarah was the confidante of the queen, this government was secure. Marlborough had been important in the negotiations for the Grand Alliance, and he was anxious to get on with the war.

The mere fact that England did not seek an agreement or remain neutral did not dampen the French king's optimism. He sent a powerful army into the lower Rhine under the command of Marshal Boufflers with instructions to do something spectacular to intimidate the German princes and make them willing to accommodate themselves to France. In his correspondence with his soldier, Louis emphasized the supposed fact that the French army of veterans would surely be superior to the raw Anglo-Dutch recruits. He was sure that Parliament's refusal to allow William to keep his army after Ryswick would guarantee an advantage for France. French intelligence had not reported the fact that "retired" (that is, unemployed) soldiers in both England and Holland had rallied quickly to the call for recruits so that Marlborough had an army, commanded by experienced officers, that enrolled a considerable number of veteran troops in the ranks.

What was more important was the fact that no one had told the king about the type of a campaign that Marlborough would wage. The Anglo-Dutch armies seized the initiative at the very outset of the war. They were not even impressed when Louis XIV sent his grandson, the Duke of Burgundy, with a commission to have Boufflers "command under his orders." Before the king's grandson and his natural son, the Duke of Maine, could win a military reputation, Marlborough tied the whole French army to a defensive position and proceeded to capture it piecemeal. Louis XIV watched with incredulous anxiety as one fortified place after another fell without allowing his soldiers to march out with the "honors of war." The predatory Englishman was intent upon capturing the French army, as well as on destroying France's defensive position in the Lower Rhineland. When he took Liège, the entire Electorate of Cologne was at his mercy, and by that time he had captured or killed more French soldiers than would normally be lost in a full-fledged battle.

With the lower Rhine in Anglo-Dutch hands, Marlborough was in a position to invade the Spanish Netherlands. It was little consolation that a French army under Villars defeated the Imperials at Friedingen; Louis of Baden's army was largely composed of detachments pulled together from the Swabian and Franconian circles. The bulk of the Imperial army was engaged in Italy and Hungary.

At this point (1702–1703) one of the most important military factors of the emerging political structure of the European world began to unfold: namely, the importance of the Straits at Gibraltar and the concomitant control of the seas. William's war (1689–1697) had taught Englishmen, who understood what was happening, how important it had been to have a naval base at Cadiz, where an Anglo-Dutch fleet could take shelter from winter storms, refit and repair the ships, and restock magazines with food, water, and munitions. Since the French had no comparable fleet to oppose them, the Anglo-Dutch squadrons could interdict communication throughout the western Mediterranean as well as in the Atlantic. In the last war, with Spain as an ally, it had been comparatively easy to establish a naval station at Cadiz and from there to control the whole Mediterranean coast of Spain, so that the French found it impossible either to take Barcelona or act against the communications between Spain and Italy. This time, however, Spain was an ally of France, and Italy was occupied by the forces of the Two Crowns. Obviously a new solution for the Cadiz base had to be found.

In 1702 the English fleet appeared before Cadiz, but its commander, who apparently did not understand what was needed, was quite unclear about his role and ineffective in his action. He apparently did not want to winter so far from England. On the way home he learned of the presence of a Franco-Spanish squadron and the Spanish Treasure Fleet in Vigo Bay; this was a target more suitable to his taste. As we have noted by this assault on Vigo Bay, the English not only captured goods and treasure, most of which belonged to Dutch merchants, but also captured or destroyed some half dozen French warships that Louis XIV could never replace. However, the action also demonstrated to the Portuguese government that English soldiers could be landed on the Iberian coast if it proved necessary to do so. This was very important, for Portugal, while technically an ally of the Two Crowns, had not yet committed any of its forces in the conflict perhaps as much because of fear that France and Spain could not protect Portuguese ships on the high seas, as of fear that Portugal would be at the mercy of Spanish powers if the Two Crowns should emerge victorious. The battle of Vigo Bay and the skill of the English ambassadors (John Methuen and his son Paul) combined to reverse the Franco-Portuguese alliance. The so-called Methuen Treaties provided for commercial agreement between England and Portugal (cloth for Port and Madera wine) that proved to be mutually advantageous as well as important for military and naval cooperation that gave the English fleet a necessary base at Lisbon from which it could patrol the Atlantic, and invade the Mediterranean.

At the same time that secret negotiations removed Portugal from the sphere of the Two Crowns, another intrigue was being pressed in the inner circle of the Duke of Savoy. Victor Amadeus had long held a grudge against his cousin, the king of France, who had treated him and his Duchy as an extension of the French kingdom, but he knew better than to allow a grudge to prevent his gaining advantages for himself and his family. In 1696 he had deserted his allies (Treaty of Turin) when it appeared that the Emperor would take France's place as Lord of Casale. However, even the advantage of marrying one daughter to the heir to the throne of France, another to the King of Spain, did not make Victor Amadeus a steadfast friend of Louis XIV; he was and remained a politician keenly aware of his place in the power balances of Italy and of his own dangerous situation between the houses of Hapsburg and Bourbon, both of which had contributed to his blood and background. When the war shaped up in 1701, with the Two Crowns fully in control of the Milanais and the Toulon fleet as the only naval power in the Mediterranean, Victor Amadeus married his second daughter to the young king of Spain and "loyally" supported his son-in-law's claim to the thrones of Spain. What else could he do? However, the march of events taught him much. He was present at the battle of Chiari; he understood what it meant when Eugene kidnapped Villeroy; he saw the whole lower Rhineland collapse, and the English navy preparing to reestablish its position as the dominant force in the straits and the western Mediterranean. In 1703 he also watched the Franco-Bavarian forces in central Europe fail to penetrate the Hapsburg lands while Eugene, with smaller forces, kept Vendôme engaged so that he could not—or at least did not—send a detachment to aid the attack in the Tyrol. Victor Amadeus had tasted English subsidies during the last war, and his sense of the way the wind was blowing told him that this one would go against the Two Crowns. Eugene of Savoy was a distant kinsman, the English were willing to pay 800,000 crowns a month, and an English squadron sailed along the coast of Italy unchallenged by the French from Toulon. Victor Amadeus finally decided to betray the Two Crowns. Although Vendôme was aware of the intrigue long before it came into the open,[28] perhaps he, like the British ambassador at Vienna, did not really believe that Amadeus would risk a shift when his lands were surrounded by the armies of the Two Crowns. However, when it became apparent that the Duke of Savoy was going to shift sides, Vendôme arrested and disarmed some 5,000 Savoyard troops and made plans to punish the Duke for his action.

Louis XIV's letter to the Duke of Savoy expressing indignation about his treason may have relieved the old king's feelings, but it could not conceal the fact that another of his allies had deserted the Two Crowns. In 1702 Cologne had been taken out of the war by military conquest; in 1703 Portugal and Savoy deserted the Franco-Spanish cause by the action of Anglo-Imperial diplomacy.

The first great military disaster, however, did not come until 1704. In 1703 Marlborough's audacity was hampered by the conservatism of the Dutch commissars attached to his army. These men, politicians and bureaucrats rather than soldiers, had been frightened by the fury of the campaign of 1702; they admitted that Marlborough had won, but they wondered whether he might not just as easily have lost the entire war in an afternoon by such aggressive tactics. In 1704 Marlborough and Eugene made common plans for the dramatic stroke that Eugene had contemplated the preceding year when the movements of the Imperial armies had forced Louis XIV to send Villars with a French army into Bavaria. Early in the spring of 1704 war supplies began to pile up on the docks of the middle Rhine as far south as Mannheim; it was a warning that some movement of the Anglo-Dutch army was about to begin. As the army moved up the Rhine, the entire French armament was frozen in place until its destination could be established, for from Mannheim, Marlborough had the choice of attacking in Flanders, in Alsace, or in Germany. When Marlborough's column turned southeast, the news came that Eugene too was on the

---

[28] Indeed, he insisted that this was the reason he did not send a detachment to aid Maximilian and Villars against the Hapsburg *Erbländer* (i.e., family holdings in the Empire).

move! Bavaria obviously was the target, and the French armies responded by moving eastward to counter the thrust.

The Anglo-Dutch forces came on. At Donauwörth (Shellenberg), Marlborough and Louis of Baden mounted a vicious attack that cost heavily in life, but opened a new line of communication into central Germany to free the Englishman of his complete dependence on the Rhine, and at the same time also placed much of Bavaria at the mercy of the Anglo-Imperial forces. At Versailles, Louis XIV believed that his ally would now "accommodate himself to the Emperor" to save "all that he valued" from capture by the Anglo-Imperials. The French army under Tallart, that thrust across the Black Forest, was prepared either to cooperate with the Duke of Bavaria or to help the other French army under Marcin return to France. Max Emanuel finally decided to take the chance against his enemies. The French argument for the campaign was cogent when it insisted that Marlborough would either have to capture several of the great fortresses of Bavaria so that he could winter in Germany, or retire without accomplishing anything. What the French had not counted upon was the audacity of their enemies. Eugene and Marlborough had no intention of wasting their time besieging a fortification; they marched against the Franco-Bavarian armies, found them encamped in a strong position at Blenheim-Höchstadt, and mounted a furious attack. The Franco-Bavarians had believed themselves too strongly posted to be attacked, but at the end of the day thousands of their soldiers were either dead or captured, and the rest in full flight toward the Rhine. This was the first time that one of Louis' marshals had been captured along with hundreds of other officers and thousands of his best soldiers. In an afternoon, the French lost Bavaria; indeed they lost everything east of the Rhine. Louis expressed the hope that "M. de Marlborough will give me a chance for revenge," but in France a shudder went through the community that is still part of French folklore and folk song.

While the Franco-Bavarians and the Anglo-Imperials faced each other in central Germany, the Anglo-Dutch fleet escorted the first allied landings in Portugal to defend Lisbon, and moved on to capture Gibraltar. The French Mediterranean fleet could not fail to respond; under the Count of Toulouse, an illegitimate son of Louis XIV, the French challenged the allied fleet off Malaga. It was a slugging match in which both fleets lost heavily in men, both were badly damaged, but neither lost a ship by capture or by sinking. The Anglo-Dutch admirals, however, were greatly embarrassed by the fact that the capture of Gibraltar had cost them so much powder and ball that their magazines were almost empty after one day's battle at Malaga. Perhaps it was fortunate for them that the French, also badly mauled, were not anxious to renew the fight. After one day of mutual observation, the French fleet returned to Toulon. It never again challenged the English navy in the Mediterranean. With bases at Lisbon and Gibraltar, it was possible the next year to land at Barcelona and hold the city. (Early in 1704 the marines had been forced to reembark after a short stay at Barcelona.) The classical role of the English navy in the structure of the balance of power in the Mediterranean was beginning to assume firm contours. The next year with the capture of the Balearic Islands and the establishment of English bases in Italy after the Imperials drove the French from the peninsula, the Mediterranean had practically become an English lake.

Following the bloody battles in Bavaria of 1704, the Dutch commissioners with Marlborough's army did everything that they could to hold him in check in 1705. They were happy that he had won his victories, but they could not forget that he could have lost the whole war in an afternoon. With these restraints, the Anglo-Dutch campaign of 1705 was not particularly brilliant. Marlborough did break the Franco-Spanish lines in the Netherlands, but when the Dutch vetoed a battle, he was unable to take advantage of the disorder in the French camp. The summer went on, marked by maneuvers and skirmishes of detachments, but no decisive battle. In Italy, too, the campaign was uneventful; Eugene and Vendôme sparred back and forth enough to prevent the French from detaching large forces to attack the Duke of Savoy, whose little army fought a hit-and-run campaign on the French supply lines while he waited in vain for an English landing to help him. In Spain the allied armies built up their forces for a campaign that would place Carlos III (Archduke Charles) on the throne, but no decisive action took place unless it was the failure of the Spanish to drive the English from Gibraltar. The next year was to be a year of more vigorous action.

Emboldened by the fact that the war had gone a little better in 1705, the French organized their campaign for 1706 in Italy to punish the Duke of Savoy by stripping him of his lands and his capital at Turin, and in Flanders for a broad sweep from the Spanish Netherlands that might intimidate the Dutch and bring them to the peace table. Suddenly all hopes for a speedy end of the war vanished. In the last week of May, Villeroy and Max of Bavaria confronted Marlborough at Ramilles; it was a great victory for the Anglo-Dutch armies. Villeroy asked to be relieved of his command, and Vendôme, who was supposed to punish the Duke of Savoy, had to hurry to Flanders to try to put some order in the remains of the dispirited French army. In Italy, Marcin persisted in his plans to besiege Turin, but Eugene slipped by the French army in the Milanais and in a series of rapid marches joined the Savoyard army and completely defeated the French forces that were trying to take Turin. In a short summer campaign the French lost Italy and the Spanish Netherlands. Nor were the disasters limited to Italy and Flanders. By the summer of 1706 the allied armies in the Iberian peninsula also seemed about to win great victories; by the end of June, Madrid was in allied hands and Archduke Charles was fully in control of Catalonia. It looked as if the cause of Philippe V were lost; many of the Spanish grandees either recognized Carlos III or were preparing to do so. However, it turned out differently for a number of reasons. The allied commanders could not agree on common action, and their soldiers revolted the Spanish by their plundering and sacrilegious behavior, while in Marshal Berwick the Two Crowns had a soldier who managed to pluck victory from the jaws of defeat. Even so after his reverses in Italy and Flanders, Louis XIV was ready to make peace on any reasonable terms, but the allies did not seem to realize that their victories in Italy and the Netherlands could not allow them to dictate peace in Spain as well.

Nor was Spain the only place where the unwise actions of the allied armies and governors failed to insure victory. The Dutch moved into the Spanish Netherlands with a desire to force their Roman Catholic cousins to pay the costs of the war. In spite of protests from the Emperor, who claimed the provinces for Carlos III, the Dutch commissioners took over the government of these provinces and quickly alienated most of the population. The next spring, Vendôme had little trouble recouping much of the losses in the Spanish Netherlands of the preceding year because he could depend upon the assistance of the local population.

In 1707 the big action again returned to the Mediterranean basin. The allied armies had two objectives: the capture of the rest of Spanish possessions in Italy and the establishment of an allied position at Toulon. Had the Germans been willing to commit all their forces for the capture of Toulon, both projects might have been successful, but the Emperor was interested in establishing his family's control over the south of Italy. The assault on Toulon, however, prevented any other French action, for Louis XIV had to draw troops from every theatre of the war to provide Marshal Tessé with the force needed to repel the invasion. The failure of the Allied armies to take that city was a bitter defeat for Eugene and the Duke of Savoy, but it was not enough to redress the military balance that was so badly tipped against the kingdom of France.

After the repulse of the allied army at Toulon, Louis XIV had hopes that his enemies would make a peace that would recognize his grandson's right to a part of the Spanish inheritance. He was quite willing to give up Italy and the Netherlands in return for the right to keep Spain and the overseas empire, or to give up Spain, the overseas empire and the Netherlands in return for Italy.

These were approximately the terms that had been written into the Anglo-Dutch Imperial alliance of 1702, but in 1707 France's enemies would hear nothing of it. Even so, the fact that Vendôme had recaptured the greater part of the Spanish Netherlands gave the French hopes that they could hold out until a compromise settlement could be made. On the allied side, there was no desire to compromise. Emperor Leopold was dead (1705) and his elder son Joseph I was on the throne. More flexible than his father, Joseph had been able to soften the Hungarian revolt, and, with his armies in full control of Italy, he could see no reason for reaching an agreement that did not give his brother, the Archduke, the thrones centered on Madrid. The Dutch and English politicians, forgetful of the treaty that they had made in 1702 that envisaged the partition of the Spanish inheritance, also had taken up the cry: "No peace without Spain."

It was a block to any agreement; the decision was left to the men with guns and sabers. Louis XIV confided his army in Flanders to the care of his grandson the Duke of Burgundy and his most famous soldier, the Duke of Vendôme. The campaign was hardly underway when these two were at odds with each other: Burgundy was cautious and defensive, Vendôme was both careless and aggressive. The king could not settle their problems from Versailles. The allied armies again planned a juncture of the Anglo-Dutch under Marlborough and the Imperials under Eugene. Without Eugene, Marlborough would have been at a numerical disadvantage; with the Imperials, the allied armies had the advantage. The first clash came at Oudenarde, where the allies forced the French to fight a running battle before either side could get into position. By evening of the first day, the French were inside a huge half-moon of fire in a terrain unsuited for cavalry action. Vendôme wanted to stand up and fight; Burgundy ordered a retreat. It was a full week before the extent of the disaster was evident; the French army had lost another major battle and all Flanders was at the mercy of the Anglo-Imperial armies.

This was a terrible blow to the old king at Versailles. The Duke of Burgundy was his favorite grandson, the hope of the dynasty; the Duke of Vendôme was a Bourbon, descending from an illegitimate line founded by Henry IV. Vendôme also was France's most prestigious soldier and the best hope for holding off the enemy. After Oudenarde these two men became enemies and their conflict spilled over into the cliques at court and upset the military action in Flanders. In the end, both of them were in disgrace.

The Anglo-Imperials, however, were unable to take full advantage of this disaster because Eugene was unwilling to leave the great French fortifications on his line of march and invade France to impose peace at Versailles. This was Marlborough's proposal, but Eugene insisted upon the siege of Lille before any invasion could begin. Old Marshal Boufflers defended Lille against Eugene while Marlborough commanded the army "of observation" that guaranteed the lines of communication. Some of the battles over the supply lines in Flanders that summer would have been ranked as full scale battles in earlier wars. The French, however, were unable to lift the siege; indeed when the season was over, of the French commanders, only Marshal Boufflers emerged with his reputation intact. He forced Eugene to pay heavily for the capture of Lille.

Then came the terrible winter of 1708–1709. The cold was bitter: trees cracked, men and animals died of the frost, even the winter wheat in the ground was largely destroyed. Before March the streets of Paris were filled with hungry people demanding bread, begging for bread. The army suffered as much as the general population. In the fall of 1708 its ranks had been badly thinned by desertion, as well as by casualties, and those soldiers who did go into winter camp were poorly clad, poorly shod, and infected with bad morale. The winter nearly put the army out of business. Louis asked Boufflers to take command to try to bring some order out of the chaos and put the kingdom in some defensive stance, but Boufflers, too, came down sick: fever, congestion of the lungs, and general weakness. After the king's personal physician visited him, Louis decided to call Villars to take his place. But the hopes at Versailles were no longer on the army; Louis and his advisors wanted peace at any price—or almost any price. France, they believed, could not sustain another campaign.

The peace party at Versailles included most of the ministers, the circle around the Duke of Burgundy, and even Madame de Maintenon, who had become convinced that God sent the terrible winter of 1708–1709 as a warning of His wrath. The king's council was convinced that France would have to accept any conditions that the enemies would impose upon the kingdom. Even before the devastation of the winter, French agents in the Netherlands were earnestly seeking peace; by February-March of 1709 they were asking for terms in language that indicated desperation. The king ceased to write to his grandson in Spain, for he knew that the treaty that he would make must deprive Philippe of his throne; he only hoped to save somthing from the wreckage to compensate Philippe for this loss. Unhappily for the mental health of the men at Versailles, the enemies well understood that France was in no position to resist. When Lille fell (December, 1708), both Eugene and Marlborough talked about marching to Versailles to dictate terms, but after the winter of 1708–1709 they no longer believed that this march would be necessary, for it seemed certain that the kingdom of France was in no condition to resist any demands that might be made upon it. When a French agent arrived in the Netherlands to secure terms, he soon learned that there was no end to the allied demands. Every day they escalated; every day they grew more and more monstrous. Finally the French foreign minister Torcy, himself went to the Netherlands to try to fix the conditions upon which the allied powers would give France peace. The peace party, that now included the king, was prepared to see all of the territory acquired by the kingdom, since the Treaty of Westphalia, and indeed, even Alsace, stripped from France. They could not believe that this would not secure peace.

The allies, however, had problems. Each member of the alliance had ambitions to deprive France of territory and influence, but their demands did not stop with conditions for France. The war was against the Two Crowns, not simply against the kingdom of France, and the allied demands of the Bourbon King of Spain were even more excessive than those upon the king of France. The recent election in England had produced a Whig government committed to the slogan "No peace without Spain." Emperor Joseph refused to consider any peace that did not place his brother Charles on the throne of Charles II as "Carlos" III. And the Dutch, as honest brokers for the alliance and protégés of the Whig statesmen, committed themselves to the proposition that all the allies must be satisfied.

The fortunes of the war, combined with the rigors of nature, had reduced the crown of France to the point at which it no longer could really hope to resist the demands of its enemies, but not so the crown of Spain. The fortunes of the war favored Philippe V. In 1709 France may have been defeated, but Bourbon Spain was not.

Indeed, quite the contrary: after the allied armies had been forced to evacuate Madrid, there was a general movement, particularly in Castile, in favor of the Bourbon king. The arrogant Protestant allied soldiers, the Portuguese looters, the general attitude of the English and Imperial officers all revolted the proud Spanish. While some of the grandees did actually rally to "Carlos" III when his military fortunes were riding high, by the winter of 1708–1709 the drift was strikingly in favor of Philippe V. For the first time he was able to free himself from the dictates of his grandfather; he had an army paid by the Spanish government and loyal to his cause. Of course Philippe was not completely independent of his grandfather's troops even in 1709, but he could better expect to be able to hold off his foes with his own forces. The war of the Two Crowns had in fact become two wars: the allies had won the war against the Bourbon crown in France, but they were far from a victory over the Bourbon Crown in Spain. This was the dilemma: could the governments of the United Netherlands and the (recently, 1707) United Kingdom of England and Scotland make peace with France and continue to fight against Spain? The peoples of these two states would be more than just critical if they saw France beginning to recover her commercial position because she was at peace, while their armies and economic energies were still involved in an impossible war in Spain. The allied negotiators were much too smart to allow themselves to fall into such a situation. A remedy had to be found. It was embodied in the famous "Preliminaries of the Hague" of 1709.

The remedy, however, made any peace impossible. What the allied negotiators demanded was an outrageous condition. To secure peace, Louis XIV must drive his grandson from the throne of Spain; if he would not go peaceably, then the king of France must use military force to compel him to give the throne to "Carlos" III. They would not even consider Louis' plaintive request that Philippe should be given a "kingdom" made up of Sicily, Naples, Sardinia, and the Tuscan ports. No, he must return to his position as Duke of Anjou—nothing more. Furthermore, the allies were only willing to grant Louis a two-month truce to accomplish the dethronement of his grandson, and that, only after he had surrendered the last of his fortifications that still defended the Netherlands frontier. Torcy was shocked. He had come to negotiate, willing to make concessions that would have deprived the kingdom of France of gains made since the days of Richelieu; he could not agree to such a monstrous proposal. On the way back to Versailles he stopped off to visit with Villars and the army that was preparing to defend the kingdom. Villars concluded that his king should place faith in the Mother of God and prepare to strike hard.

The military situation of the spring and summer of 1709 deserves considerable attention. When Boufflers became sick, the king sent Villars to take his place at the head of an army that lacked almost everything. Happily for Villars, while he often lacked the bread needed to feed his troops, he still had more bread than many of the villages and towns of the kingdom, and the desertion rate de-clined as the troops realized that they had a better chance to evade starvation in the army than as deserters. Villars was a tough soldier, and he knew what had to be done. The kingdom could be saved by "lines"—field fortifications that would allow a numerically inferior army to fight against a larger enemy with a good chance of success. The fact that Eugene and Marlborough believed that France would have to surrender anyway led them to postpone the beginning of their campaign in the spring of 1709, and thereby gave Villars enough time to make his field fortifications formidable. When the Anglo-Imperials got around to opening the campaign, their commanders decided on a siege of a French fortification rather than an attack of the lines and a march to Versailles. Louis and Villars were jubilant, but Villars could not leave it at that: by the middle of July he was writing to the king that there were only two alternatives: accept the peace terms or try for success in battle. There was not enough bread to keep the army alive, and unless the enemy were made "docile" by a battle, he could not hope to defend the kingdom. Finally Louis consented, and Villars moved into a position that he hoped would provoke Marlborough and Eugene to attack him. The result was the battle of Malplaquet.

Europe had to wait a hundred years to see another battle as bloody as Malplaquet. Before the battle was joined, Louis sent Boufflers to be on the scene in case Villars should be put out of action. The two men understood and respected each other, and the senior, Boufflers, was willing to work under Villars. Together they set up a defensive position and received the Anglo-Imperial attack. This was just the affair that Dutch commissars had been afraid of ever since Marlborough's campaign of 1702. The Dutch infantry regiments were cut down like grain and left in heaps on the field: a casualty rate of close to 80 percent. A line of some forty French cannons enfiladed their foes with terrible results. It was true that Villars was badly wounded and that Boufflers had to call for retreat, but the enemy was in no condition to follow up a supposed victory. Eugene and Marlborough had lost almost twice as many men as the French, and the French army withdrew from the field in good order, ready to defend itself in case the enemy should wish to renew the battle. Villars was not far wrong when he wrote the king that "If God would allow the enemy to defeat us in one more such battle, the enemy army would cease to exist." Malplaquet did not end the war, but it did give pause to the allied plans to march on Versailles and dictate peace. The allies continued to make outrageous demands upon France, but their commanders were cautious not to give Villars another chance to fight them in an open field battle.

In the winter of 1709–10, despite the battle of Malplaquet, France's position remained desperate. While Louis continued to talk about the necessity of giving his grandson a kingdom based upon Naples and Sicily, and steadfastly refused to accept the responsibility for driving Philippe from Madrid, he did propose that the kingdom of France would pay the allies a subsidy so that they could accomplish this feat. This suggestion, like the one that Philippe should be compensated by an Italian kingdom, fell on stony ground; the allies were sure that they had the force to compel the kingdom of France to accede to their complete demands, and indeed, in the summer of 1710, one after another of Vauban's fortresses fell as Marlborough and Eugene stripped the kingdom of its ability to resist. They would not allow Villars to provoke them into a battle: they believed that would not be necessary.

At this very moment, however, events in England were about to undermine the solid front of the alliance and open at least a crack of the door to a more reasonable peace.

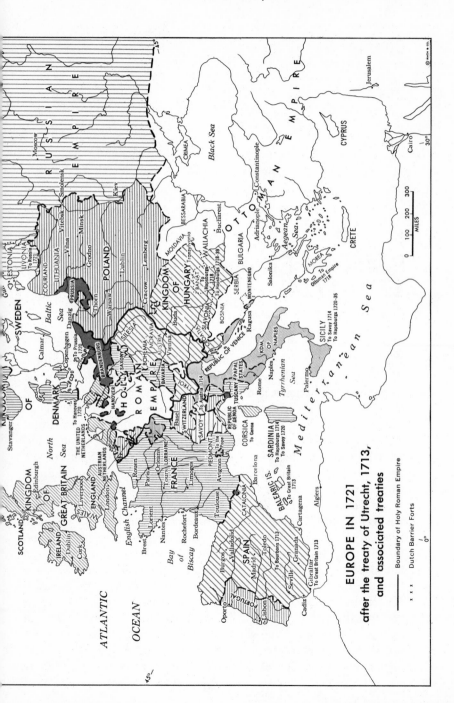

EUROPE IN 1721
after the treaty of Utrecht, 1713,
and associated treaties

—————  Boundary of Holy Roman Empire

x x x   Dutch Barrier Forts

# Chapter 8

# Peace for Europe:
# 1710–1714

The conference at Gertruydenberg in the spring of 1710 failed; the allies, pressured by the Whig statesmen, confident in the strength of their armies, and convinced of French weakness, refused to budge from the conditions of the Preliminaries of the Hague that the French king considered not only impossible but monstrous. This was the demand that the French surrender their frontier fortifications to the allies and send their own troops to Spain to dethrone Philippe V. The allies would agree that their troops in Spain would cooperate in this enterprise, but, if it were not completed at the end of two months, the allies reserved the right to reopen the war against France from the bases that had been surrendered to them. From the allied point of view this demand made sense, for they had committed themselves not to make a peace that did not place the Archduke on the Spanish throne, and yet they knew that the English and Dutch people would become highly critical and restless if France were granted peace while their own armies still had the task of driving Philippe from Spain. From the French point of view it was impossible: the king of France would not make war on his own grandson to satisfy his enemies! And yet there were men in the entourage at Versailles who were convinced that, in the end, they would be forced to do just that. At Gertruydenberg the French negotiators offered to give up Alsace and to pay the allies a subsidy as long as they were forced to fight in Spain, but they could not agree to the use of French troops against Philippe V. The offer was rejected: the English were convinced that they could impose their will upon France, and their insistence kept their allies in line.

For his part, Philippe V, his back stiffened by his wife and the Princesse des Ursins, announced that he would not leave Spain alive, and, even though he no longer had support from French troops, it looked as if he might be able to maintain himself, for the Spanish (Castile in particular) were rallying to his cause. The allies prepared an expedition for an assault on Spain in the summer of 1710. It reached Madrid, and again Philippe V seemed about to become an exile, but Louis XIV, distraught over the failure of the conference at Gertruydenberg, sent Vendôme with a small French force to command Philippe's armies. Vendôme's task was lightened by the actions of the Anglo-Dutch-Imperial armies. Their hostility toward the Catholic Church in Spain led them again to outrage the sensibilities of pious Spaniards and thereby swell the support of the Bourbon king. But perhaps even more important, by pushing on to Madrid without having fully prepared the way, they found themselves in a difficult position and had to retreat. Vendôme knew how to take advantage of both their divided command and the embarrassment that their lack of supplies created. He pushed on after them, not even allowing Philippe to celebrate the liberation of Madrid. By the end of December the fate of Spain was decided: the best part of the Anglo-Imperial armies was in prison pens; the debris of that force was locked up in Barcelona utterly dependent upon the English fleet for its survival. It should have been clear to everyone that Philippe had won his right to occupy the throne in Madrid.

This victory came in December; it could not have been foreseen in June when the war in Flanders again riveted attention on the problem of peace. In the Spring of 1710, the French army was still in bad shape, but there was more food, and the summer harvests refilled the grain bins so that Villars could hope to fight with at least as much success as he had the previous August at Malplaquet. That battle had been a rude shock to the Anglo-Dutch-Imperial commanders and statesmen. The "butchers bill" seemed excessive to many politicians in England and the United Netherlands, and it convinced both Marlborough and Eugene that Villars was a dangerous man and that they must not let him entice them into another such engagement. The soldiers could argue that another such battle was not necessary: the French could not prevent their taking one fortification after another until they had stripped France of all its defenses; then the road to Versailles would be open. And indeed this was the case, for Villars could not force them to fight, nor could he prevent their capturing the lines of fortifications that defended the kingdom. By the fall of 1710 only a thin defense still remained, and Villars, suffering from his wound, could not obey the king's orders to bring the enemies to a battle. At this moment when it again seemed that Louis XIV would finally be forced to accept any terms offered to him, there came a break that would widen with Vendôme's victory in Spain, and finally unhinge the alliance that so adamantly insisted upon its right to dictate terms. The peace would be negotiated after all.

The allies at Gertruydenberg seemed to present a solid front, but in reality the alliance was already in some trouble. The Dutch would have gladly accepted the terms that Louis was willing to offer, but had, in fact, lost control over their own policy. By 1709–10 the United Netherlands was in desperate financial shape; without important agricultural or industrial resources, the United Netherlands largely depended upon commerce for the livelihood of its people, and the war severely limited commerce while the costs of war piled new taxes upon old until no resources were left. Two things held the Dutch in line: first their recognition of their economic and military dependence upon England, as well as the fear of the much superior English fleet, and secondly, the promises that the Whig politicians who governed England in 1709 had given them. A treaty assured the Dutch control over some sixteen of the most important towns in the Spanish (to become Austrian) Netherlands as well as Upper Guelders and an important share with England in the commerce of the Spanish Colonies. Dependence on English power and greed for control over the rest of the Netherlands made the Dutch into a "cat's paw" for the Anglo-Imperials. They carried the brunt of the negotiations at Gertruydenberg quite against their own interests. Little did they understand how easily the situation in England could change and leave them in the lurch.

The English political problem was a complicated one. The last elections to Parliament had returned a Whig majority. Marlborough and Godolphin were not party men, but like the Whigs, they wished to continue the war to its ultimate conclusion. They agreed to the formula: No peace without Spain! No peace without securing the interests of all of the allies. In 1709 and again in 1710 the Whig politicians were adamant in sheer determination to force France to submit totally. They held all the trump cards in the game, and they were going to play them. But England, like the rest of Europe, suffered from the great frost of 1709. It did not produce the starvation that came to France, but the price of bread went higher and higher as wheat had to be imported from abroad, and with high prices came grumbling. Then came Malplaquet. Like the Dutch burghers who saw their regiments cut to pieces, many Englishmen were aghast at the cost in blood, and irritated when the government resorted to enforced enlistments to refill the ranks of the army. There also was much gossipy talk in the back lanes of England about the way the Dutch were waxing rich at the expense of their Catholic cousins in the Spanish Netherlands, how the Germans were not carrying their share of the war, and how Marlborough was filling his own pockets at the expense of the English taxpayer. Furthermore, taxes were high—too high—and the Whig money men in London were becoming rich on war profits. Much of this sentiment irrationally hardened when the government brought Dr. Sacheverell before the House of Lords on a treason trial because of a sermon that seemed to involve the war and the revolutionary settlement of 1689. It was the Whig ministry that really came under fire.

The story of the reversal of the Whig-Marlborough-Godolphin ministry in England in 1710 is too complex to tell in a short account like the present one. England, and most of all those Englishmen who were paying the taxes, were weary of the war; Marlborough and his wife Sarah made the mistake of antagonizing Queen Anne; the Tory leaders understood how to take advantage of the changing public mood as well as of the Queen's shifting loyalties. The ministry was attacked piecemeal: first Marlborough's son-in-law, and finally Godolphin himself. New elections were held and a Tory majority confirmed the fact that England had greatly shifted its political axis. It did not take long for the shift to be known in France and finally in Europe.

Other events crowded in to emphasize the changing political

climate. In December, Vendôme's victories in Spain forced men to
see that Archduke Charles probably could never hope to capture
the throne in Spain. He had never been much more than an English
puppet; when the English army was defeated and made prisoners
of war, even his puppet status was in question. Then a few months
later came other news that affected Charles and his chances for the
Spanish throne: his brother, Emperor Joseph I, died without direct
heirs, and Charles mounted the thrones of the Danubian monarchy
and that of the Empire as Charles VI. Who in England, or for that
matter in the United Netherlands either, would seriously fight to
establish him as king in Spain as well? The Tory politicians made
their first tentative approach to the court at Versailles early in the
fall of 1710; by mid-winter 1711 the negotiations to discover terms
for peace were fully under way even if still secret. The English
statesmen were in a ticklish position: their favor rested upon the
will of the queen, but she was old and sick, and if she should die,
the heir to the throne of the United Kingdom of England and Scotland was George of Hanover. Prince George was the comrade in
arms of Marlborough, and he probably would favor the Duke and
the Whigs. Thus the Tories had to move cautiously to be sure that
whatever they might do could be defended as being in the interests
of the kingdom so that they would not face the loss of their offices
and perhaps their heads, should the Queen die. It turned out that
the Queen lived long enough for the kingdom to profit enormously
from their desertion of their allies, and when the Whigs returned
to power with the accession of George I, no one was willing to give
up England's advantages in the treaties that the Tories had made
because of loyalty to Dutch or German allies.

Viscount Bolingbroke and Robert Harley (later Lord Oxford)
were the architects of the agreement with France. They wanted
first of all to convince the important people in the City of London
that Tory statesmen could look out for English commercial interests
as well as the Whigs had done; they also had to satisfy the country
gentry and squires that the kingdom would not be sacrificed to
the interests of foreigners, indeed that its global interests would be
assured. This meant, in effect, that they had to devise a treaty that
would guarantee their country a central role in the future government of the western world. The two wars fought since 1689 clearly
indicated that the one most important position to be achieved was
control over naval bases that would allow the British navy to act

effectively in both the Atlantic and the western Mediterranean: in effect this meant the acquisition of bases at the Straits of Gibraltar, in the western Mediterranean, at Nova Scotia, and in the Antilles. It also meant recognition of the British claims to Newfoundland and Hudson's Bay as well as trading privileges in the Spanish colonial empire, at least as good as those that Charles III promised the Whigs in 1709. While they were prepared to recognize Philippe V as king in Spain, they also required the assurance that the thrones of Spain and France would never be united. At the same time they needed to have French and Spanish recognition of the revolutionary settlement of the succession to the throne in England. These Tory statesmen would probably have preferred James Edward, the Stuart pretender, to George of Hanover as heir to Queen Anne, but they knew that the Stuart pretender's unwillingness to compromise his Catholicism, even to obtain a throne, made it unlikely that he could ever wear the crown.

If they could secure all this for themselves, they would be willing to consider the interests of their allies, but the Tories were less than anxious to fulfill the inter-allied treaties, let alone the moral obligations that their predecessors had undertaken. They were much interested in the Spanish Netherlands, but the feeling in England that the Dutch were becoming rich by their exploitation of those provinces—to the exclusion of English interests—made them less willing to listen to Dutch demands for control of all the border fortifications and cities. As for the Emperor's ambitions, the English felt that he should be satisfied with the share in the partition of the Spanish Empire that they felt was his due. The "legitimate pretensions" of the Empire and the German princes, like those of the Emperor, also seemed somewhat less important to them than these things had been for the Whigs. Indeed they were quite ready to desert their erstwhile allies, to force them to agree to terms. This attitude led to charges of "perfidy" that followed English diplomacy for years to come.

While British conditions were stiff, they were in no way as difficult for France as the preliminaries of the Hague had been. When the Anglo-French negotiations got under way in the spring of 1711, the war in Flanders slowed down to a walk. Both Marlborough and Villars had orders not to fight a general engagement. Marlborough also was well aware that his command would soon be taken away from him. The soldiers stood guard and the diplomats took the stage: by October 1711 the preliminaries of London were completed and France and the United Kingdom (England and Scotland) were now ready to draw up a general peace. In January, 1712 the belligerents were invited to Utrecht to write a treaty.

However, this plan for the partition of the Spanish Empire satisfied none of the other parties. Philippe V did not want to give up Italy; the Emperor did not want to give up Spain. He had so long regarded himself as "Carlos" III and so identified his interests with Spain that neither the accession to the thrones in Germany and the Danubian lands, nor the defeat of his army in Spain, could convince him that he must accept a partition of the Empire. Furthermore, his military position was considerably strengthened by the pacification of Hungary (Szathmar, 1711) which allowed him to transfer more troops to the Rhine. Thus, even though he knew of the desperate plight of the Catalonians loyal to his cause, he refused to believe that he would be forced to accept the Anglo-French solution. The Dutch and also the Empire felt that their interests had been cavalierly treated, but they were more dependent upon England than they wanted to believe, and like the Germans, soon discovered that their pleas to Queen Anne to remember England's pledged word had no effect on the progress of events. For his part, Philippe V could not resist his grandfather's will.

In February, 1712, crises arose that threatened to break the Anglo-French understanding when the Duke of Burgundy, his wife, and his eldest son died within a few weeks of each other. The year before when the Grand Dauphin (Louis XIV's son) died, there had not been a political ripple, since three lives still stood between the throne of France and Philippe V. But by March, 1712 only a sickly little boy, who also seemed destined to have an early death, was left. The French were willing to put an article in the treaty barring Philippe V from the throne, but they pointed out that the Parlement of Paris probably would pay no attention to it. It was now important to have a declaration from Philippe V waiving his and his children's rights to the throne of France, and Philippe did not want to make such a declaration. He had the impossible hope that one of his sons could become king of Spain, the other, king of France. For a while the negotiations waivered, and the English army, under a new commander, was poised to take its place beside the allies. Then Bolingbroke hit on a scheme: let Philippe V choose whether he would remain king of Spain and waive all right to the throne of France, or turn Spain over to the Duke of Savoy (an English client) and become ruler of Naples, Sicily, and Savoy with the chance of bringing Savoy to France should he ever mount the throne at Versailles. Louis XIV favored the latter solution, but Philippe decided that he had become a Spaniard and would remain in Madrid. When this decision was about to be made, the English withdrew their army from the coalition; it marched away leaving Eugene with the Dutch, Imperial, and German troops (heretofore paid by England, now by the Dutch) to face Villars. They had to attempt to secure a military decision that would reverse or modify the Anglo-French agreement.

Eugene was in a strong position even without the English army, but he was not overwhelmingly superior to the French. He moved to besiege Landrecies, one of the last remaining fortifications still in French hands. At Versailles emotions ran high; Villars was ordered to fight. The decisive action came at Denain, July 24, 1712, when the French army overran the position before Eugene could bring up detachments to support the fortification. It was a disaster for the allies; for the Dutch, a catastrophe, since the flower of the Dutch army, some twenty-seven regiments that had escaped Malplaquet, was cut to pieces at Denain. Both noble and bourgeois families in the United Netherlands again mourned their sons; no one asked what the little people thought.

Villars quickly followed up his advantage. He was on Eugene's lines of communication, and on July 30 he reversed the relative positions of the two armies by capturing Marchennies where he found a huge magazine of war materials: over a hundred cannons, immense supplies of powder and shot, quantities of cheese, bread, and grain. Eugene not only lost his ability to continue the siege of Landrecies, now he was on the defensive. In short order the French recaptured Fort de la Scarpe, Douai, and Quesnoi where they found another hundred cannons. Without supplies, Eugene was forced to fall back on Brussels while Villars reestablished the lines that assured the defense of the kingdom.

This military situation had immediate political repercussions: at Utrecht, the United Netherlands, Portugal, and Savoy (the latter two were protégés of England) were ready to talk seriously about peace. The Emperor and the Empire still held out, but western Europe went on to make peace without the Germans.

The Peace of Utrecht is a complex of eleven separate treaties between the several belligerents; in a short account it would not be useful to try to separate them since they were in fact intertwined in the agreement that was finally hammered out in 1713. These were the last of the "partition treaties" solving the crisis created by the failure of the Spanish House of Hapsburg to produce an heir. Although the kingdom of France also was required to surrender some of the border cities that it had recently acquired on the frontier with the Spanish Netherlands, as well as certain colonial positions, it was not the French but the Spanish crown that was forced to pay the bill; Spain gave up territories in Italy and the Netherlands that had been ruled from Madrid for almost two centuries.

Even though they did insist that their allies be paid by the partition of the Spanish empire, the British statesmen secured the "lion's share" for themselves. The very cornerstone of British interests centered around the acquisition of Gibraltar and Minorca. The Whigs had secured a treaty from Charles "III" assuring them these territories; the Tories were careful to have their cession appear in the final treaties. This gave the British navy the dominant position in the western Mediterranean and the northeastern Atlantic as long as men depended upon sails for power. The acquisition of French Arcadia (Nova Scotia) with Port Royal (Annapolis) and the recognition of British rights over Newfoundland and Hudson's Bay completed the chain of naval stations that assured the British predominance in the northwestern Atlantic. This splendid situation was further strengthened by the acquisition of the entire island of Saint Christopher. Charles "III" had promised the Whigs extensive commercial privileges in the Spanish Empire; the Tories secured as much or more by obtaining the right of the *Asiento* which allowed them to sell slaves in the Spanish New World colonies as well as the right to send a trading ship each year to traffic with the colonial merchants. This trade was not worth as much as it had been a century earlier when the mines were still producing precious metals and when smuggling had not yet reached the status of "business as usual"; nonetheless, it was regarded as a plum plucked for the merchants of London. Another clause in the Anglo-French treaty provided for the destruction of the fortifications of Dunkirk from which French privateers had preyed on allied commerce during the preceding two wars. Finally, in spite of the French suggestion that the Parlement of Paris would probably pay no attention to a treaty statement, one clause of the treaties excluded Philippe V and his heirs from the throne of France. French historians in our time insist that this was an attempt to elevate the principle of the Revolution of 1688, by which men rather than the act of God regulated succession to the throne, to the status of international law. In France the Salic law was the very foundation of the principle of the divine right of kings; the settlement of 1689, as of Utrecht, set aside God's will in favor of mundane arrangements for the regulation of succession.

Both the French and the British had a protégé whose interests they were bent upon protecting. For the French, this was the Duke of Bavaria. Of all the allies that had joined the Two Crowns in 1701, only Max Emanuel had remained faithful, even at the loss of his inherited estates in Bavaria. For a very long time, sovereignty over the Spanish Netherlands had been held up to him as a possible reward, and, indeed, throughout the war Louis XIV had unsuccessfully attempted to persuade his grandson to invest Max with this territory. Only after it was too late did Philippe V act to give his uncle these provinces. The Dutch, as might be expected, wanted no French puppet satellite in control of the Spanish Netherlands, nor were the English willing to support any such proposal. Louis XIV sought compensations elsewhere for the Duke of Bavaria, but in the end he was fortunate to recover his family lands in central Europe. The English protégé was the Duke of Savoy; he emerged from the treaties much more fortunate than did the Duke of Bavaria. By 1713 his "treason" of 1695 was forgotten; the English realized that they could use the Duke of Savoy, who had happily also "betrayed" Louis XIV in 1703, to assure their own position in the central Mediterranean. Not only did he secure "modifications" of his mainland frontiers in the Piedmont, but he was also given the island of Sicily and the title "King of Sicily and Piedmont." (A few years later he exchanged Sicily for Sardinia.) He also was placed next in line after Philippe V and his descendants, in the succession to the Spanish throne.

The Dutch were interested first of all in the fate of the Spanish Netherlands. Differences in religion and commercial rivalry, envy, and hostility separated the peoples of the two Netherlands; those of the United Provinces, with good Calvinist self-assurance, believed themselves superior to their relatives to the south whose speech was hard to understand and whose supine acceptance of

Hapsburg power seemed cowardly or slavish. The southerners shared this mutual dislike. They had seen the northerners shut off the commerce of Antwerp in order to strangle a rival and use their military power to force the south to pay for a large part of the costs of the war. Their Catholicism as well as the considerable number of French-speaking Walloons added other dimensions to the problems between the two Netherlands. The Spanish Netherlands wanted nothing to do with their northern cousins; they preferred Catholic Hapsburg rule to government from Amsterdam. The United Provinces understood that the south could not be "ruled" from the north like a conquered province, but in treaties made with the Whig statesmen (1709), they had been assured that, while the sovereignty over the provinces would remain in Hapsburg hands (Charles III in Spain), they would be allowed to garrison a strong "barrier" system of fortifications so as to assure both military and economic control over the land. This promise had kept the Dutch firm in the negotiations of Gertruydenberg. At Utrecht they got somewhat less. The Spanish Netherlands were ceded to the United Netherlands with the understanding that they would be turned over to Emperor Charles VI as soon as he had agreed to make peace. The French ceded Furnes, Ypres, Menin, and Tournai to strengthen the "barrier," but the number of fortifications given over to the United Netherlands was sharply reduced. There was some satisfaction in the knowledge that the Emperor would be morally and politically committed to the defense of the "Austrian Netherlands" and that England could also be counted upon to oppose any French aggression in that area, but this did not make up for the smaller "barrier" nor for the fact that the Tory politicians did not allow the Dutch to share the commercial advantages in the Spanish Empire. Finally Upper Guelders, which had been promised to them, was given to the King of Prussia, whose favor it was now time for the British to court.

The King of Prussia was the only German prince to sign at Utrecht. His title of king was generally recognized, and in addition to Upper Guelders in the Rhineland, he also acquired Neuchatel and Vallangen, a succession that had been in contest between the house of Hohenzollern and the French family of Longueville for about a decade. The king of Portugal also signed the treaties, but his compensation was largely English willingness to continue the treaties of alliance and commerce that had been negotiated a decade before. English favor and the English market for Portuguese wines were more important than the minor revision of the frontier between the Portuguese colony in the new world and French Guiana.

Emperor Charles refused to sign the treaties even though they reserved for him Naples, the Tuscan ports, Sardinia, the Milanais, and the now "Austrian" Netherlands. Charles VI wanted also to be "Carlos" III, but without the English navy to sustain the Catalonian "Carlists" and without the soldiers paid by England and the Dutch, he could not hope to secure that throne in Madrid. Even so, the war between France and the Empire continued, but now it was Eugene's turn to retreat before Villars. In 1713, the French took Landau and Freiburg, and established themselves on both sides of the Rhine: even Charles VI "got the message." In February, Villars and Eugene settled down at Rastadt to discuss peace. The Frenchman had the military advantage, but Eugene had the psychological one. They finally made peace only after exchanging instructions so that each could see what had to be done to end the war.

The treaty of Rastadt essentially spelled out the terms that had already been made earlier. The French got Landau and kept Strasbourg, but the eastern frontier of France was about the same as that created at Ryswick. This treaty was also presented to the Empire for ratification by the Diet at Ratisbon. The last of the ratifications was exchanged in December 1714.

# Chapter 9

# Epilogue:
# The Balance of Power in 1715

It is probably no accident that the first real proposal for a government for Europe to maintain general peace had to wait until after 1713–1714. And even then, the Abbé de Saint Pierre's proposal probably deserved Cardinal Fleury's admonition that he should organize a band of missionaries to convert the hearts of princes if he wished his plan actually to germinate. However, what the good Abbé saw was a world in which the government depended upon the balance of power between the states of Europe, and since in human affairs no "balance" can really exist because human affairs are always more or less unstable, what actually had happened was that the government of Europe was now dependent upon a system which had the sword as the ultimate guardian of European peace and liberty. In the succeeding centuries, after Europeans fought other great wars on the scale of those of 1683–1713, other plans would be proposed: the Holy and the Quadruple Alliances (1814–15); the League of Nations (1919); and the United Nations (1945). Each of these also fundamentally rested upon the balance of power created by the conflicts that had preceded them, and each left as the ultimate resort of an aggrieved party, the appeal to the sword. But as warfare has become more and more of a disaster for all men, more and more curbs have been erected to stave off this appeal to heaven as the arbiter of political affairs in the world. In 1715 it was not even possible to create institutions with the pious platitudes of the Holy Alliance as a check on the free play of states' interests; only the balance of power restrained the egotism of states and dynastic ambitions.

By 1715, the traditional alliance systems suggested the structure of the European power balances. It was clear to everyone that the Emperor alone was no military match for France, but Germany supported by the Netherlands and England had proven its ability to place bounds upon French ambitions. On the other hand, the French alliances, potential and actual, in turn could place bounds on the ambitions of the Emperor, the Netherlands, and England. For the Empire was no monolithic block; thus the king of France could find in Bavaria or, even better, Brandenburg-Prussia, balances within the Empire; and in Europe, Bourbon Spain, perhaps Savoy, and possibly Poland or Sweden could help to right the weights against France. Furthermore, everyone knew that alliances were unstable: France and England had combined to write the treaty of Utrecht; they could and would cooperate on other projects. What was evident was the fact that there were three great military powers in western and central Europe: the kingdom of France, the united British kingdom, and the Hapsburg Imperial complex governed from Vienna, that drew its force basically from the Danubian crowns. On a second level, there was Spain and the United Netherlands. Both had slipped from the power status they had had earlier; Bourbon Spain had become more or less dependent upon France, and the United Netherlands on the United Kingdom. A step below these two, but struggling to achieve status, was the new kingdom of Piedmont-Sicily (soon to be Piedmont-Sardinia) which could still play the important role as "porter" in the Alps and Northern Italy between the king of France and the emperor at Vienna.

The interesting, and in a real way disturbing, developments of 1715 were located in the east rather than the west. In 1700, war had broken out between Sweden on the one side and Denmark, Russia, and Poland-Saxony on the other. The three states were attempting to partition the Swedish Empire only to discover that they had chosen as an antagonist young Charles XII whose natural talent as a military leader took them by surprise. Denmark was forced out of the war immediately; then Charles sailed for the

Baltic with some 8,000 troops, attacked the Russians at Narva and completely defeated them. The odds were between five and seven to one against him, but the Russians had no understanding of war. The next seven years Charles spent campaigning in Poland against August I. It was a futile, wasteful sort of war that neither could win. In the meantime Peter I of Russia reorganized his armies, began the remodeling of his state, and invaded the Swedish Baltic provinces, but in spite of his propaganda about the power and the new strength of Russia, no one in the West took him seriously. It was not realized in western Europe, nor in the entourage of Charles XII, that Peter was really rebuilding the military capacity of his country: his reforms were reforms aimed at the creation of a Russian military establishment, armed with modern weapons, drilled in modern exercises, and commanded by men who would understand modern strategy.

After Charles XII invaded Saxony (1707) and dictated peace to Augustus I, he turned on Russia to make Peter pay both for his temerity in making war on the Swedish Empire and his invasions of the Swedish Baltic provinces. The campaign ended with the battle of Poltava (1709) in which the Swedish army was defeated, many of its men killed, and nearly the entire remaining army was made prisoners of war. Charles escaped to the Ottoman Empire where he managed to embroil Russia with the Turks. His success, however, was frustrated when the Vizier made peace with Peter I rather than destroying him and his army (Peace of Purth, 1711). Thus Peter's Russia, after promising not to disturb the Turks, was able to concentrate on the North. The time again seemed ripe for the partition of the Swedish Baltic Empire.

Curiously enough, this war in the Baltic and the Polish borderlands did not become involved in the conflict over the Spanish succession. There were several reasons. Both Peter I and Charles XII were hostile to France; both were friendly to the Sea Powers.[28] Augustus of Saxony-Poland was a protégé of the Emperor, but when Charles invaded Germany to punish him, the Swedish king had no intention of playing the part of Gustavus Adolfus; he wanted only to punish Augustus and be off to Russia to make Peter I pay for his actions. The general Francophobia shared by all the combatants in the Northern War probably would not be enough in

---

[28] England and the United Netherlands.

itself to explain the fact that the Northern War and the war in the west remained separated. Distances also played a role; Poland and Russia were desperately far away from Western Europe in 1715; indeed the two wars were almost on separate continents. And while the Anglo-Dutch commercial and naval interests were involved in the Baltic, the French were unable to reach that sea, so there was not a problem involving the commercial interests of belligerents of both wars at the same time. The battle of Poltava, capped by Peter's lucky escape through the treaty of Purth, changed the problem somewhat, for now it became evident that the partition of Sweden's Baltic empire, which had not been possible in 1700, was imminent. The king of Denmark, the king of Brandenburg-Prussia, and the future king of England, Elector George of Hanover, suddenly all became involved in the problems of the Baltic. Since both Prussia and Hanover were closely allied in the coalition against Louis XIV, and the king of Denmark, although not directly involved, had hired his best cavalry regiments to the English government, it was not a situation that Louis XIV could use effectively to split his foes. The Treaties of Utrecht were written without interference from the Baltic problems.

Only after 1714 when Charles XII returned to Sweden from Turkey, did the situation became more pregnant with problems involving the whole community of Europe, but since France was too weak, too impoverished, too worn out to play an active role, the solution of the Northern War unrolled without any general European involvement. However, a central fact did emerge. The Baltic had a new master. After 1714, Russian warships controlled that sea; Russian marines were even landed on Swedish soil; and the Russian Baltic bases assured the Tsar's fleet of future control over those waters. Furthermore, the "revolution" in Russia, for Peter's reforms were in fact a revolution, had created a Russian army of 100,000 men; they may not have been a match for their contemporaries in the French or Austrian armies, but they could no longer be brushed aside with a sneer. The Russians had modern arms, they had good artillery, they were properly drilled; Russia was in the process of becoming a first class military power. So, even though Peter "the Great" was not invited to help write the Treaties of Utrecht, in the future his state and his diplomacy would have to figure in the European balance of power.

The arrival of Russia to the status of a great power is simple evidence of the fact that the "balance of power" is not a physical "scale" or mechanical model; it is rather an evolving process in which instabilities are introduced by the growth or decay of states, by new military techniques, by economic forces, and by other changes in the politics of the world. The process that we call the balance of power does have an inner government that seeks to maintain the characteristic forms and patterns that have brought it into being and that make it useful to the political community. Until some superstate, which will have the ability to coerce all members of the community, can come into existence, this characteristic balance of power will surely continue to play an important role in the relations between states, and will be the central factor in the government of international society.

# Bibliography

Since this little volume is intended primarily for English-speaking students with only a slender knowledge of other languages, I have largely omitted books other than in English. The exceptions are books that will provide a bibliography for anyone who is able to explore the subject in other languages.

Robert G. Albion, *Forests and Sea Power, The Timber Problem of the Royal Navy, 1652–1862*, Cambridge, 1926.

Louis André, *Louis XIV et l'Europe*, Paris, 1950.

Paul W. Bamford, *Forests and French Sea Power*, Toronto, 1956.

Thomas M. Barker, *Double Eagle and Crescent*, New York, 1967.

Stephen Baxter, *William III*, London, 1966.

G. N. Clark, *The Dutch Alliance and the War Against French Trade, 1688–1697*, London, 1923.

*War and Society in the Seventeenth Century*, Cambridge, 1958.

*The Seventeenth Century*, 2nd Ed., 1954.

Julian Corbett, *England in the Mediterranean, 1603–1703*, 2 vols., London, 1904.

Charles W. Cole, *Colbert and a Century of French Mercantilism*, 2 vols., Columbia, 1939.

C. J. Friedrich, *The Age of the Baroque, 1610–1660*, New York, 1954.

J. F. C. Fuller, *Military History of the Western World*, Vol. II, New York, 1955.

Pieter Geyl, *The Netherlands in the 17th Century*, Part Two, 1648–1715, Barnes and Noble, 1964.

Hajo Holborn, *A History of Modern Germany, 1648–1840*, Knopf, 1963.

Walther Hubatsch, *Das Zeitalter des Absolutismus, 1600–1789*, Braunschweig, 1962.

Max Immich, *Geschichte des Europäischen Staatensystems*, Munich, 1905.

Philip A. Knachel, *England and the Fronde*, Cornell Univ. Press, 1967.

A. D. Lublinskaya, *French Absolutism, The Crucial Phase (1620–1629)*, Cambridge, 1968.

Robert Mandrore, *Nouvelle Clio, La France aux XVII⁰ et XVIII⁰ Siecles*, Paris, 1967

C. J. Marcus, *A Naval History of England,* Boston, 1961.

David Mayland, *Europe in the Seventeenth Century,* New York, 1966.

Friedrick Meinecke, *Machiavelism; The doctrine of Raison d'État and its place in Modern History* (Praeger paperback), 1965.

*New Cambridge Modern History,* Vol. V, *The Ascendency of France,* Cambridge, 1961.

F. L. Nussbaum, *The Triumph of Science and Reason, 1660–1685,* New York, 1953.

George M. Trevelyan, *England under the Stuarts,* London, 1912.

*The English Revolution, 1688–1689,* New York, 1939.

*England under Queen Anne,* 3 vols., London, 1930–34.

Orest Ranum, *Richelieu and the Councillors of Louis XIII,* London 1963.

John Roach, *A Bibliography of Modern History,* Cambridge, 1968.

H. H. Rowen, *The Ambassador Prepares for War,* The Hague, 1957.

George A. Rothrock, (ed.) Vauban's *A Manual of Siegecraft and Fortification,* Ann Arbor, 1968.

J. B. Wolf, *The Emergence of the Great Powers, 1685–1715,* Harper and Row, 1951.

*Louis XIV,* Norton, 1968.

"The Reign of Louis XIV; A Selected Bibliography of Writings Since the War of 1914–1918," *Journal of Modern History,* XXXVI (1964), pp. 127–144.

Gaston Zeller, *Histoire des Relations Internationales,* (P. Renouvin Ed.) Vol. I, *De Christophe Colomb à Cromwell,* Paris, 1955.

Vol. II, *De Louis XIV à 1789,* Paris, 1955.


For a more complete bibliography see E. Préclin and V-L. Tapié, *Clio, Le XVIIe Siècle, 1610–1715,* Paris, 1949.

# Index

Printed in U.S.A.